T0319749

Economic Instruments of Pollution Control in an Imperfect World

This book is dedicated to the memory of my mother, Jiang Guiying

Economic Instruments of Pollution Control in an Imperfect World

Theory and Implications for Carbon Dioxide Emissions Control in China

Tingsong Jiang

The Australian National University and Centre for International Economics, Australia

Edward Elgar
Cheltenham, UK • Northampton, MA, USA

Published by
Edward Elgar Publishing Limited
Glensanda House
Montpellier Parade
Cheltenham
Glos GL50 1UA
UK

Edward Elgar Publishing, Inc.
136 West Street
Suite 202
Northampton
Massachusetts 01060
USA

A catalogue record for this book
is available from the British Library

Library of Congress Cataloguing in Publication Data

Jiang, Tingsong, 1964–
    Economic instruments of pollution control in an imperfect world:
theory and implications for carbon dioxide emissions control in
    China/Tingsong Jiang.
        p. cm.
    Includes bibliographical references and index.
    1. Air—Pollution—Economic aspects—China. 2. Air—Pollution—
Government policy—China. 3. Carbon dioxide mitigation—China.
4. Carbon dioxide—Economic aspects—China. I. Title.
HC430.A4J5   2004
363.738'746'0951—dc22

                                                        2003049441

ISBN 1 84376 625 6

Printed and bound in Great Britain by MPG Books Ltd, Bodmin, Cornwall

Contents

Figures

Tables

Acknowledgements

It would not have been possible to complete this book without the generous assistance and unfailing support of many individuals and institutions. I would like to express my sincere gratitude to them all.

This book is based on my PhD dissertation at the Australian National University (ANU). I have been particularly fortunate with my advisory panel of Warwick McKibbin, Ben Smith and Yiping Huang. Warwick has been a wonderful encouraging supervisor, combining acute attention to detail with a breadth of vision and penetrating insight. I benefited greatly from all our discussions. I have also benefited from discussions with Ben, and his feedback was prompt and helpful. Yiping, a long time friend, suggested I apply for the PhD study at ANU, and was usually the first person from whom I sought help during the early days of my PhD course.

I would like to thank other staff members of the Economics Division at ANU's Research School of Pacific and Asian Studies, especially Prema-Chandra Athukorala, Ronald Duncan, George Fane, Peter Drysdale, Mardi Dungey, Ross Garnaut, Chris Manning, Ross McLeod, Xin Meng, Ligang Song and Mei Wen, for their helpful comments, suggestions and friendship. Discussions, and even sometimes arguments, with my fellow students Alexandra Sidorenko, Kanhaiya Singh, Qun Shi, Chia-Hung Sun and Yuyu Chen were also fruitful and helpful. I am in debt to Carol Kavanagh, for her help with editing of the manuscript.

Most parts of this book have been presented at various occasions, including the regular PhD seminar series held in ANU's Asia-Pacific School of Economics and Management, the 6th Biennial Meeting of the International Society for Ecological Economics, the 29th Annual Conference of the Economic Society of Australia, the 2000 PhD Conference in Economics and Business. I would like to thank all the participants at these seminars and conferences for their valuable comments and suggestions. Special thanks go to Peter Dixon from Monash University and Dr David Stern from ANU's Centre for Resource and Environmental Studies for providing valuable discussion on my work.

I would like to thank the *Australian Journal of Agricultural and Resource Economics* (published by Blackwell Publishing), *Environment and Development* (published by Cambridge University Press) and the Asia Pacific

Press at the Australian National University for permitting me to include some of my previous works in this book.

I would like to thank Jeremy Warford and Stein Hansen from the Environmental Economics Working Group of the China Council for International Cooperation on Environment and Development for helping me set the tone and structure of the book and for suggesting sources of information. I would also like to thank Prodipto Ghosh from the Asian Development Bank for providing me with the background information of China's CO_2 emissions, and the Institute of Environmental Studies, Japan, for allowing me to use their database for CO_2 emission projections.

I would especially like to thank the Australian Government and the Australian National University for providing me with scholarship funding, without which it would not have been possible for me to complete this book. Some ideas about the book were first developed during my stay at the Department of Economics at the University of Queensland. I am sincerely grateful to Clem Tisdell and the Department and the University for providing me with academic and financial support. I would also like to thank the Centre for International Economics for providing support when I finalised this book.

I would like to thank Francine O'Sullivan and other staff of Edward Elgar, who carried out the numerous tasks involved in editing and producing this book.

This book is dedicated to the memory of my mother, Jiang Guiying, who passed away before the book was completed. She was a great mother, always placing her children and grandchildren above herself. I am also sincerely grateful to my father, Sun Xingben, for his understanding and encouragement. My younger brother, Tingyou, and sister, Fenghua, took over my responsibility for supporting the family. Without their support, I would not have been able to focus on my studies.

Finally, but not least, my love and thanks go to my wife, Qiwen Lin, and daughter, Shufan, for their love and support.

Tingsong Jiang
Canberra, 2003

Abbreviations

$2 \times CO_2$	Doubling of atmospheric CO_2 concentration
AAU	assigned amount unit
ADB	Asian Development Bank
AEEI	Autonomous Energy Efficiency Index
AGE	Applied General Equilibrium
AIM	Asian Pacific Integrated Model
ASF	Atmospheric Stabilization Framework Model
BAU	Business As Usual
BTU	British Thermal Unit
CAC	Command And Control
CDM	Clean Development Mechanism
CER	certified emission reduction
CES	Constant Elasticity of Substitution
CET	Constant Elasticity of Transformation
CETA	Carbon Emissions Trajectory Assessment model
CGE	Computable General Equilibrium
COD	Chemical Oxygen Demand
COP	Conference Of Parties
CRTM	Carbon Rights Trade Model
DGE	Dynamic General Equilibrium
DICE	the Dynamic Integrated model of Climate and the Economy
EI	Economic Instrument
EMF	Energy Modeling Forum
EPA	Environmental Protection Agency (of the United States)
ERU	emissions reduction unit
ESAM	Extended Social Accounting Matrix
FAO	Food and Agriculture Organization of the United Nations
FSU	Former Soviet Union
FSU/EE	Former Soviet Union and East Europe
FUND	climate Framework for Uncertainty, Negotiation and Distribution
GCM	General Circulation Model
G-Cubed	Global General Equilibrium Growth Model
GDP	Gross Domestic Product
GEF	Global Environmental Facility
GFDL	Geophysical Fluid Dynamics Laboratory
GHG	GreenHouse Gas

GISS	Goddard Institute for Space Studies
GNP	Gross National Product
GREEN	GeneRal Equilibrium ENvironment model
IEA	International Energy Agency
IEW	International Energy Workshop
IIASA	International Institute of Applied Systems Analysis
IMAGE	Integrated Model to Assess the Greenhouse Effect
I/O	Input–Output
IPCC	Intergovernmental Panel on Climate Change
IS92	IPCC Scenarios 1992
JI	Joint Implementation
LATC	Labour Augmented Technical Change
MAPSS	Mapped Atmosphere-Plant-Soil System
MARIA	Multiregional Approach for Resource and Industry Allocation
MBI	Market-Based Instrument
MESSAGE	Model for Energy Supply Strategy Alternatives and their General Environmental Impact
MiniCAM	Mini Climate Assessment Model
MPI	Max-Planck Institut für Meteorologie
NEPA	National Environmental Protection Agency of China
OSU	Oregon State University
PNNL	Pacific Northwest National Laboratory
RFF	Resource For the Future
RICE	Regional Integrated model of Climate and the Economy
RMU	removable unit
ROW	Rest Of the World
SAR	Second Assessment Report (of IPCC Working Groups)
SEPA	State Environmental Protection Administration of China
SEPC	State Environmental Protection Commission of China
SOE	State-Owned Enterprise
SRES	Special Report on Emission Scenarios
SSB	State Statistical Bureau of China
TFP	Total Factor Productivity
TVE	Township and Village Enterprise
TVM	Terrestrial Vegetation Model
UKMO	United Kingdom Meteorological Office
UKMOH	High-Resolution UKMO Model
UNDP	United Nations Development Programme
UNEP	United Nations Environmental Programme
UNFCCC	United Nations Framework Convention on Climate Change
WB	World Bank
WG	IPCC Working Group
WRI	World Resource Institute

Preface

One of the key issues of the twenty first century is how China will address its environmental problems. As incomes rise in China, the value of environmental quality will become an increasingly important part of the development debate in China. China is also a large and critical participant in the debate on global environmental issues such as climate change policy. This important book, *Economic Instruments of Pollution Control in an Imperfect World* by Dr Tingsong Jiang, presents a framework for analysing the policies needed to tackle China's myriad of local as well as global environmental problems. It is a rigorous and innovative volume covering theoretical and empirical issues as well as focusing the results of the research directly into current debates on environmental policy in China.

The first part of the book presents the economics of pollution control policy in an uncertain world – a particularly important issue for China. Concepts such as the theory of optimal environmental taxation are presented. One innovative aspect of the approach presented here is the idea that earmarking of revenue from environmental taxation for specific purposes can have important implications for the optimality of environmental taxes. This part also considers the theory of equilibrium pollution presenting a model of the demand and supply of pollution. This model is then econometrically estimated focusing on water pollution, air pollution and solid wastes using data from a range of Chinese provinces. The results are used to assess the effectiveness of government intervention in historically addressing these pollutants. A key result from this analysis is that, although various measures of pollution continue to rise in China, they have been rising less quickly than otherwise would be the case, as a result of government policy intervention. This is an important result because it suggests that China has already begun the difficult task of addressing local pollution problems – and the measures used, despite their imperfections in practice, have actually been effective. The standard approach of focusing on the absolute increase of pollution to evaluate the effectiveness of policy is misleading in a country like China where rapid economic growth is likely to be associated with rising pollution.

The second part of the book focuses on China's potential contribution to global climate change and policies to address climate change. As a large country with enormous growth potential and vast reserves of fossil fuels,

China is a key country in the climate change debate. Despite this fact, insufficient detailed work has been done on China. This book develops a theoretical framework for addressing China's role in global climate change. This model is then developed into a dynamic general equilibrium model of China and the rest of the world, extending the approach of the G-Cubed multi-country model. Using this model, a number of scenarios are developed for future Chinese emissions of carbon dioxide and a number of alternative policies are evaluated. These policies include uniform global taxes versus differential taxes across countries, and emission permit trading.

This book covers a wide range of critical environmental issues currently facing China. The development of a clear theoretical framework and rigorous empirical analysis makes this book an essential reference point for researchers in environmental policy design. The applications to China clearly indicate the contribution of the research but the frameworks developed in the book have far wider applications for all countries, particularly developing countries, facing environmental problems.

Warwick J. McKibbin
Professor and Head of Economics
Research School of Pacific and Asian Studies
The Australian National University
and Co-Director of the Climate Change Program
The Brookings Institution, Washington DC, USA

1. Economic Instruments of Pollution Control: An Introduction

This chapter gives a brief introduction to the economic instruments (EI) and related problems and sets the scope of the book. It is organised as follows. The first section raises the questions this book tries to answer. Section 1.2 gives a textbook description of economic instruments and identifies some factors affecting their success. Section 1.3 introduces EI practices in China and their applications in the area of global warming policy. It is followed by a discussion on choosing economic instruments in certain circumstances. Finally the structure of this book is described and a brief conclusion of the findings is given.

1.1 RESEARCH QUESTIONS

Environmental policies usually consist of two components: setting a goal and choosing instruments to achieve that goal. Policy instruments in turn take two forms: 'command and control' (CAC) and economic (or market-based) instruments.[1] Conventionally, authorities tend to set specific standards for firms in order to achieve certain environmental goals. These standards are either technology-based, that is, specifying methods or even equipment that firms should employ; or performance-based, that is, setting specific control targets for firms while allowing them to decide how to achieve these targets (Stavins 2000a, 2000b). As these instruments allow very little flexibility in the means of achieving environmental goals, they are often referred to as command and control instruments.

In contrast, economic instruments (EIs) provide firms and/or individuals with higher flexibility of compliance. If properly designed and implemented, they can achieve the environmental objectives with least cost and provide incentives for firms and/or individuals to comply with environmental regulations based on their self-interest. Because of these advantages, recent years have witnessed growing popularity for economic instruments.

However, the use of EIs does face some limitations in institutional and organisational capacity, information availability and so on. Moreover, different types of EIs may have different consequences under certain circumstances, that is, uncertainty, pre-existing distortion, and income transfers across agents. So choosing an appropriate instrument is an important issue of policy design. This book analyses the instrument choices under imperfections, with special references to China's environmental policy instruments and to the climate change policies. More specifically, it attempts to answer the following questions:

What are the consequences if the possibility of earmarking pollution charges for environmental activities is considered? Many economic instruments, for example, emission taxes and auctioned emission permits, generate revenues for the government. However, the existing literature overlooks the use of such revenues, except the 'double-dividend hypothesis' that suggests using such revenues to replace existing distortional taxes. This book suggests another use of such revenues: earmarking them for environmental activities. It analyses the impact of earmarking on optimal emission tax rates and compares this arrangement with the double-dividend hypothesis.

What is the appropriate policy instrument under uncertainty? The existing literature develops the rule of choosing instruments under uncertainty in a partial equilibrium setting, that is, the so-called Weitzman's rule. This book analyses this issue in a general equilibrium setting and asks: is Weitzman's rule applicable in a general equilibrium setting? If not, what restrictions should be imposed to validate it?

Are China's environmental policies, especially the pollution levy system, effective and efficient? China's environmental policies have been criticised as being ineffective and inefficient. This book presents a quantitative analysis on this issue and concludes that China's pollution levy system has been effective in the sense that firms respond well to effective levy rates, but not efficient because the government sets environmental controls without reference to the preferences of households.

What are the appropriate economic instruments for global warming policy? One complication of choosing economic instruments emerges in the arena of international cooperation like global warming policy because there may be huge income transfers across different countries. This has not been paid due attention in the existing literature. This book examines several instruments – a tradable permit system, an international uniform emission tax and a differential emission tax – in this context.

What will China's future carbon dioxide emissions be? Despite the fact that there have been many projections about China's future CO_2 emissions, this book revisits the issue by formulating scenarios about China's economic, demographic and technological development based on a new data set and a new economic model of China.

What are the appropriate policy options of carbon dioxide emission control for China? The existing literature has been focusing on the instruments for achieving a certain CO_2 emission control target in China. This book tries to find an appropriate policy target for China in addition to the policy instruments to achieve such a target.

Before answering the above questions, it is useful to give a brief introduction to economic instruments.

1.2   ECONOMIC INSTRUMENTS FOR POLLUTION CONTROL

1.2.1   A Textbook Interpretation of Economic Instruments

Economic instruments are regulations that encourage behaviour through market signals rather than explicit directives regarding pollution control levels or methods (Stavins 2000a, 2000b). The idea of economic instruments is closely related to the theory of externality. An economic instrument tries to internalise the externality into private decision procedure.

As shown in the upper panel of Figure 1.1, the benefits of emitting pollutants could be depicted by a downward sloping marginal benefit

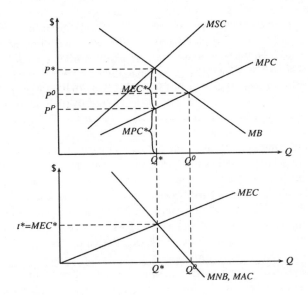

Figure 1.1   Private, external and social costs

schedule.[2]   Discharging pollutants may incur private cost to firms, for example, transportation costs of wastes, costs of building and operating pipelines and so on.   In addition, pollution causes environmental damage. Therefore, the full cost of pollution, the marginal social cost (*MSC*), is the sum of marginal private cost (*MPC*) and marginal external cost (*MEC*).[3] Without governmental intervention, firms would operate at a situation with over-polluting, Q^0. Taking account of full costs, the socially optimal pollution would be Q^*.

The same idea is shown in the lower panel of Figure 1.1, where the marginal external cost is depicted against firms' marginal net benefit (*MNB*) or marginal abatement cost (*MAC*). *MNB* is the difference between *MB* and *MPC* depicted in the upper panel.   If *MNB* incorporates behaviour adjustments by firms as the pollution level changes, the schedules of *MNB* and *MAC* are identical (Perman et al. 1996, p.204).[4] Again, firms would emit pollution of Q^0 without governmental intervention, while the socially optimal pollution level is Q^*. A well-designed economic instrument would let market forces induce firms to emit the socially optimal level Q^*.

To that end, a tax or charge at the rate of $t^* = MEC^*$ could be imposed on emissions.   Figure 1.2 illustrates this idea.   Two firms, with individual marginal abatement costs MAC_1 and MAC_2, respectively, operate in the economy. Without any intervention, firm 1 would emit pollution up to q_1^0, and firm 2 q_2^0.   The socially optimal pollution is Q^* which is less than the sum of emissions from the two firms. With the tax, firms will determine their emissions (or abatement level in other direction) based on the marginal condition: $MAC^* = t^*$.   At the margin, a firm has two options: paying tax $t^* = MEC^*$ without further abatement, or abating emissions at the cost of MAC^* to save tax. If the *MAC* is lower than the tax rate, the firm would abate pollution. On the other hand, if the *MAC* is higher than the tax rate, the firm

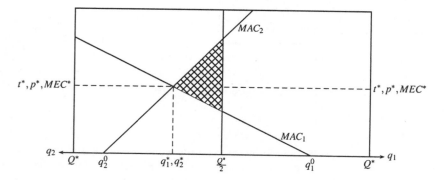

Figure 1.2   Economic instruments of pollution control

would be willing to pay the tax for an additional unit of emission. Eventually, all firms will have an identical marginal abatement cost which is equal to the tax rate, although their pollution or abatement level may be different. Figure 1.2 shows that this leads to the lowest total abatement cost, while CAC arrangements, such as equal pollution cap, usually incur higher abatement costs (the cross-hatched triangle).

Alternatively, permits totalled Q^* could be issued and a market created to allow firms to trade their permits. Suppose each firm is allocated with half the optimal number of pollution permits in a two-firm economy as shown in Figure 1.2. Initially, firm 2's marginal abatement cost is higher than firm 1's, therefore it pays for firm 2 to buy the additional permit from firm 1 at a cost no higher than $MAC_2(Q^*)$, and firm 1 is willing to sell the permit at a price no less than $MAC_1(Q^*)$. Eventually, if trade costs are negligible, the same optima q_1^* and q_2^* are reached. Furthermore, Coase's (1960) Theorem says that if trade is allowed and costs of trade are negligible and in the absence of significant income effects, the optima q_1^* and q_2^* will be achieved no matter how the permits are initially allocated.

The above discussion illustrates two important characteristics of EIs. First, economic instruments are efficient in the sense that they can achieve particular environmental goals with least cost. They not only reduce compliance costs of firms, but also administrative burdens (Huber et al. 1998).[5] Second, EIs provide powerful incentives for firms to develop and employ better and cheaper pollution-control technologies because to do so can increase their profits. The experience of economic instruments in many countries has demonstrated these characteristics (for example, see Panayotou 1994, 1995; Industry Commission 1997; James 1997; OECD and NEPA 1997; Huber et al. 1998; Stavins 2000a, 2000b).

1.2.2 Factors Limiting the Success of Economic Instruments

Although economic theory assures the cost-effectiveness and incentives of economic instruments, there are counter-arguments. The use of EIs will not automatically result in least cost solutions, and there is evidence that poorly designed EIs can cost as much as CACs (Hufschmidt et al. 1983). As regards incentives, if environmental control costs do not represent a large proportion of total cost, there may be little incentive for firms to respond to price signals (James 1997). Moreover, EIs have been criticised as resulting in little environmental gain, weaker regulatory controls, and legitimising pollution by providing a licence to pollute, especially when the pollution charge is not high enough or permits are grandfathered. Although these criticisms may be a *misconception* about EIs, they do represent some of the major factors limiting their successful implementation (Industry Commission 1997).

Even a well-designed instrument may not guarantee its success. One important cause is that firms are simply not well enough equipped internally to make the decisions necessary to fully utilise EIs. Since EIs have only been used on a limited basis, and firms are not certain about their endurance, most have chosen not to reorganise their internal structure to fully exploit the cost savings these instruments offer (Stavins 2000a).

EIs may be information demanding and result in higher administrative costs. The design of EIs needs to identify and value environmental damage costs, and sometimes, firms' abatement costs. These tasks are usually complex and surrounded by uncertainty, and impossible in some cases. Some critics argue that administrative costs will be increased because of an additional outlay of regulation, and also direct regulations required to support the use of EIs (James 1997).[6]

Economic instruments are also facing constraints due to limited institutional capacity to oversee them. Experience in many countries has shown that local authorities and strong institutional support play an important role in the success of economic instruments (Huber et al. 1998). This is especially important for developing countries and transitional economies which may adopt EIs designed in developed countries with different institutional arrangement (Panayotou 1995).

Some of these limitations will be explored later in the discussion of difference between price-based and quantity-based instruments and their selection.

1.2.3 Categories of Economic Instruments

Economic instruments can take many forms, for example, OECD (1989) identifies more than 100 different types of economic instruments. These instruments can be divided into two broad categories: price instruments and market creation (Table 1.1), or roughly equivalent, price-based and quantity-based instruments.[7]

Originated from Pigou's ([1920], 1938) idea of taxing or subsidising externality-generating activities, economic instruments in the first category directly change price signals. These instruments include pollution charges, levies, fees or taxes, subsidies, tax differentiation and so on. Financial instruments, such as soft loans, grants, and subsidised interest rates, are also in this category because they provide incentives for firms to take on environmentally-friendly activities through changing the price of financial goods.

A special case of pollution charges is a deposit-refund system, whereby consumers pay a surcharge when purchasing potentially polluting products and receive a refund when returning them for recycling and disposal. A

Table 1.1   *Economic instruments for environmental protection and natural resource management*

Category	Sub-category	Instruments
Price instruments	Charge systems	Pollution charges; user charges; betterment charges; impact fees; access fees; road tolls; administrative charges
	Fiscal instruments	Pollution taxes (effluent taxes, emission taxes); input taxes; product taxes; export taxes; import tariffs; tax differentiation; insurance premium taxes; royalties and resource taxes; land use taxes; investment tax credits; accelerated depreciation; subsidies
	Financial instruments	Financial subsidies; soft loans; grants; location/relocation incentives; subsidised interest rates; hard currency at below equilibrium exchange rate; revolving funds; sectoral funds; ecofunds/ environmental funds; green funds
	Bond and deposit-refund systems	Environmental performance bonds; land reclamation bonds; waste delivery bonds; environmental accident bonds; deposit-refund systems; deposit-refund shares
Market creation	Tradable permit systems	Tradable emission permits; tradable catch quotas; tradable development quotas; tradable water shares; tradable resource shares; tradable land permits; tradable offsets/credits; credit programmes; cap-and-trade programmes
	Property rights	Ownership rights (land titles, water rights, mining rights); use rights (stewardship, licensing, concession/bidding, turfs); development rights
	Reducing market barriers	Liability rules; information programmes (product labelling, reporting)

Sources: Panayotou (1995), Huber et al. (1998) and Stavins (2000a).

parallel instrument for firms is an environmental performance bond system. Another important variant of pollution charges is a 'presumptive tax'. A firm is compelled to pay the tax based on a presumed level of pollution, and no specific monitoring is conducted. If the firm wishes to reduce its tax burden, it must conduct monitoring at its own expense to demonstrate that its actual pollution loads are less than the presumed level (Huber et al. 1998).

The most notable instrument in the market creation category is the tradable permit or quota system. It can be traced to Coase's (1960) discussion of negotiated solutions to externalities. The example in Figure 1.2 has shown how it operates. Another important instrument of market creation is defining and assigning property rights. It is used to address the excessive resource depletion and environmental degradation resulting from the absence (or thinness) of markets in resource and environmental assets (Panayotou 1995). Tradable permit can also be viewed as a special type of property rights. Market creation also includes measures reducing market barriers, for example, liability rules that encourage firms to consider the potential environmental damage of their decisions; and information programmes such as product labelling (Stavins 2000a).

1.3   APPLICATION OF ECONOMIC INSTRUMENTS

Economic instruments have wide application. In many cases, they are not designed to replace existing CAC instruments, but to complement them and enhance their effectiveness. The main motivation behind many economic instruments has been to raise revenue for environmental management rather than to achieve environmental quality goals, and to reduce environmental impacts, or improve the cost-effectiveness of existing regulations (Huber et al. 1998). Rather than discussing a broad application of economic instruments worldwide, this section focuses on EI practices in China and their application in the field of global warming policy.

1.3.1 Economic Instruments for Environmental Policy in China

Almost every category of EIs can be found in China (Table 1.2), but the most notable economic instrument for environmental policy is the pollution levy system which is administered by the State Environmental Protection Administration (SEPA).[8] It aims to achieve two objectives: (1) provide firms with incentives to economically use energy and resources and reduce pollutant discharges; (2) collect funds for pollution treatment and disposal (Yang et al. 1998).

China's pollution levy system dates from the late 1970s. Clause 15 of China's Environmental Protection Law (Provisional) promulgated in 1979 specifies that 'in a case where the discharge of pollutants exceeds the limit set by the state, a pollution levy shall be charged according to the quantities and

Table 1.2   Economic instruments for environmental policy in China

Category	Sub-category	Instruments	Coverage
Price instruments	Charge systems	Pollution levy (excess discharge based on volume)	National
		SO_2 charge	Regional
		User charge for sewage network	National
		Wastewater treatment charge	Regional
		Ecological destruction compensation	Regional
		Mineral resource compensation	Regional
	Fiscal instruments	Resource taxes	National
		Tax differentiation for treatment, reuse and recycling of waste	National
		Financing pipeline for environmental protection	National
		Subsidy to environmental protection projects	National
	Bond and deposit-refund systems	Deposit for the 'Three Simultaneous Steps'	Regional
		Deposit for clean-up operations	Regional
		Deposit for solid wastes	National
Market creation	Tradable permit system	Tradable permits	Regional
		Waste-trading market	Regional

Source: Wang and Lu (1997), Table 1, p. 17.

concentration of pollutants released.'[9] The nationwide implementation of this system began in 1982 when the 'Provisional Regulations for Collection of Compensation Fees for Pollutant Discharge' was issued by the State Council. In the beginning, only 'excess discharge'[10] of wastewater, waste gas and solid wastes were subject to the levy. After several amendments, with the most significant in 1991, the system now covers 113 pollutants in five media – wastewater (both excess discharge and total volume), waste gas, solid wastes, noise and radiation. Several regions have also collected fees for SO_2 discharged from industrial coal burning since 1992. Approximately 650 000 factories have been charged for their emissions, and about 5 billion RMB yuan of levies were collected per year in recent years (Tables 1.3–1.5). About 80 percent of the funds have been used to finance industrial pollution prevention and control, accounting for about 15 percent of total investment in these activities (NEPA 1994, 1993–1997).

Table 1.3   *Number of firms charged with pollution levy in China*

Year	Total	Metall.	Chem.	Light	Textile	Power	Coal	TVE[*]	Other
1985	89 246	2 425	4 928	13 397	3 913	831	1 707	15 945	45 982
1986	108 645	4 557	5 674	14 955	4 534	845	2 039	24 377	51 064
1987	135 837	3 400	6 013	16 507	4 547	880	1 977	34 217	68 296
1988	160 383	3 546	6 480	17 375	4 731	880	2 034	46 840	78 497
1989	183 256	4 070	6 838	17 501	4 872	886	2 447	58 197	88 465
1990	188 142	3 890	3 387	18 132	4 687	940	2 838	58 934	92 034
1991	205 892	3 971	3 882	19 112	4 563	1 054	3 116	63 690	103 080
1992	223 655	4 886	7 994	19 443	4 853	1 081	3 438	72 098	109 862
1993	254 274	n.a.	n.a.	n.a.	n.a.	n.a.	n.a.	n.a.	n.a.
1994	300 437	n.a.	n.a.	n.a.	n.a.	n.a.	n.a.	n.a.	n.a.
1995	368 213	6 134	11 143	24 497	4 959	1 345	5 024	119 662	195 449
1996	496 324	n.a.	n.a.	n.a.	n.a.	n.a.	n.a.	n.a.	n.a.
1997	563 488	n.a.	n.a.	n.a.	n.a.	n.a.	n.a.	n.a.	n.a.

Notes:
[*] Township and village enterprises.
n.a. Not available.

Sources: Yang, Wang et al. (1998); Editorial Committee of China Environmental Yearbook (1993–98).

Table 1.4   Pollution levy from different media in China (RMB million yuan)

Year	Total	Excess discharge					Waste Waster	Other*
		Water	Gas	Solid	Noise	Radiat'n		
1984	756	504	224	15	4	1	1	7
1985	929	594	251	23	11	1	0	50
1986	1 190	711	329	25	19	1	8	97
1987	1 428	821	380	34	24	1	21	147
1988	1 610	869	441	33	31	1	29	206
1989	1 674	858	453	33	36	1	32	261
1990	1 753	900	448	31	34	1	52	287
1991	2 006	996	494	40	41	1	62	372
1992	2 381	1 181	510	33	87	1	83	486
1993	2 681	1 228	561	38	119	1	126	608
1994	3 098	1 319	647	33	155	1	201	742
1995	3 713	1 504	743	48	190	2	254	972
1996	4 096	1 551	818	37	214	2	288	1 185
1997	4 543	1 642	902	50	244	2	305	1 398
1998	4 902	1 637	1 170	44	264	1	283	1 503

Note: *The so-called 'four small items', including revenue from (1) raising levy rates for firms who failed to meet the discharge standard within three years after the collection of pollution levy; (2) doubling levy rates for newly established firms who failed to meet the standard; (3) overdue fines; and (4) fines for firms violating standards and causing damages.

Sources: Yang et al. (1998); Editorial Committee of China Environmental Yearbook (1993–98).

11

Table 1.5   Pollution levy from different sectors in China (RMB million yuan)

Year	Total	Metall.	Chem.	Light	Textile	Power	Coal	TVE*	Other
1985	931	172	184	175	79	38	22	35	226
1986	1 190	217	231	216	101	55	25	60	281
1987	1 427	233	285	277	112	64	31	72	353
1988	1 610	252	326	312	119	77	35	102	387
1989	1 675	256	346	309	115	79	42	117	411
1990	1 752	212	370	311	116	83	42	132	425
1991	2 006	308	407	345	120	96	51	169	510
1992	2 379	353	446	418	129	105	55	231	642
1993	2 680	890	389	330	106	89	46	252	580
1994	3 098	634	412	387	112	117	466	343	627

Note: * Township and village enterprises.

Source: Yang et al. (1998).

China's pollution levy system has its peculiar characteristics. On the collection side, the government sets an emission standard for the firm and the firm is subject to an emission levy if its emission violates the standard.[11] The system uses a 'markup' based on the percentage deviations from discharge standards for effluent concentrations. If one source discharges multiple pollutants, levies are charged only on the pollutant which incurs the highest levy from each source. As this pollutant is cleaned up, the levy will shift to the next pollutant in order of levies.

On the outlay side, the revenue collected is earmarked for environmental protection. Initially 80 percent of the fee was freely returned to individual enterprises contributing to finance pollution abatement activities. The authority moves to collectively subsidise some 'important' projects, and gradually turns the subsidy into a loan, although it is exempt of repayment in certain circumstances.

This system has received heavy critiques. For example, it is argued that the levy rate is too low to give firms an incentive to comply with the environmental regulation. Thus, from some critics' point of view, the levy is merely a local financing mechanism and ineffective as a regulation instrument. Moreover, the strictness of enforcement is thought to vary widely, so factories in different regions may face very different penalties for polluting (Qu 1991; NEPA 1994; Shibli and Markandya 1995; Wang and Lu 1997). However, some studies show that the pollution levy system has played an important role in protecting China's water environment from further deterioration (Dasgupta et al. 1996, Wang and Wheeler 1996). The econometric analysis in Chapter 4 of this book also confirms the effectiveness of China's pollution levy system.

1.3.2 Economic Instruments for Global Warming Policy

Before discussing economic instruments for greenhouse policy, several characteristics of the global warming problem should be mentioned. The first is that 'it is a global problem'; and the second is that 'both the extent of any climate change and the nature of its effects are uncertain' (Fisher et al. 1996). In addition, it is a dynamic process and has very long time horizons. These features have important implications for global warming policy. Because global warming policy can be classified as national, regional and global policies, almost all the economic instruments mentioned in Table 1.1 can be candidates to address the issue. However, only those frequently discussed instruments are introduced in this subsection.

International carbon tax
Two types of carbon taxes have been proposed to tackle the global warming problem. First, an international agency would be established to collect taxes

from nation states according to an international agreement. For reasons of cost-effectiveness in achieving CO_2 emissions target, the tax rate should be equal across countries (Fisher et al. 1996). As the tax is collected by an international agency, national sovereignty and tax revenue distribution are big concerns. Therefore, the second type, a harmonised domestic carbon tax system is proposed, that is, all countries could levy a domestic carbon tax at the same rate. This arrangement could eliminate the problem of allocating the tax revenues to participating countries under the first system. However, a uniform carbon tax system may have different effects on individual countries' economic development, although it may achieve cost-effectiveness for a certain environmental target. That is, taking account of the indirect cost of the carbon tax, a uniform tax may not be an optimal choice. Chapter 5 of this book takes a closer look at this issue.

Tradable emission permit

Carbon dioxide emission permit trading is a well ploughed area of global warming policy, for example, see Tietenberg et al. (1999) for a collection of literature on this issue. Article 17 of the Kyoto Protocol explicitly states that parties from Annex B countries could 'participate in emissions trading for the purpose of fulfilling their commitments under Article 3.' It is also proposed that non-Annex B countries could participate in the trading if they agree to cap their emissions to a certain level.

Simulations show that CO_2 emission trading could effectively reduce the costs of abatement, especially when more countries, including developing countries, participate in the trading (McKibbin and Wilcoxen 1994, Zhang 2001). However, there are at least two practical questions related to the implementation of CO_2 emission trading.

First, emission trading would cause large cash flows between countries, thus heavily affecting international trade and financial markets (McKibbin and Wilcoxen 1997). Second, because a tradable permit system could have huge distributional effects on countries, how to allocate the permit is a heavily debated issue and little consensus has been achieved, especially when the developing countries are included.[12] While scholars from developing countries argue that such permits should be allocated on the basis of equal per capita emissions (Gupta and Bhandari 2000), this is objected to by developed countries. Moreover, the Protocol does not define how to allocate permits at the sub-national level. Zhang (1999) argues that individual governments should be free to devise their own methods of allocating the permits due to concerns about international competitiveness. McKibbin and Wilcoxen (2000) also suggest that it should be up to individual governments to determine how to allocate permits (in their proposal, such permits are termed emission endowments).

Joint implementation and clean development mechanism

Although joint implementation (JI) is not specifically defined by the United Nations Framework Convention on Climate Change, its Article 4.2(a) is often referred to as the provision of JI: '... developed country Parties and other Parties included in Annex I ... may implement such policies and measures jointly with other Parties and may assist other Parties in contributing to the achievement of the objective of the Convention ...'

In the Kyoto Protocol, the concept of JI was narrowed down to refer to joint activities carried out among Annex I countries (Article 6), while the activities involving both Annex I and non-Annex I countries were referred to as the clean development mechanism (CDM, Article 12).

The Marrakesh Accords, adopted by the Seventh Conference of Parties (COP7) held in Marrakesh in October and November 2001, define four types of emissions permits associated with JI or CDM. A JI host country converts an appropriate number of its assigned amount units (AAUs), which are determined by its commitment, to emissions reduction units (ERUs) on a one-to-one basis, which can be transferred to the investing country. On the other hand, CDM projects generate certified emission reductions (CERs). The fourth one, removal units (RMUs), is generated by the enhancing 'sinks' of carbon dioxide – forests or other mechanisms that remove carbon dioxide from the atmosphere.

Joint implementation and the clean development mechanism can be broadly defined as an attempt to reduce the overall cost of achieving a given level of global greenhouse gas emission abatement. There are three possible ways to implement JI or CDM. First, countries could pool their resources in a fund, from which investment would then be made. Second, investment arrangements could be made directly between countries on a bilateral or multilateral basis. Third, investment could be made by private sectors to meet emission targets set by national governments (Jones 1994). In some sense, JI and CDM can be viewed as a barter trade of CO_2 reduction credits, with countries making investment in exchange for credits of net emission reduction in host countries.

Theoretically, JI and CDM could greatly save developed countries' abatement cost (Barrett 1992; Burniaux et al. 1992a). Developing countries could also benefit from JI and CDM through increased access to more advanced pollution control technologies and funds. JI and CDM also help reduce carbon emission leakage that can result from unilateral abatement actions (Jones 1994). It seems a flexible instrument that avoids the distribution problems associated with tradable emissions permits or taxation.

However, because of asymmetric information, participants (both investing and host countries) in JI or CDM projects have an incentive to misreport emission reductions. As a result, hypothetical reductions may be large while actual reductions are most likely to be small (Wirl et al. 1998). In addition, although CDM seems a win–win–win instrument for developed and developing countries and the environment, developing countries are concerned about (1) lack of capacity to negotiate fair contracts with CDM investors from Annex I countries; (2) using up all low-cost abatement options while leaving them only high-cost options when they are required to reduce their own emissions; (3) offsetting reductions in current development aid budgets; and (4) effects on national sovereignty as developed countries may use CDM to interfere in their internal affairs (Zhang 2000a). In addition, as CDM involves searching out partners, negotiating terms and getting approval from certain international agencies, it may incur high transaction costs.

In addition to the above pure forms of economic instruments, some hybrid policies have been proposed. For example, McKibbin and Wilcoxen (2000) advanced the so-called McKibbin–Wilcoxen Proposal to address the issue of encouraging participation by developing countries. They suggest a coordinated but decentralised system of national permit trading systems with a fixed internationally negotiated price for permits. A permanent endowment of emission right is allocated to each country; beyond the endowment, the government of each country could sell an annual emission permit to firms at the negotiated price, that is, the permit price is equivalent to a tax on additional emissions. The endowment for developing countries could be set far higher than the current amount they emit. Therefore developing country firms would not need to buy additional permits in the short or medium run. However, the endowment has a positive present price, because the holders of the endowment foresee that as long as the countries keep growing, the endowment will eventually become a binding constraint. This gives incentives for carbon abatement in developing countries through price signals without imposing large short- or medium-term costs in these economies.

1.4   SELECTION OF ECONOMIC INSTRUMENTS

Theoretically, price-based instruments (represented by the emission tax system) and quantity-based instruments (represented by the tradable permit system) could achieve exactly the same results. As illustrated in Figure 1.2, if the government imposes a pollution tax at the rate of t^*, firms will discharge the optimal pollution q_1^* and q_2^*, and total optimal pollution Q^* can be achieved. Alternatively, if the government issues emission permits totalled Q^* and allows firms to trade their permits, firms will end with pollution levels of q_1^* and q_2^*, and the permit price p^* will be the same as the tax rate t^*. However, in reality, these two types of instruments may have different requirements and result in different consequences. As a result, choosing appropriate instruments is an important issue in environmental policy-making. Moreover, the first-best outcome – welfare maximisation – is usually not attainable because of uncertainty, pre-existing distortions and other imperfect conditions. Some such factors are discussed as follows.

1.4.1 Information Requirement and Uncertainty

The first difference between price- and quantity-based instruments is their requirement for information. Environmental policies are often specified by a set of quantitative requirements, for example reduction in emissions. To design a quantity-based instrument, a government need only transform the environmental goal into operational quantitative rules,[13] that is, total permits and initial allocation of permits, and let the market do the rest. On the other hand, designing a price-based instrument requires information on firms' behaviour in order to establish the relationship between tax or charge and the required quantity target, which is often costly.[14]

Although designing quantity-based instruments seems to require less information, in many cases there is a high degree of uncertainty regarding the appropriate quantity target. In the case of global warming, opinions about the future trend and impact of CO_2 emissions and climate change have been very diverse. Chapter 7 of this book will show the different CO_2 emission projections and impact estimations. Because of these uncertanties, the CO_2 emission control target is a highly debatable issue.

Uncertainties about the benefits and costs of reducing CO_2 emissions bring about different outcomes under these two types of instruments. A tradable permit system could maintain the benefit within a certain range by controlling the total amount of permits while leaving the cost of achieving the target very uncertain. On the other hand, an emission tax may give a clear signal of abatement costs to firms, but leave the resultant emissions uncertain. Weitzman (1974) and Fishelson (1976) find that the relative advantage of instruments depends on the curvature of marginal cost and marginal benefit of reducing emissions. If the marginal benefit curve is steeper than the marginal cost curve, a quantity-based instrument is preferred because deviation from the desired quantity could result in huge damage; by contrast a steeper marginal cost curve favours a price-based instrument because fixing quantity could cause very uncertain abatement costs. This result is termed Weitzman's Rule. If only the benefits of abatement are subject to uncertainty, both instruments would be identical. However, if uncertainties to marginal benefit and cost are related, Stavins (1996) finds that uncertainty of benefits also matters. Specifically, a positive (negative) correlation tends to favour the quantity (price) instruments and, theoretically, these effects can overwhelm the recommendation based on relative-slopes. However, these findings are based on partial equilibrium settings, thus they need to be examined in a general equilibrium framework, which will be the task of Chapter 3.

1.4.2 Pre-existing Distortions and Use of Pollution Charges

Difference also arises from the revenues generated from both types of instruments and their uses. From the aspect of revenue-generation, only a permit trading system with initial permits auctioned could be equivalent to a tax system. Because revenues from emission taxes can be used to replace existing distorting taxes, they can obtain 'double dividend', that is, less distortion and less environmental damage (Pearce 1991). By contrast, a permit trading system, except for auctioned permit trading, usually does not have revenue to generate such effects. This issue will be explored in Chapter 2 more broadly, that is, considering the possibility of earmarking pollution charges.

Moreover, tax and permit trading systems have different distributional effects. Different allocation of initial permits may bring about different cost burdens on firms. In the case of an emission tax, the revenues can be used in different ways which leads to different consequences for various players in an economy. This will be more obvious in the case of international cooperation like global warming policy where income flows across country borders, which will be discussed in more detail in Chapter 5.

1.4.3 International Cooperation

In addition to the distributional effects mentioned above, national sovereignty should be taken into account when choosing instruments of international cooperation in the field of environmental protection. From this aspect, a more decentralised instrument such as the harmonised domestic tax or even differential domestic tax and the decentralised permit trading scheme proposed by McKibbin and Wilcoxen (2000) might be superior to those centralised instruments such as international tradable permits or the first type of international emission tax, as will be seen in Chapters 5 and 8. It should be borne in mind that 'policy instruments that appear impeccable from the vantage point of research institutions, but consistently prove infeasible in real-world political institutions, can hardly be considered "optimal"' (Stavins 2000a).

1.5   THE STRUCTURE OF THE BOOK

This book aims at refining the theory of environmental policy choice and developing feasible and efficient instruments to control carbon dioxide emissions in China, taking account of some imperfections, especially the uncertain world environment. It consists of two parts: a general analysis of economic instruments, and the application in CO_2 emission control.

The first part presents the discussion of pollution control policies in general equilibrium settings. The focus of this part is on the comparison of pollution taxes and tradable permits in certain kinds of circumstances with imperfections. It consists of three chapters – Chapters 2 to 4.

Chapter 2 systematically discusses the consequences of different uses of pollution charges. In addition to examining the 'double-dividend' hypothesis, the possibility of earmarking pollution charges (and permit sales revenues) for environmental projects and its implication on the optimal tax rate are also considered. Conditions of justifying different uses of pollution charges are developed.

Chapter 3 considers environmental policy choices under uncertainty in a general equilibrium framework. Weitzman's rule is examined and re-established under certain conditions, namely, risk neutrality and utility separability. Further complications such as risk aversion and earmarking are also considered.

Chapter 4 reviews China's environmental policy, especially the pollution levy system. Two questions are asked: are China's environmental policies effective in the sense of giving incentives for firms to reduce their emissions? Are they efficient in the sense that they are formulated according to welfare maximisation principles? To answer these questions, two methods are employed. First, the changes in pollutant discharges are decomposed to find the possible causes of such changes. Second, using a panel data model, a system of demand and supply functions of pollution rights based on the theory of equilibrium pollution is estimated to capture the behaviour of firms and governments.

The second part of the book brings the discussion into the area of global warming policies. It consists of four chapters – Chapters 5 to 8.

Chapter 5 discusses a number of schemes of global warming policies. Tradable permits, harmonised domestic tax and differential tax are discussed in a theoretical general equilibrium model, and simulated with a simplified numerical model.

Chapter 6 develops a dynamic general equilibrium model, G-Cubed-T, for the purpose of analysing proper policy choices of CO_2 emissions control in China, and describes its structure and parameter estimation and calibration. The model is composed of three regions: China, the United States and rest of the world. It is based on a reduced version of the G-Cubed model of McKibbin and Wilcoxen (1999). For this book, a new database for China is used, and more importantly, a feedback from climate change to real economic activity is included in the model.

Using the model, Chapter 7 develops several scenarios about China's future CO_2 emissions based on different assumptions about China's future economic, demographic and technological paths.

Chapter 8 investigates two issues. First, what is the appropriate target of CO_2 emission control for China? Second, how to achieve this target? Different policy alternatives for China are simulated using the G-Cubed-T model.

The final chapter concludes the findings in this book and provides suggestions for future work.

To conclude this introduction, a summary of the main results of this book is provided as follows. This book argues that the use of pollution charges is an integral part of environmental policy-making. Earmarking such revenues for environmental activities could be a better choice if marginal utility of the environment is high and the amount of revenues small. It is found that the conventional interpretation of Pigouvian tax is not correct if the possibility of earmarking is taken into account. An optimal tax rate is not necessarily equal to the marginal damage cost of pollution. It is also found that Weitzman's rule is not directly applicable in a general equilibrium setting unless under strong assumptions – risk neutrality and utility separability. Contrary to the usual criticism, the empirical result in this book shows that China's environmental policy has been effective.

In the arena of global warming policy, a differentiated emission tax is a better choice than a uniform tax to achieve the second best outcome, and an emission trading system could improve the welfare further. Simulations of the G-Cubed-T model confirm this argument. Model projections show that China will become the world's largest CO_2 emitter in the next 20 to 50 years, although the per capita level is still quite low. Moreover, given the current information, it is not likely that China will emit less CO_2 than the current level over a fairly long period of time, for example 50 years. In terms of emission control target, one based on the per capita emissions standard seems the most favourable target for China, while a target based on the equal-burden principle is the minimum that China should accept if it is to join an international agreement for targeting CO_2 emissions.

NOTES

1. Huber et al. (1998) divide policy instruments into three categories: control-oriented, market-oriented and litigation-oriented instruments based on decentralisation and flexibility in individual decision-making. Control-oriented instruments are the most centralised system and have the lowest flexibility, while

litigation-oriented instruments are at the other end. In addition to CAC and economic instruments, Industry Commission (1997) suggests another type of instrument: suasive measures, that is, addressing environmental problems through education, training, social pressure and negotiation.

2. This is mainly determined by two factors: diminishing marginal product at firm level and downward sloping demand curve at market level.

3. MEC should be interpreted in a broader way, including both marginal environmental damage cost, and marginal user cost in the case of using non-renewable resources (Pearce and Warford 1993; Panayotou 1994, 1995).

4. This can be shown as follows. Suppose the benefit of polluting is $B(Q)$ where Q is the amount of pollutant discharged, and the private cost of shipping the pollutant is $C(Q)$, then the net benefit is $B(Q) - C(Q)$. If the firm is allowed to discharge pollutant up to the amount of $\overline{Q}$, it has to abate the pollution at the cost of $AC(Q-\overline{Q})$ for any pollution Q above the allowed $\overline{Q}$. A profit maximisation firm would operate such that $B'(Q) - C'(Q) - AC'(Q-\overline{Q}) = 0$, that is, $MB - MPC - MAC = 0$, or $MNB = MAC$.

5. Theoretically, CAC instruments could achieve cost-effectiveness by specifying a desired pollution target for each firm. However, doing so requires very detailed information which, in general, is not available to the government. The costs of gathering such information would be prohibitively high.

6. This argument does not contradict the previous statement that EIs require less information and lower administrative cost than CACs. The previous statement is established in the case where both EIs and CACs are required to achieve the social optimum. However, if comparing an EI with an existing CAC which does not intend to achieve the social optimum, it might be the case that the EI requires more information and incurs higher administrative cost.

7. There is little consensus in the literature about categories of economic instruments. For example, Panayotou (1994, 1995) divides the instruments into seven categories: property rights, market creation, fiscal instruments, charge systems, financial instruments, liability instruments, and performance bonds and deposit refund systems; Industry Commission (1997) distinguishes five categories: charges and taxes, subsidies and tax concessions, financial enforcement incentives, deposit refund systems, and property rights and market creation; Stavins (2000a, 2000b) identifies four categories: pollution charge, tradable permits, market barrier reductions and government subsidy reductions. The classification in the text is close to that in Huber et al. (1998).

8. SEPA, with the ministerial authority in the central government, was restructured in 1998 from the National Environmental Protection Agency (NEPA), signalling China's serious concern about environmental issues.

9. The formal China's Environmental Protection Law promulgated in 1989 specifies similar requirements in Clause 28.

10. 'Excess discharge' refers to pollutant discharge that violates the effluent or emission standard, that is, exceeding the limit set by the standard.

11. It is not an offence to discharge pollutants exceeding the limit set by standards. SEPA regulations specify variations in effluent standards by sector and fees by pollutant. With the approval of SEPA, local authorities may raise both standards

and fees above the nationally-mandated level.

12. Presumably the allocation of permits among Annex B countries has been specified in the Kyoto Protocol – their quantified emission limitation or reduction commitment is defined in Annex B to the Protocol.

13. Experiences show that absolute baselines, rather than relative ones, should be used as the point of departure for tradable permit systems to avoid 'paper trades' (Stavins 2000a).

14. Another closely related factor is transaction costs, or administrative costs, among which the cost of obtaining information is one item. Obviously the two types of instruments have different transaction costs and incidence on governments and firms. It seems that governments bear more administrative costs under an emission tax system, while firms bear more costs under a tradable emission permit system. Stavins (1995) and Conrad and Kohn (1996) find that transaction costs tend to lower the trading volume. Contrary to Coase's Theorem, Stavins (1995) finds that the equilibrium will be affected by the initial allocation of permits because of transaction costs. Concerning the impact of transaction costs and market power on the efficiency of the permit market, Bertram (1992) argues that a tradable permit regime to combat atmospheric pollution is likely to work better at a global than at a national level, whereas carbon taxes are likely to succeed at a national level. Schmutzler and Goulder (1997) show that the first-best can be achieved with a pure emissions tax only if perfect monitoring can be conducted. However, given the fact that perfect monitoring is very costly, a pure emission tax is not optimal if monitoring cost is an increasing function of the output level.

PART I

Economics of Pollution Control Policy

2. Earmarking of Pollution Charges and the Sub-optimality of the Pigouvian Tax*

2.1 INTRODUCTION

One of the textbook approaches to internalise the negative externality of economic activities is to impose the so-called Pigouvian tax on such activities. As illustrated in Figures 1.1 and 1.2, the standard Pigouvian solution calls for 'a tax (subsidy) per unit on the externality-generating activity equal to its marginal external damage (benefit)' (Baumol and Oates 1988, p. 55). Under this tax scheme, the social cost is embodied in the private cost so that the social optimum can be achieved in a competitive market with private ownership. However, this standard version of Pigouvian tax overlooks the question of how to use the tax revenue. It treats the tax as if the revenue vaporises after it is collected. In his classical work *The Economics of Welfare*, Pigou ([1920] 1938) presented at least two different revenue schemes. On the one hand, he seems to assume externality taxes are fiscal taxes equivalent to the damage imposed; on the other hand, he indicates that they work as 'extraordinary restraints' and are to be earmarked for a special purpose. Later he clarifies that the taxation of negative externalities raises revenues to be spent on the provision of positive externalities (Pigou [1928] 1949, p. 99):

> When maladjustments have come about ... it is always possible, on the assumption that no administrative costs are involved, to correct them by imposing appropriate rates of tax on resources employed in uses that tend to be pushed too far and employing the proceeds to provide bounties, at appropriate rates, on use of the opposite class.

Strangely many environmental economists neglect Pigou's point of view, although they often label a pollution charge in his name. Perhaps Mikael Skou Andersen is the only exception. He writes (Andersen 1994, p. 37):

> It is surprising that modern externality theory hardly deals with the question of what should happen to the revenue from externality taxes, and that Pigou's tax-bounty scheme has largely been neglected. Externality taxation is instead treated

in terms of a partial equilibrium analysis, where its implications for marginal costs are analysed extensively, but without considering whether or not it makes a difference if the revenue is earmarked or not. In fact the possibility of earmarking has been subject to much criticism.

In contrast to earmarking the pollution charges in the environment, some economists propose the use of such revenues in reducing pre-existing distortions. This idea is called 'double-dividend hypothesis', which suggests that increasing taxes on polluting activities can provide two kinds of benefit. The first is an improvement in the environment, and the second an improvement in economic efficiency from the use of these revenues to reduce other taxes, such as income taxes that distort labour supply and savings (Pearce 1991).[1] Another related topic is the Solow–Hartwick rule for the use of resource rents (Hartwick 1977, 1978; Solow 1974a, 1974b). If exhaustible resources are being extracted efficiently and all rents from resources go to capital accumulation, it is possible for the economy to have positive and constant consumption over time. Although it may lead to intergenerational equity, the rule itself and the constant utility criterion are too restrictive to be efficient in distributing intertemporal resources and thereby welfare (Asako 1980). Asako (1980) shows that introduction of pollution-abatement investment may cure the problem of non-feasible solutions in some cases. However, the pollution charges are not explicitly discussed in these works.

According to the above discussion, at least three taxation programmes are at hand. Firstly, under a *pure pollution tax scheme*, the revenue from taxing polluting activities is used as a lump-sum transfer to the public, with no spending on the environment. This is suggested by the conventional Pigouvian tax scheme. Secondly, by contrast, under a *(fully) earmarked pollution levy scheme*, the whole of the revenue is used for environmental purposes. Lastly, a *general tax-income scheme*, or following Pigou, a *tax-bounty scheme*, does not impose these prior restrictions on spending. This chapter attempts to examine these arrangements in both partial and general equilibrium settings, and to find the optimal pollution tax scheme. The rest of the chapter is organised as follows: the next two sections analyse these schemes in static partial and general equilibrium settings; the discussion then moves into a dynamic general equilibrium analysis of the tax schemes; and the final section summarises the findings.

2.2   STATIC PARTIAL EQUILIBRIUM ANALYSIS

2.2.1   Pollution Tax/Levy Imposed on Product

It is easier to begin the analysis by assuming that the pollution tax or levy has the form of a product tax or levy. Suppose a firm's cost function is $C = C(q)$, where q is the quantity of its product, with the property that $C' \geq 0$ and $C'' \leq 0$. The damage caused by pollution from the production process is $D = D(q)$ with the property that $D(0) = 0$, $D' \geq 0$ and $D'' \leq 0$. The price of the product is p, and the government imposes a product tax on the firm at the rate of t to internalise the external cost. To maximise its profit, $\pi = (p - t)q - C(q)$, the firm should meet the following first order condition:

$$p - t = C'(q). \qquad (2.1)$$

Therefore the firm's response function to a given tax rate t can be written as $q = q(t)$. A reasonable property of this response function is $q' \leq 0$. The social planner is to maximise the net social benefit, $pq(t) - C(q(t)) - D(q(t))$, by choosing an appropriate tax rate. And the first order condition gives:

$$p - D'(q) = C'(q). \qquad (2.2)$$

Comparing eq. (2.1) and (2.2) gives the optimal tax

$$t^* = D'(q^*).$$

This is the origin of the Pigouvian tax: the tax rate should be equal to the marginal damage cost. In the above social planner's problem, the collected tax revenue is treated as a lump-sum transfer from the firm to the general public, and the net social benefit is not changed by this use of the revenue. However, if the revenue can be used on pollution control activities, the optimal tax rate may be different.

For simplicity, it is assumed that the pollution eliminating function is $E = E(S)$, where S is the spending on pollution control, and E is the reduction in damage in monetary terms.[2] It is assumed that $E(S)$ has the following properties:

$$E' \geq 0, \ E'' \leq 0, \ E(0) = 0, \ E'(0) \geq 1. \qquad (2.3)$$

Under this assumption, a pure pollution tax scheme is not optimal because the marginal net benefit of environmental spending is positive at least over some range of spending. Therefore the social planner has to choose an appropriate level of environmental investment in addition to the tax rate. Suppose the levy rate is τ, the firm's response function to a certain levy rate can be derived as in the pure tax case, $q = q(\tau)$. Hence the social planner's problem becomes:

$$\max_{\tau,S} \quad pq(\tau) - C(q(\tau)) - D(q(\tau)) + E(S) - S$$
$$\text{s.t.} \quad S \le \tau q(\tau)$$

The Lagrangian for this problem can be written as:

$$\pounds = pq(\tau) - C(q(\tau)) - D(q(\tau)) + E(S) - S + \lambda(\tau q(\tau) - S).$$

From this Lagrangian, it is clear that a pure pollution tax cannot be a better solution because it adds one more constraint, $S = 0$, to the problem. The Kuhn–Tucker conditions are therefore:

$$pq'(\tau) - C'(q)q'(\tau) - D'(q)q'(\tau) + \lambda(q(\tau) + \tau q'(\tau)) = 0 ; \qquad (2.4)$$
$$E'(S) - 1 - \lambda = 0; \qquad (2.5)$$
$$\lambda(\tau q(\tau) - S) = 0, \quad \lambda \ge 0 \text{ if } S = \tau q(\tau) . \qquad (2.6)$$

There are two possible solutions: the budget constraint is binding or sluggish. If the constraint is binding, a fully earmarked levy scheme is optimal, $S = \tau q(\tau)$ and $\lambda \ge 0$ according to eq. (2.6),[3] which, in turn, implies $E' \ge 1$ from eq. (2.5). Using $p - C'(q) = \tau$, eq. (2.4) becomes

$$\tau q'(\tau) - D'(q)q'(\tau) + (E' - 1)(q(\tau) + \tau q'(\tau)) = 0.$$

And the optimal tax rate can be written as

$$\tau^* = \frac{dD}{dq} - (E' - 1)\frac{d(\tau q(\tau))}{dq} = \frac{dD}{dq} - \frac{d(E - S)}{dS}\frac{dS}{dq}$$

The above expression reflects two effects of the changes in production: the impact on the pollution damages and the impact on tax revenues. The first effect is captured by marginal damage cost, dD/dq, and the second effect is relevant because the environmental spending is financed by a pollution tax which is affected by the quantity of product. Note that E' is the marginal direct benefit of environmental investment, and $E' - 1$ is the marginal net benefit; while $d(\tau q)/dq = dS/dq$ is the marginal tax revenue of production. Therefore, $(E' - 1)d(\tau q)/dq$ or dS/dq is the marginal net benefit of environmental spending caused by changes in production. Thus the above formula just repeats the usual doctrine: the optimal tax rate is equal to the marginal (external) cost.

To clearly see the difference between this formula and Pigouvian tax, the optimal tax rate can be rewritten as:

$$\tau^* = \frac{D'}{E' + (E' - 1)/\varepsilon}$$

where $\varepsilon = q'(\tau)\tau/q(\tau)$ is the output elasticity of the pollution levy rate. It can be seen that the usual Pigouvian tax rate is not likely to be justified even in this static partial equilibrium setting. If $E' > 1$, that is, excluding the case discussed in note (3), the optimal tax/levy rate is not equal to the marginal damage cost, unless $\varepsilon = -1$. If $\varepsilon > -1$, that is, the output is inelastic to the tax/levy rate, the social planner can get more revenue by raising the tax rate, therefore the optimal tax rate is above the marginal damage cost. By contrast, if the output is elastic, the optimal tax rate will be below the marginal damage cost. However, the tax rate can not be zero or negative as $E' + (E' - 1)/\varepsilon > 0$ when $\varepsilon < -1$. Intuitively, if there was no revenue used for environmental investment, it would be back to the usual problem where the solution is that the tax rate equals the marginal damage cost.

These discussions can be summarised in the following theorem.

Theorem 2.1 *If condition $E'(0) > 1$ holds, a pure Pigouvian pollution tax is not optimal. In addition, if $E'(S) \geq 1$, when $S = \tau q$, a fully earmarked pollution levy scheme is optimal. In this case, if $E'(S) > 1$, the optimal tax/levy rate is larger than, equal to or less than the marginal damage cost if the output is inelastic, unit-elastic or elastic to tax/levy.*

Proof. See above discussion. ∎

When the budget constraint is sluggish, $\lambda = 0$ according to eq. (2.6). And using $p - C'(q) = \tau$, conditions (2.4) and (2.5) become:

$$\tau^* = D'(q) \text{ and } E'(S) = 1.$$

Because the budget constraint is now not binding, the decision in environmental investment has no effect on the production side. Therefore the optimal tax rate has the usual form. In this case, only a part of the tax/levy revenue is used for environmental purposes. Therefore neither a pure tax scheme nor a fully earmarked levy scheme is optimal. However, if the net benefit of spending all levy revenue is positive, that is, $E(\tau q) > \tau q$, an earmarked levy system is better than a pure tax system. In combination with Theorem 2.1, the following result can be derived:

Result 2.2 *If $E(S) > S$ holds when $S = \tau q$ and the tax can be treated as a pure transfer, an earmarked pollution levy is always better than a pure* *pollution tax.*

The above result may seem trivial, however, it is very important to policy makers. In the real world, there may not be sufficient information to decide the optimal tax/levy rate and optimal amount of revenue being used for environmental purposes. The theorems suggest they could be determined by analysing individual pollution control projects. This was a popular practice in European countries during the 1960s and 1970s: '... the authorities have employed schedules of fees that generate revenues sufficient to cover the costs of public pollution-abatement programs', and criticised as 'a most unsatisfactory method for the determination of fee schedules, for it is not based on any goal for the changes in behaviour that the fees are presumably designed to induce' (Baumol et al. 1979, p.375). However, according to the discussion here, it is not totally groundless.

In China, only part of the pollution charges (about 80 percent) goes to specific pollution control projects, and the remainder goes to local environmental protection authorities for subsidising some environmental protection personnel and purchasing related equipment. This practice is still preferable to a pure pollution tax system, which can be seen by rewriting the objective function:

$$W(\tau) = pq(\tau) - C(q(\tau)) - \alpha\tau q(\tau) + E(\alpha\tau q(\tau)) - D(q(\tau))$$
$$= V(\tau) + E(\alpha\tau q(\tau)) - \alpha\tau q(\tau),$$

where α is the fraction of pollution charges used for environmental projects, $0 < \alpha \le 1$. As long as $E(\alpha\tau q) \ge \alpha\tau q$, it always gives $W(\tau) \ge V(\tau)$.

2.2.2 Pollution Tax/Levy Imposed on Emissions

This subsection tries to emphasise two points. First, the above derived propositions are independent of the forms of emission tax/levy. This is obvious because there are no other distortions in the production. A levy or tax on product can be transformed into a levy or tax on emissions. Second, from the discussion of a levy/tax on emissions, it becomes clearer that, if earmarking of tax/levy revenue for environmental purpose is considered, the pollution damages need not be fully internalised into the producers' decision-making process under certain circumstances. A formal discussion is given below.

Given pollution tax rate t, the firm chooses an output level to maximise profit, $pq - C(q) - tD(q)$. The first order condition of the firm's profit maximisation problem is $p - C'(q^*) - tD'(q^*) = 0$, which gives the firm's response function to the tax, $q = q(t)$. Under the pure tax scheme, the social planner chooses a tax rate to maximise $pq(t) - C(q(t)) - D(q)$. The corresponding first order condition is $(p - C'(q) - D'(q))q'(t) = 0$.

Comparing these two first order conditions, and assuming $q'(t) \neq 0$, gives $t^* = 1$, which is equivalent to the Pigouvian tax: the tax rate is set at a level so that the damage caused by pollution is fully embodied in the firm's decision-making process. However, following the same reasoning, as long as condition (2.3) holds, this scheme cannot be optimal. The social planner should adopt the general tax-income scheme to maximise the net benefit, so that the problem can be written as:

$$\max_{\tau,S} \quad p(\tau) - C(q(\tau)) - D(q(\tau)) + E(S) - S$$
$$\text{s.t.} \quad S \leq \tau D(q(\tau))$$

As before, the condition for a binding constraint is $E'(S) \geq 1$ when S is equal to all tax revenue. In this case, a fully earmarked levy scheme is optimal. Denote the pollution elasticity of tax/levy as

$$\eta = \frac{dD(q(\tau))}{d\tau} \frac{\tau}{D} = \frac{D'q'\tau}{D},$$

and the optimal levy rate can be written as

$$\tau^* = \frac{1}{E' + (E' - 1)/\eta}.$$

If $E' > 1$, that is, strictly binding constraint, the optimal tax rate is larger than, equal to, or less than, one when the pollution is inelastic, unit-elastic, or elastic. This result has a strong implication: if the tax/levy revenue is required to be fully earmarked for an environmental purpose, an optimal tax/levy programme does not necessarily suggest the pollution damage should be fully internalised into the producer's decision-making process.

2.3 STATIC GENERAL EQUILIBRIUM ANALYSIS

In the previous section, the consumption is suppressed and the objective function does not fully capture the social welfare, taking consideration only of the firm's profit and environmental impacts. This section extends the investigation to an economy-wide analysis of pollution charges. First a general equilibrium framework is formally set up, and then the optimal pollution tax/bounty scheme is explored, followed by comparison of pollution

taxes and emission permits and discussion of the pollution control policy with
pre-existing distortions.

2.3.1 The Model

There are three agents in the economy: a firm, a consumer and a government.
Their behaviour is described as follows.

Firm

The firm employs labour (L), and environmental capacity whose use may
produce harmful pollutants that have negative effects on the household's
utility. The unit is carefully chosen such that the environmental factor used in
the firm can be represented by the pollutant emissions (D). For simplicity, as
the model is static at this stage, capital is not considered and will be included
later in a dynamic model. However, it can be shown that including capital
and other input factors will not affect the analytical result. Thus the
production function can be written as $Y = f(L, D)$,[4] which has the usual
properties:

$$f_L > 0, \ f_{LL} < 0, \ f_D > 0, \ f_{DD} > 0, \ f_{LD} = f_{DL} > 0,$$

where a subscript denotes the partial derivative, for example, $f_L = \partial f(L,D)/\partial L$, $f_{LL} = \partial f_L(L,D)/\partial L$, and so on.

Supposing a pollution tax or levy is imposed at the rate of t, and
normalising the output price, the firm's profit maximisation problem is:

$$\max_{L,D} \quad f(L,D) - wL - tD,$$

where w is the real wage rate. The first order conditions for the firm's profit
maximisation problem are:

$$f_L(L,D) = w, \quad f_D(L,D) = t. \tag{2.7}$$

Household

A representative household maximises its utility subject to the budget
constraint. The utility comes from the consumption good (C), leisure ($\tilde{L}$),
and amenity of the environment (E). Leisure is defined as the difference
between total time endowment ($\bar{L}$) and supply of labour (L). Therefore the
utility function can be written as:

$$U(C, \bar{L} - L, E) \tag{2.8}$$

It is assumed that the utility function has the usual properties, that is,

$$U_C > 0, \ U_{CC} < 0, \ U_{\tilde{L}} > 0, \ U_{\tilde{L}\tilde{L}} < 0, \ U_E > 0, \ U_{EE} < 0.$$

It is also assumed that the household owns labour and the firm, therefore its income comes from labour income (wL) and profit of the firm (π). It also receives transfers from government (G). Thus the household's utility maximisation problem is to choose C and L to maximise (2.8) subject to

$$C \leq \pi(w,t) + wL + G . \tag{2.9}$$

And the first order conditions are:

$$U_C = \lambda, \ U_{\tilde{L}} = \lambda w , \tag{2.10}$$

where λ is the Lagrangian multiplier of constraint (2.9).

Government
The government maximises social welfare which could be represented by the household's utility function (2.8) through various government instruments. One of them is the exertion of state ownership over the environment, that is, it decides the supply of environment. The government has two options to do this: setting the amount of environmental supply and letting the market decide the price of the environmental good; or setting the price – environmental tax – and letting the market determine the quantity. They are equivalent in this model with complete information. The case where uncertainty exists will be discussed in the next chapter. The government also decides how to allocate the environmental charge revenue on the environment and whether to transfer to the household.

In a similar way to leisure, environmental quality is defined as the difference between environmental endowment ($\overline{E}$) and supply of environmental absorption capacity of pollution (D). Investment in environment can also increase the environmental amount. Therefore,

$$E = \overline{E} - D + e(S) , \tag{2.11}$$

where S is the spending on environmental projects, and $e(S)$ the pollution abatement or environment improvement function. It is assumed that $e(0) = 0$, $e' > 0$ and $e'' < 0$.

In line with the above mentioned pollution tax schemes, the government's budget constraint has three forms:

1. As the pure tax scheme suggests, all revenue is transferred to the household. In this case, the budget constraint is: $G = tD$ and $S = 0$.
2. All revenue from supplying environmental capacity is earmarked for the environment, thus the budget constraint becomes: $S = tD$ and $G = 0$.
3. Following the general tax-income scheme, there are no specific prior restrictions on spending on consumption goods and the environment. The budget constraint is therefore: $S \geq 0$ and $S + G \leq tD$. Note that this constraint could end up with $S > tD$, therefore the transfer G could be negative. This case will be discussed in detail later.

It is clear that both the pure tax scheme and the fully earmarked levy scheme are actually special cases of this general arrangement. The pure tax scheme is reached by imposing one more constraint, namely, $S = 0$; similarly, under the earmarked levy scheme, a different constraint, $S = tD$, is imposed. According to the optimisation theory, if more constraints are imposed on a maximisation problem, that is, the feasible set for choice variables becomes smaller, and the optima of the objective function can not be increased. Therefore this gives the following result.

Theorem 2.3 *The optima of a pure pollution scheme and a fully earmarked levy scheme are no better than the optimum of the general pollution tax-income scheme.*

It could be made clearer if a centralised model is constructed. Under the general tax-income scheme, a social planner chooses C, L, D and S to maximise $U(C, \overline{L} - L, \overline{E} - D + e(S))$ subject to $C + S \leq f(L, D)$. Under the pure tax scheme, one more constraint is imposed: $S = 0$, which is replaced by $S = tD$ under the fully earmarked scheme. Appendix 2.A discusses the equivalence and difference between decentralised and centralised models.

2.3.2 The Optimal Pollution Tax-Bounty Scheme

Outlay of pollution tax/levy

The government's problem can be formally written as:

$$\max_{D,S,G} U(C, \overline{L} - L, \overline{E} - D + e(S))$$
$$\text{s.t.} \quad S + G \leq tD$$
$$C = \pi + wL + G$$
$$S \geq 0, \ G \geq 0$$

Government transfer (G) is set as a choice variable because the government anticipates that G affects the household's income, thus affecting its utility. The second constraint is added in line with this fact. The Lagrangian is:

$$\mathcal{L} = U(C, \overline{L} - L, \overline{E} - D + e(S)) + \lambda_1(tD - S - G)$$
$$+ \lambda_2(\pi + wL + G - C) + \lambda_3 S + \lambda_4 G$$

The corresponding first order conditions are:

$$U_E = \lambda_1 t, \ U_E e'(S) = \lambda_1 - \lambda_3, \ \lambda_1 = \lambda_2 + \lambda_4, \ \lambda_3 S = 0, \ \lambda_4 G = 0 \qquad (2.12)$$

Note that both λ in eq. (2.10) and λ_2 here are the marginal utility of increasing the budget to the household, and therefore should be equal.

A general tax-income scheme sets no limitation on S, that is, the constraint $G \geq 0$ could be dropped from the above problem, which is equivalent to $\lambda_4 = 0$. If an interior solution exists under a general scheme, $\lambda_3 = 0$. Thus the above conditions become:

$$U_E = \lambda_1 t, \ U_E e'(S) = \lambda_1, \ \lambda_1 = \lambda_2 = \lambda \qquad (2.13)$$

If there exists a corner solution in the general tax-income scheme, that is, $S = 0$, the pure tax scheme is justified. In this case, $\lambda_3 \geq 0$ and $\lambda_4 = 0$ as $G = tD > 0$, the first order conditions thus become:

$$U_E = \lambda_1 t, \ U_E e'(S) \leq \lambda_1, \ \lambda_1 = \lambda_2 = \lambda \qquad (2.14)$$

Theorem 2.4 *A pure pollution tax scheme is optimal if all of the following conditions are satisfied:*

(1) $U_E e'(0) \leq U_C = U_{\widetilde{L}} / f_L(L, D)$; and
(2) $1/e'(0) \geq f_D(L, D) = t$.

Proof. Using conditions (2.7), (2.10) and (2.14).   ∎

The above conditions make sense and are intuitive. Because spending on the environment will reduce the spending on consumption, the first part of condition (1) in Theorem 2.4 states that it is not optimal to invest in environmental projects if the marginal utility of environmental quality derived from environmental spending, $U_E e'(S)$, is less than the marginal utility of consumption.

Condition (1) in Theorem 2.4 also compares the marginal utility of environmental investment and the marginal utility of leisure. As spending on the environment increases, the household may want to supply more labour to increase its whole income to support a certain amount of consumption, and thus enjoy less leisure. $f_L(L,D)$ is the marginal product of labour, $1/f_L(L,D)$ is therefore the amount of labour needed to produce an extra (infinitesimal) unit of product or income. Thus this condition says it does not pay for society to invest in the environment if the resulting marginal utility is less than the marginal utility of leisure forgone to recover the extra unit of income, $U_{\tilde{L}}/f_L(L,D)$.

Condition (2) in Theorem 2.4 deals with the efficiency of environmental investment. $e'(S)$ is the marginal environmental output of spending on environmental projects, so $1/e'(S)$ is the marginal cost of environmental goods, while $f_D(L,D)$ is the marginal product or income of the environmental factor. Certainly it is not optimal to invest in the environment if the former is greater than the latter.

It is known that $e'(0)$ is a large number because $e'(S) > 0$ and $e''(S) < 0$, therefore the marginal utility of the environment (U_E) should be sufficiently low so that condition (1) holds. According to the property of the utility function, a very low U_E in turn implies that E should be very large, that is, environmental quality should be very good or environmental resources should be abundant. Unfortunately, this is not the case at present. The environmental problem has become a global issue and caused great concern, therefore the conditions are not likely to be satisfied in the real world.[5] As a result, a pure pollution tax system may not be optimal.

There is one problem with the general tax-income scheme. Theoretically, optimal spending on the environment could be larger than the tax revenue from pollution. Because the government has no other taxation revenue, this leads to $G < 0$, that is, there is a net lump sum transfer from the household to the government. In a model as simple as the one presented here, it seems that transfers from the household to the government do not cause much trouble. However, in the real world, the government should find a cost-free way to raise revenue beyond the pollution taxation revenue. If it fails to do so, it may be better to set a budget constraint for the government, that is, $S \le tD$. Clearly this will be a second-best option.

If the fully earmarked scheme is considered, $S = tD$, which implies $\lambda_3 = 0$. From $S + G = tD$, this is equivalent to $G = 0$, which implies $\lambda_4 \ge 0$. Therefore the condition (2.12) becomes

$$U_E = \lambda_1 t, \ U_E e'(S) = \lambda_1, \ \lambda_1 \ge \lambda_2 = \lambda. \tag{2.15}$$

The conditions justifying a fully earmarked pollution levy scheme are summarised in the following theorem.

Theorem 2.5 *All pollution tax/levy revenue should be used in environmental projects if all of the following conditions are satisfied:*

(1) $U_E e'(tD) \geq U_C = U_{\tilde{L}}/f_L(L,D)$;

(2) $U_E/U_C \geq f_D(L,D) = t$; and

(3) $U_E/U_{\tilde{L}} \geq f_D(L,D)/f_L(L,D) = t/w$.

Proof. Using conditions (2.7), (2.10) and (2.15).   ∎

Condition (1) in Theorem 2.5, which is opposite to condition (1) in Theorem 2.4, shows that it pays for the society to increase investment in the environment if the marginal utility of the environment resulting from environmental investment is larger than the marginal utility of consumption, or the marginal utility of leisure forgone to recover expenditure on the environment. Conditions (2) and (3) in Theorem 2.5 show that the marginal rate of substitution of consumption or leisure for environmental amenity is larger than the related marginal rate of transformation.

If some of the above three conditions are violated, the constraint for the government's budget is not binding. It turns out that the fully earmarked levy scheme is not optimal.

These three conditions are likely to be satisfied when the marginal utility of the environment is high, the pollution tax/levy or related income is small (thus the marginal output of environmental spending is high) and the marginal utility of consumption is also small. To apply these conditions, the world can be divided into several groups along three dimensions: abundance or scarcity of environmental resources; strength of pollution control; and degree of development. A rough idea is presented in Table 2.1. China falls into the group with scarce environmental resources, low pollution levy revenue and lower-medium development degree, and is therefore most likely to earmark all pollution levy revenue into environmental use.

Optimal pollution tax/levy rate
Until now the focus has been on the outlay of pollution tax/levy revenues. It is time to turn to another side of the issue: the optimal tax rate. From the first order conditions in (2.7), (2.10) and (2.13), the optimal tax rate under a general tax-income scheme can be derived as:

$$t^* = f_D = U_E/U_C = w^* U_E/U_L = 1/e'$$

Most of the above equations merely repeat the usual doctrines, and are thus not worth repeating here, except $t^* = 1/e'$, that is, the optimal tax rate

Table 2.1   Application of conditions for earmarking

Environmental resources	Development degree	Pollution tax /levy revenue	Fully earmarking?	Sample country
Abundant	Low	Low	Ambiguous	Some African countries
		High*	Not likely	
	High	Low	Ambiguous	
		High	Not likely	
Scarce	Low	Low	Likely	China
		High*	Not likely	
	High	Low	Likely	
		High	Ambiguous	

Note: *Not likely to happen in the real world.

should be equal to the marginal cost of public environment-improving or pollution-cleansing activities. It shows that the usual interpretation of the Pigouvian tax is conceptually incomplete. Typically, a Pigouvian tax rate is set according to the marginal cost of pollution damage and, when implemented, leads to an identical marginal cost of pollution abatement across firms. However, it does not say anything about the public environmental activities. Moreover, the relationship derived here has an important implication for policy-making, as discussed in partial equilibrium analysis. There is an impression that valuing environmental benefit or measuring pollution damage is highly subjective and very difficult. However, it is easier to account for the cost of environmental projects. Policy-makers may be more confident in policy design if they can plan projects according to certain environmental targets and set the pollution tax rate based on the cost analysis of these projects. It seems that most governments in the world follow this approach, although it was doubted by some environmental economists (for example, see Baumol et al. 1979).

The above relationships may be changed if there exist corner solutions where pure tax or earmarking schemes are justified. If a pure pollution tax scheme is justified, most of the relationships are maintained except that

$$t^* = 1/e'(0).$$

This has been indicated by condition (2) of Theorem 2.4. Because the marginal cost of public environment-improving or pollution-cleansing activities is very high, no tax revenue should be used in such activities, therefore the optimal tax rate is no higher than the marginal cost of environmental projects.

If a fully earmarked pollution levy scheme is justified, it is true that

$$t^* = f_D = 1/e'(tD),$$

but $\qquad t^* \leq U_E/U_C = w^* U_E/U_{\tilde{L}}.$

These have been virtually explained in the discussion of Theorem 2.5, but it is worth emphasizing two points. Firstly, analogous to the case where $S = 0$, it would be expected that $t \geq 1/e'(tD)$ because there is an upper limit put on the environmental spending. However, tD is not a fixed point like 0. The government chooses both D (therefore t) and S to maximise the objective function, and thus achieve the identity between the optimal tax rate and the marginal cost of the environmental project. Secondly, the fact that the government can manipulate both environmental supply (or tax) and spending results in an imbalance between the optimal tax rate and the marginal rates of substitution (U_E/U_C and $w^* U_E/U_{\tilde{L}}$). Unlike the pure tax scheme, where $S = 0$ is a fixed value, the government has the incentive to increase the tax revenue if the constraint on its environmental spending is binding.

2.3.3 Pollution Tax versus Emission Permit

In the current one-firm, one-household and one-government model, there are no transaction costs or uncertainty, therefore the price control mode and quantity control mode are equivalent (Weitzman 1974). The government can tax the firm at an appropriate rate to get the optimal amount of pollution, or it can directly issue this amount of emission permits. However, there are still some problems with the permit scheme in the real world.

First, if there are multiple firms the permit should be tradable. The administrative cost might be prohibitively high if the government tries to issue an appropriate number of permits to individual firms. Therefore a tradable permit system should be developed to ensure that permits are allocated efficiently across firms. However, a tradable permit scheme may have higher transaction costs than a levy/tax scheme. The government has to monitor firms' compliance and bear similar costs in both schemes. But firms may bear different costs. Generally speaking, the permit price is equal to the tax/levy rate. However, individual firms have to search for trading partners and bargaining for trade deals in a tradable permit scheme. If there are a large number of firms involved, the trading cost could be very large. Therefore a tax/levy scheme has advantages over a tradable permit system in this sense.

Second, the method of issuing permits may make a difference. As the model implies, the household may not be willing to invest in the environment. If the income goes to the household, it will presumably be spent on consumption goods. If the emission permits are grandfathered, firms do not have to pay for obtaining the permits. In this case, firms may have higher profit and the profit in turn becomes households' income which will be used for consumption. Therefore a grandfathered emission permit system works in the same way as a pure pollution tax scheme. On the other hand, if the permits are auctioned by the government, firms have to pay a price to buy permits and the government receives the revenue of permit auctions. This means that a tradable permit system with permits auctioned may follow the optimal general tax-income scheme.

2.3.4 Pre-existing Taxes and 'Double-Dividend'

The analysis is complicated by pre-existing taxes. Before a pollution tax/levy scheme was introduced, the government taxed labour income at the rate ϖ to finance some public goods $\overline{G}$. With this $\overline{G}$, the utility function now becomes:

$$U\left(C,\overline{L}-L,\overline{E}-D+e(S),\overline{G}\right). \tag{2.16}$$

It is also assumed that there is no control over pollution at the beginning. Now the government introduces a pollution tax/levy to tackle the environmental problem. To keep things simpler, and more realistic, it is assumed that tax revenues, pollution tax or labour income tax, are used to finance the production of public goods and are not transferred to the household. This assumption is not untrue because if the government had surplus revenues, it would have lowered the labour income tax rate. Therefore the household's budget constraint becomes:

$$C \leq \pi + (w - \varpi)L.$$

And the new first order conditions of utility maximisation are:

$$U_C = \lambda, \ U_{\tilde{L}} = \lambda(w - \varpi), \tag{2.17}$$

where λ is the Lagrangian multiplier of the new constraint.

The government chooses $\varpi, \overline{G}, D$ and S to maximise (2.16), subject to

$$\overline{G} + S \leq \varpi L + tD,$$
$$C = (w - \varpi)L + \pi(t, w),$$

$$0 \le S \le tD$$

The second constraint is added because the government anticipates that the selection of ϖ affects the household's budget and behaviour. The Lagrangian for this problem is,

$$\mathcal{L} = U\left(C, \overline{L} - L, \overline{E} - D + e(S), \overline{G}\right) + \lambda_1\left(\varpi L + tD - \overline{G} - S\right)$$
$$+ \lambda_2\left(\pi(t, w) + (w - \varpi)L - C\right) + \lambda_3 S + \lambda_4(tD - S).$$

And the corresponding Kuhn–Tucker conditions are:

$$U_{\overline{G}} = \lambda_1, \ U_E = \lambda_1 t + \lambda_4 t, \ \lambda_1 = \lambda_2 = \lambda,$$
$$U_E e'(S) = \lambda_1 - \lambda_3 + \lambda_4, \ \lambda_3 S = 0, \ \lambda_4(tD - S) = 0. \tag{2.18}$$

The relationship $\lambda_1 = \lambda_2$ is derived by setting the partial derivative of Lagrangian with respect to ϖ to be zero. It represents the fact that a rise in the government's budget due to changing ϖ leads to an equivalent decline in the household's budget. The relationship $\lambda_2 = \lambda$ comes from the fact that both λ_2 and λ are the multiplier of the household's budget constraint when maximising the same objective function.

One corner solution of the above problem is $S = 0$, that is, the whole pollution tax revenue should be used to replace the distortional income tax. The above Kuhn–Tucker conditions give the following theorem.

Theorem 2.6 *With pre-existing labour income tax, the whole of the pollution tax/levy revenue should be used to replace the income tax if all of the following conditions are satisfied:*

(1) $U_E e'(0) \le U_{\overline{G}} = U_C = U_{\widetilde{L}}/(f_L - \varpi)$; *and*

(2) $1/e'(0) \ge t = f_D$.

Proof. $S = 0 < tD$ implies $\lambda_3 \ge 0$ and $\lambda_4 = 0$. Using $f_L = w$, (2.17) and other conditions in (2.18) gives the result.   ∎

The first condition is similar to condition (1) in Theorem 2.4, except that the effect of labour income tax and the utility of public good are now considered. Because the public good and environmental investment are jointly financed by environmental and income tax, a rise in environmental spending would reduce the funds available to the public good. Therefore, if the marginal utility from infinitesimal environmental spending is less than the marginal utility of public good, no tax revenue should be used in environmental projects, that is, all the revenue from pollution tax should be used to replace the labour income tax. Because of the existence of income tax, the marginal income of labour received by the household should be adjusted by extracting the tax rate ϖ, and $U_E e'(0) \leq U_{\tilde{L}}/(f_L - \varpi)$ states that if the marginal utility of infinitesimal environmental spending is less than the marginal utility of leisure forgone to recover that extra unit of income, the environmental spending is not justified, thus all pollution tax revenue should be used to replace labour income tax.

Another corner solution is $S = tD$. If this is justified, a fully earmarked scheme is required, and is likely to finance environmental spending by increasing income tax. The conditions are given in the following theorem.

Theorem 2.7 *With pre-existing labour income tax, the whole of the pollution tax/levy revenue should be earmarked for environmental purposes if all of the following conditions are satisfied:*

$$(1) \quad U_E e'(tD) \geq U_{\overline{G}} = U_C = \frac{U_{\tilde{L}}}{f_L - \varpi}; \text{ and}$$

$$(2) \quad \frac{U_E}{U_C} = \frac{U_E(w - \varpi)}{U_{\tilde{L}}} = \frac{U_E}{U_{\overline{G}}} \geq t = f_D.$$

Proof. $S = tD > 0$ implies $\lambda_3 = 0$ and $\lambda_4 \geq 0$. Using $f_L = w$, (2.17) and other conditions in (2.18) gives the result.   ∎

These conditions are similar to those given in Theorem 2.5, except that the marginal labour income is adjusted due to income tax and the marginal utility of public good is considered. The new conditions in Theorem 2.7 state that a fully earmarked pollution levy scheme is justified if the marginal utility from environmental spending is larger than the marginal utility of public good and if the marginal rate of substitution of environmental good for public good is larger than the marginal product of environmental good.

Checking the real situation against the conditions, it may be found that those in Theorem 2.6 are more likely to be violated, whilst those in Theorem 2.7 are more likely to be satisfied. Therefore the basis for the 'double-dividend hypothesis' is eroded.

However, another version of the 'double-dividend hypothesis' may be proposed. Even without using the revenue to replace pre-existing taxes, an environmental tax might help reduce the distortion of labour income tax through the substitution effect. After an environmental tax is imposed, the environmental factor is more expensive than before, so the firm may demand more labour, that is, the income tax base is enlarged, given $\overline{G}$, which leads to a less distortional labour income tax rate.

Hypothesis 2.1 (New Version of Double-Dividend) *In addition to reducing pollution, an environmental tax may help lower the distortional pre-existing tax rates, as the higher price of environmental factors induces the firm's demand for a larger amount of other previously taxed factors.*

2.4   DYNAMIC GENERAL EQUILIBRIUM ANALYSIS

In the real world, the environment is a stock of certain elements and provides flows of services of which absorbing pollutants is one. More importantly, the environment itself has the capacity of natural assimilation over time, which may affect earmarking in environmental projects. Therefore the above results should be examined in a dynamic setting.

2.4.1   The Model

The framework is a modified Ramsey model with environment arguments in both production and utility functions.

Firm
The firm employs three factors: labour, capital and environmental absorption capacity. The effective labour is increasing with an exogenous, constant rate n. And economy-wide variables are normalised by this effective labour level.[6] Capital is accrued by investment (i) made by the firm, and depreciated at a constant rate δ:

$$\dot{k}_t = i_t - (\delta + n)k_t .\qquad (2.19)$$

For simplicity, the installation cost is not considered here. Assuming the production function is constant returns to scale, the output per effective unit of labour is

$$y_t = f(k_t, d_t) .$$

Assuming a pollution tax is imposed at rate τ, the firm's instantaneous profit is

$$\pi_t = f(k_t, d_t) - i_t - w_t - \tau_t d_t .$$

The firm chooses i and d to maximise its intertemporal profit

$$\int_t^\infty \pi_t e^{-(R(s)-n)(s-t)} \mathrm{d}s \,,$$

subject to the constraint as given in (2.19). The discount rate may vary over time, that is,

$$R(s) = \frac{1}{s-t} \int_t^s r(x)\mathrm{d}x \,.$$

Household

The representative household owns the firm, supplies labour, and receives dividends and government transfers. It can also borrow and lend at the rate r to finance its spending on consumption. The dynamic budget constraint is therefore

$$\dot{a}_t = (r-n)a_t + w_t + v_t - c_t \,, \tag{2.20}$$

where a is the household's assets and v is government transfer. And the household's debt should also meet the No-Ponzi-Game condition

$$\lim_{t \to \infty} a_t e^{-(r-n)t} \geq 0 \,. \tag{2.21}$$

The household chooses consumption path (c_t) to maximise its intertemporal utility

$$\int_t^\infty e^{-(\theta-n)(s-t)} u(c_s, e_s) \mathrm{d}s \,, \tag{2.22}$$

where θ is the household's rate of time preference, subject to (2.20).

Government

The government collects pollution tax from the firm and allocates it to environmental spending and transfers. It is assumed that government does not accrue any asset or debt, that is,

$$s_t + v_t = \tau_t d_t \,. \tag{2.23}$$

The environmental stock is eroded by pollution, and improved by environmental investment, while the environment itself has natural assimilation ability. Therefore the change of environmental stock can be given as:[7]

$$\dot{e}_t = h(e_t) + g(s_t) - ne_t - d_t, \tag{2.24}$$

where e is environmental stock, d is pollutant discharge, $h(\cdot)$ is the natural assimilation function of the environment, and $g(\cdot)$ is the provision function by environmental investment. It is assumed these functions have the usual property.

The government chooses paths of d_t, s_t and v_t to maximise the inter-temporal social welfare represented by (2.22) subject to (2.20), (2.23) and (2.24). Constraint (2.20) is included because the government anticipates its spending on the environment affects the household's budget and, thus, utility.

2.4.2 Analytical Results

The current-value Hamiltonian and first order conditions for the above model are reported in Table 2.2. Using these results, the conditions to justify pure tax and fully earmarked schemes are derived.

Table 2.2   First order conditions for dynamic problem

Agent	Current-value Hamiltonian	First order condition
Firm	$f(k,d) - i - w - \tau d$ $+ \lambda_0[i - (\delta + n)k]$	$f_d = \tau,\ f_k = r + \delta,\ \lambda_0 = 1,$ $\dot{k}_t = i - (\delta + n)k$
Household	$u(c,e) + \lambda[(r-n)a + w$ $+ v - c]$	$u_c = \lambda,\ \dot{\lambda} = (\theta - r)\lambda,$ $\dot{a} = (r-n)a + w + v - c$
Government	$u(c,e) + \lambda_1(\tau d - s - v)$ $+ \lambda[(r-n)a + w + v - c]$ $+ \lambda_2[h(e) + g(s) - ne - d]$ $+ \lambda_3 s + \lambda_4 v$	$\lambda_1 \tau = \lambda_2,\ \lambda_1 = \lambda + \lambda_4,$ $\lambda_1 = \lambda_2 g' + \lambda_3,$ $\lambda_3 s = 0,\ \lambda_4 v = 0,$ $\dot{\lambda}_2 = (\theta - h')\lambda_2 - u_e,$ $\dot{e} = h(e) + g(s) - ne - d$

Conditions for pure tax and earmarked levy schemes
From the results presented in Table 2.2, the conditions to justify a pure tax scheme, or a fully earmarked levy scheme in dynamic setting, can be derived.

Theorem 2.8 *Along the optimal path, a pure tax scheme is adopted if $\lambda_1 \tau g'(0) = \lambda_2 g'(0) \le u_c$ and $1/g'(0) \ge f_d(k,d) = \tau$ at every time; and a fully earmarked scheme is optimal if $\lambda_1 = \lambda_2 g'(s)\big|_{s=\tau d} \ge u_c$, and $\tau = 1/g'(s)\big|_{s=\tau d}$ at every time.*

Proof. $S = 0$ implies $\lambda_3 \geq 0$ and $\lambda_4 = 0$, and $s = \tau d$ implies that $\lambda_3 = 0$ and $\lambda_4 \geq 0$. Using other conditions gives the result. ∎

These conditions are virtually the same as those in the static model. Note that λ_1 is the marginal value of objective function (the marginal utility) if the government budget is increased exogenously by one infinitesimal unit, λ_2 is the marginal utility of environmental stock, $g'(s)$ is the marginal environmental product of environmental spending, therefore $\lambda_2 g'(s)$ and $\lambda_1 \tau g'(s)$ are the marginal utility of environmental spending, with the former through a direct increase in environmental stock, and the latter through savings in government spending. It is clear that no tax revenue should be used in the environmental project if the marginal utility of such spending is less than the marginal utility of spending it on consumption. And if the condition is reversed, even when all pollution tax revenue is used in an environmental project, a fully earmarked scheme is justified.

It should also be pointed out that these conditions do not imply that government should stick to one particular scheme along the optimal path. It is possible for the government to shift from one to another. However, the policy change may follow a smooth path, that is, from one extreme (pure tax or fully earmarking) to another via the general scheme.

The steady state and stability

The steady state is summarised in Table 2.3. In deriving these results, the following relations are used:

$$w_t = f(k_t, d_t) - f_k k_t - \tau d_t, \text{ and } a_t = k_t .$$

The first in the above relations comes from the assumption of constant returns to scale production. The second comes from the fact that in

Table 2.3　　*Steady state of general tax/income scheme*

$s = 0$	$0 < s < \tau d$	$s = \tau d$
$1/g'(s) \geq f_d(k,d)$	$1/g'(s) = f_d(k,d)$	$1/g'(s) = f_d(k,d)$
$u_c f_d = u_e/(\theta - h')$	$u_c f_d = u_e/(\theta - h')$	$u_c f_d \leq u_e/(\theta - h')$
$u_c \geq u_e g'/(\theta - h')$	$u_c = u_e g'/(\theta - h')$	$u_c \leq u_e g'/(\theta - h')$
$f_k = \theta + \delta$	$f_k = \theta + \delta$	$f_k = \theta + \delta$
$f(k,d) = (\delta + n)k + c$	$f(k,d) = (\delta + n)k + c + s$	$f(k,d) = (\delta + n)k + c + s$
$h(e) = ne + d$	$g(s) + h(e) = ne + d$	$g(s) + h(e) = ne + d$

equilibrium, aggregate private asset (or debt) must always be zero: although each household assumes it can freely borrow and lend, in equilibrium there is neither lending nor borrowing (Blanchard and Fischer 1989, p. 50).

Because a pure pollution tax can only reduce demand for the environment, rather than increase its supply, it may be unstable in the dynamic process. However, environmental investment can increase the environmental stock and thus may help improve stability, and be likely to achieve sustainable growth. Therefore the following hypothesis is proposed.

Hypothesis 2.2 *Spending pollution tax/levy on environmental projects may improve the system stability.*

It is difficult to prove this hypothesis formally. Rather a simple example is presented to demonstrate its validity. Suppose the environmental regeneration function is $h(e) = \beta e$ with $0 < \beta < n$. According to (2.24), if there is no environmental investment, e will decrease forever, and a steady state cannot be found where e is constant. However, when environmental investment is made, the steady state is possible.

Adjustment path
From the first order conditions, it can be seen that the Keynes–Ramsey rule becomes

$$(u_{cc}/u_c)\dot{c} = \theta + \delta - f_k - (u_{cc}/u_c)\dot{e},$$

or
$$\varepsilon_{11}\dot{c}/c = \theta + \delta - f_k - \varepsilon_{12}\dot{e}/e,$$

where ε_{11} and ε_{12} are elasticities of marginal utility with respect to consumption and environment, respectively. It is clear that the movement of consumption and environment is related. However, if utility separability of consumption and environment is assumed, ε_{12} is zero, and the above expression reverts to the usual Keynes–Ramsey rule.

2.5 CONCLUSION

This chapter demonstrates that the usual interpretation of the Pigouvian tax is incomplete. An optimal pollution tax/levy programme should include the possibility of spending the revenue on environment-improving or pollution-cleansing projects. A pure tax scheme can not do better than a general tax-income or tax-bounty scheme, and, in fact, is not sufficient for an optimum. This chapter also finds the conditions for a pure tax system and for earmarking all pollution tax/levy revenues into environmental projects. A pure tax system might be an optimum only if the marginal utility of environment is sufficiently small, that is, environmental resources are abundant. However, this situation is rare in the current world. By contrast, a fully earmarked system is likely to be a better choice when the marginal utility of environment is high, relative to that of consumption, and the pollution tax/levy revenue is small.

Usually, a Pigouvian pollution tax rate is equal to the marginal damage cost of this negative externality. However, it is found that this is not necessarily the case if the tax revenue can be used for environmental purposes. In the general equilibrium setting, under the general tax-income scheme, the optimal pollution tax rate should be equal to the marginal cost of producing environmental goods and services. This may imply that less information is required than thought to design a tax policy. Even in a partial equilibrium setting, if all revenue is to be used in an environmental project, it is not necessary to fully internalise pollution damage to reach an optimum, and the optimal rate might be different from the marginal damage cost.

In the case with pre-existing distortional taxes, using all the pollution tax/levy revenue to replace the distorting taxes is usually not an optimum. At least some of the revenue from the pollution tax/levy should be used in environmental activities. And, considering the current situation, it is most likely optimal to earmark the whole pollution tax/levy revenue for environmental projects.

These static results survive in the steady state of a dynamic setting. Moreover, because a pure pollution tax can only reduce the demand for environment, rather than increase its supply, it may be unstable in the dynamic process. However, environmental investment may help to improve stability, and be likely to achieve sustainable growth.

APPENDIX

2.A   Decentralised versus Centralised Models

Combining household and government together

Because the objective of government is to maximise the household's utility, it is natural to consider the legitimacy of combining household and government together. It is now assumed the household can exert the function of government, that is, decide the supply of environmental good and collect and allocate pollution tax/levy revenue.

Static general equilibrium Now the household/government chooses C, L, D and S to maximise (2.8) subject to (2.11), $C + S \leq \pi(w,t) + wL + tD$, and

$0 \le S \le tD$. And the Lagrangian is:

$$\mathcal{L} = U\big(C, \overline{L} - L, \overline{E} - D + e(S)\big) + \lambda\big(\pi(w,t) + wL + tD - C - S\big)$$
$$+ \lambda_1 S + \lambda_2 (tD - S),$$

which leads to the following first order conditions:

$$U_C = \lambda, \ U_{\overline{L}} = \lambda w, \ U_E = (\lambda + \lambda_2)t, \ U_E e'(S) = \lambda - \lambda_1 + \lambda_2.$$

Under the general tax-income scheme, $0 < S < tD$ implies that $\lambda_1 = \lambda_2 = 0$, the above conditions are equivalent to those given by (2.10) and (2.13). If a pure tax scheme is required, that is, $S = 0$, it gives $\lambda_1 \ge 0$ and $\lambda_2 = 0$, which transforms the above conditions to those in (2.14). If a fully earmarked scheme is justified, that is, $S = tD$, it gives $\lambda_1 = 0$ and $\lambda_2 \ge 0$, which are the same as those in (2.15). Therefore combining household with government is the same as separating them in this case.

Static general equilibrium with pre-existing income tax With pre-existing labour income tax, the combination of household and government makes a difference. In the separation case, the wage rate the household receives is only $w - \varpi$, and the labour supply is governed by (2.17). However, in the case of combining household and government together, labour income tax ϖ, which is just an internal transfer, does not play any role in determining the agent's behaviour: the new entity receives the whole wage rate w, therefore the labour supply is governed by the old relationship represented by (2.10). Because of this, the results are different no matter how the model is constructed. The following example illustrates the difference.

Suppose the household/government chooses C, L, D, S, $\overline{G}$ and ϖ to maximise (2.16) subject to $C + S + \overline{G} \le \pi + wL + tD$ and $0 \le S \le tD$.[8] And the Lagrangian is:

$$\mathcal{L} = U\big(C, \overline{L} - L, \overline{E} - D + e(S), \overline{G}\big) + \lambda\big(\pi + wL + tD - C - S - \overline{G}\big)$$
$$+ \lambda_1 S + \lambda_2 (tD - S)$$

which leads to the following first order conditions:

$$U_c = \lambda, \ U_{\overline{L}} = \lambda w, \ U_E = (\lambda + \lambda_2)t, \ U_E e'(S) = \lambda - \lambda_1 + \lambda_2, \ U_{\overline{G}} = \lambda.$$

It is clear that these results are different from those in (2.17) and (2.18).

However, there exists one possibility of equivalence. Suppose the household understands that its contribution to public goods via income tax may enhance its welfare, and knows government's behaviour, then its problem could be represented by the following Lagrangian:

$$\mathscr{L} = U\left(C, \overline{L} - L, \overline{E} - D + e(S), \varpi L + tD - S\right) + \lambda\left(\pi + (w - \varpi)L - C\right)$$

The first condition of labour supply is:

$$-U_{\widetilde{L}} + U_{\overline{G}}\varpi + \lambda(w - \varpi) = 0$$

Knowing that the government set $U_{\overline{G}} = \lambda$, the household will supply labour according to $U_{\widetilde{L}} = w\lambda$, which is identical to the above case.

This possibility is based on the assumption that both household and government have full knowledge about each other's behaviour. If there were only one household, the government and household could achieve the result simply by negotiation. However, as in the real world there are many households, the game will be far more complicated, and will be played not only between households and government, but also amongst individual households. In this case, an individual can not presume others will follow its thinking, and there is no authority to prevent others from cheating. Or the household will presume its share in the labour market is so tiny that its rational behaviour has no effect on the whole world. Therefore it supplies labour simply according to the after-tax wage rate.

Dynamic general equilibrium The household/government's dynamic budget constraint becomes:

$$\dot{d}_t = (r - n)a_t + w_t + \tau_t d_t - c_t - s_t, \tag{2.A.1}$$

which should also meet the No-Ponzi-Game condition (2.21). The new entity chooses the path of consumption (c_t), environmental supply (d_t) and environmental spending (s_t) to maximise the intertemporal utility (2.22) subject to (2.24) and (2.A.1). The current-value Hamiltonian is thus:

$$\mathscr{H} = u(c,e) + \lambda[(r - n)a + w + \tau d - c - s]$$
$$+ \lambda_1[h(e) + g(s) - ne - d] + \lambda_2 s + \lambda_3(\tau d - s)$$

The corresponding first order conditions are:

$$u_c = \lambda, \ (\lambda + \lambda_3)\tau = \lambda_1, \ \lambda + \lambda_3 = \lambda_1 g'(s) + \lambda_2, \ \dot{\lambda} = (\theta - r)\lambda,$$
$$\dot{\lambda}_1 = (\theta - h'(e))\lambda_1 - u_e, \ \lambda_2 s = 0, \ \lambda_3(\tau d - s) = 0.$$

These are essentially the same as those given in Table 2.2, except for different symbols for the Hamiltonian multiplier, leading to the same conditions in Theorem 2.8. Therefore combining the household with government is equivalent to separating them in the dynamic setting.

Centralised model

In a centralised model, the three agents, firm, household and government, are combined into one social planner. This kind of model is close to a partial equilibrium analysis. In the centralised model, all prices are implicit, that is, the distribution of income, or payment to factors, are through internal lump-sum transfers; while in the decentralised model, all agents make their decisions assuming the prices they face are given, that is, they cannot influence the prices, and permit the market equilibrium to determine prices. This may have different consequences, which are stated as follows.

Result 2.A *Decentralised and centralised models are different when environmental spending is bounded by pollution tax revenue, or when the pollution tax interacts with pre-existing taxes. As differences arise, a decentralised model is required.*

It has been shown that combining household and government together leads to different results when a labour income tax exists. The difference should also persist with a more centralised model. Therefore the following discussion focuses on the first circumstance in the above statement.

Static general equilibrium A social planner chooses labour supply (L), environmental supply (D), consumption (C) and environmental spending (S) to maximise utility (2.8) subject to (2.11), $C + S \leq f(L, D)$, and $0 \leq S \leq f_D D$. The corresponding Lagrangian is:

$$\mathscr{L} = U(C, \overline{L} - L, \overline{E} - D + e(S)) + \lambda(f(L, D) - C - S) + \lambda_1 S + \lambda_2(f_D D - S),$$

and first order conditions are:

$$U_C = \lambda, \; U_{\widetilde{L}} = \lambda f_L + \lambda_2 f_{LD} D, \; U_E = (\lambda + \lambda_2) f_D + \lambda_2 f_{DD} D,$$
$$U_E e'(S) = \lambda - \lambda_1 + \lambda_2, \; \lambda_1 S = 0, \; \lambda_2(f_D D - S) = 0.$$

It can be seen that they are different from the results derived from the decentralised model when $S = f_D D$, but the same as the results when $0 \leq S \leq f_D D$ (see Table 2.A for details). The difference arises from the fact that the social planner has the ability to change the pollution tax rate when s/he faces a binding constraint on environmental spending, while the government has to treat the tax rate as given in the decentralised model.[9]

Table 2.A   Centralised versus decentralised models[a]

Case	Decentralised model	Centralised model	Comment
$S = 0$	$U_{\tilde{L}}/U_C = f_L$ $U_E/U_C = f_D$ $1/e'(S) \geq f_D$	$U_{\tilde{L}}/U_C = f_L$ $U_E/U_C = f_D$ $1/e'(S) \geq f_D$	Equivalent
$0 < S < tD$	$U_{\tilde{L}}/U_C = f_L$ $U_E/U_C = f_D$ $1/e'(S) = f_D$	$U_{\tilde{L}}/U_C = f_L$ $U_E/U_C = f_D$ $1/e'(S) = f_D$	Equivalent
$S = tD$	$U_{\tilde{L}}/U_C = f_L$ $U_E/U_C \geq f_D$ $1/e'(S) = f_D$	$U_{\tilde{L}}/U_C = f_L$ $\dfrac{U_E}{U_C} \genfrac{}{}{0pt}{}{<}{>} f_D$ if $\epsilon_{Dt} \genfrac{}{}{0pt}{}{<}{>} 1$[b] $1/e'(S) \geq= f_D$	Different

Notes:
[a] Static general equilibrium models.
[b] $\varepsilon = -(\partial D/\partial t)(t/d)$, the elasticity of environmental demand with respect to tax rate.

Dynamic general equilibrium In this case, the motion of capital is determined by

$$\dot{k}_t = f(k_t, d_t) - (\delta + n)k_t - c_t - s_t, \qquad (2.A.2)$$

and the model is restructured as: the central planner chooses proper paths for c, d and s to maximise (2.22) subject to constraints (2.A.2) and (2.24). The current-value Hamiltonian is:

$$\mathcal{H} = u(c,e) + \lambda_1[f(k,d) - (\delta + n)k - c - s] + \lambda_2[h(e) + g(s) - ne - d]$$
$$+ \lambda_3 s + \lambda_4(f_d d - s).$$

The first order conditions for this problem are:

$$u_c = \lambda_1; \quad (\lambda_1 + \lambda_4)f_d = \lambda_2 - \lambda_4 f_{dd} d; \quad \lambda_1 + \lambda_4 = \lambda_2 g' + \lambda_3;$$
$$\lambda_3 s = 0, \ \lambda_3 \geq 0 \text{ if } s = 0; \quad \lambda_4(f_d d - s) = 0, \ \lambda_4 \geq 0 \text{ if } s = f_d d;$$
$$\dot{\lambda}_1 = \lambda_1(\theta + \delta - f_k) - \lambda_4 f_{kd} d; \quad \dot{\lambda}_2 = \lambda_2(\theta - h') - u_e;$$
$$\dot{k} = f(k,s) - (\theta + n)k - c - s; \quad \text{and} \quad \dot{e} = h(e) + g(s) - ne - d.$$

Like the static general equilibrium analysis, the centralised model differs from the decentralised model when $\lambda_4 \neq 0$, that is, a fully earmarked scheme is justified. Again the difference arises from the fact that the social planner can influence the (shadow) pollution tax rather than assume it as given.

NOTES

* This chapter draws heavily from Jiang (2001), 'Earmarking of pollution charges and the sub-optimality of the Pigouvian tax'. Permission to use the material by Blackwell Publishing is acknowledged.
1. This hypothesis has attracted heavy criticism. Fullerton and Metcalf (1997) argue that if the tax only replaces current command and control regulations (that is, environmentally neutral), there is no first dividend. Goulder et al. (1996) point out that the second dividend is not generally guaranteed, because the revenue-recycling effect may well be eroded by the tax-interaction effect. However, their numerical result does show that, if the proceeds of an environmental tax are used to reduce pre-existing taxes, the gain from the revenue-recycling effect is larger than the loss from the tax-interaction effect, implying a net gain in addition to environmental improvement. Similar results can be found in studies by Goulder et al. (1999), Parry et al. (1996) and Parry and Williams (1999). But Bovenberg and Goulder (1996) report that the substitution of environmentally motivated taxes for traditional income taxes involves a gross cost: the double dividend does not materialise. However, both proponents and critics of this hypothesis neglect the possibility of earmarking.
2. Usually the pollution eliminating activity is affected by the pollution level. As the model does not specify the pollution level, D may be used as a proxy, that is, the E function could be written as $E = E(S, D)$. If so, the optimal tax rate becomes $\tau^* = (1 - E_D)D'/(E_S + (E_S - 1)/\varepsilon)$, where E_D and E_S are, respectively, the partial derivative of E with respect to D and S, and ε is the output elasticity of the pollution tax. It is clear that the qualitative result from the simplified model does not change, although the marginal cost of pollution is adjusted to include the effect on pollution elimination.
3. Accurately speaking, $S = \tau q(\tau)$ and $\lambda = 0$ are not conditions of binding constraint because the interior solution happens to be at the corner. However, as all revenues are used for environment, the discussion is included in the fully earmarked scheme.
4. The usual approach to model a firm's pollution and abatement activity assumes that pollution is a useless by-product of the production process, and under certain environmental policies, the firm is forced to abate the pollution to some extent at its cost. The approach in the text also captures these properties, although the firm's abatement activity is not explicitly modelled.
5. Curious readers may find that condition (2) is likely to be satisfied in the real world, for example in some badly polluted regions. In those regions because a huge amount of environmental resources – the pollution absorption capacity – are used in production, the marginal product of environmental factor is very low,

while the marginal cost of cleansing is very high due to heavy pollution. However, condition (2) alone can not justify the pure pollution tax scheme, which requires that all conditions are satisfied.

6. Following convention, lower case letters are used to denote these normalised variables.

7. The reason why pollution stock is not used as the state variable is that, at steady state, the total pollution stock will increase at the rate n, which is not a desirable result.

8. It seems that the constraint $0 \leq \overline{G} \leq \omega L$ should be included. However, as the problem originates from the discussion of replacing income tax by a pollution tax, such a constraint would exclude the possibility at the first instance.

9. One might be tempted to replace the constraint $0 \leq S \leq f_D D$ by $0 \leq S \leq tD$ and assume that t is exogenous. This treatment would lead to the same results as in the decentralised model. However it is inappropriate because t is endogenous and should be linked to other variables in the model.

3.   Stochastic General Equilibrium and Environmental Policy Choice

3.1   INTRODUCTION

Like other processes, because of natural, technical and political reasons, uncertainties about the benefits and costs of pollution control are a perpetual feature. '... [T]he degree of fuzziness could be reduced by research and experimentation, but it could never be truly eliminated because new sources of uncertainty are arising all the time' (Weitzman 1974). 'The true costs will only be known when the production is actually underway' (Weitzman 1978).

The importance of uncertainty to the selection of policy instruments was addressed by Weitzman (1974) for the first time. He argues that in an environment of complete knowledge and perfect certainty there is a formal identity between the use of prices and quantities as planning instruments, as long as quantities or prices are such that the marginal benefit is equal to the marginal cost.[1] But in the presence of uncertainty, these two instruments will generate different consequences.

Weitzman (1974) defines the relative advantage of price control over quantity control as the difference of expected net benefit between these two control policies. He assumes that the benefit and cost functions of one product have quadratic form around some critical quantity:

$$B(q,\varepsilon) \cong a(\varepsilon) + [B' + \alpha(\varepsilon)](q - \hat{q}) + \frac{B''}{2}(q - \hat{q})^2,$$

$$C(q,\theta) \cong b(\theta) + [C' + \beta(\theta)](q - \hat{q}) + \frac{C''}{2}(q - \hat{q})^2.$$

where $a(\varepsilon)$, $\alpha(\varepsilon)$, $b(\theta)$ and $\beta(\theta)$ are stochastic functions and B', B'', C' and C'' are fixed coefficients. B'' is the slope of the (linear) marginal benefit (or demand) curve, C'' is the slope of the (linear) marginal cost (or supply) curve. This specification assumes additive shocks to marginal benefit and marginal cost. It is also assumed that these two types of shocks are independent. Based on these assumptions, he derives the following rule to determine the relative advantage of price control over quantity control:[2]

$$\Delta \approx \frac{\sigma^2(B'' + C'')}{2(C'')^2},$$

where σ^2 is the variance of vertical shifts in the marginal cost (or supply) curve.

Two important conclusions can be derived from the above rule. First, the uncertainty in benefit or demand does not appear in the expression. 'To a second approximation, it affects price and quantity modes equally adversely.' Second, the relative advantage depends on the slopes of marginal cost (supply) and marginal benefit (demand) functions. If the demand curve is steeper than the supply curve ($B'' + C'' < 0$), the quantity mode is preferred; by contrast a steeper supply curve favours the price control mode.

Adar and Griffin (1976) present a model of linear marginal benefit and cost with symmetric multiplicative disturbances and show that the choice of the optimal instruments depends on more parameters in addition to relative slopes. Following their idea, Watson and Ridker (1984) use nonlinear marginal cost and benefit functions with multiplicative asymmetric errors to analyse the control instrument of air and water pollution. Yohe (1976) introduces substitution between clean factor and pollutant in production to study the effect of uncertainty. He finds that, as the elasticity of substitution increases, the quantity mode becomes more preferred. If they are perfect substitutes, the benefit losses of changes in output level would disappear, and a quantity mode would be unambiguously favoured.

Stavins (1996) argues that Weitzman's assumption of independent uncertainties in supply and demand is not realistic in many cases. He finds that the uncertainties in both demand and supply affect the relative advantage of price control over quantity control if they are correlated. In this case, the rule becomes

$$\Delta \approx \frac{\sigma_C^2(B'' + C'')}{2(C'')^2} - \frac{\sigma_{BC}^2}{C''} = \frac{\sigma_C^2}{C''}\left(\frac{B'' + C''}{2C''} - \frac{\rho_{BC}\sigma_B}{\sigma_B} \right),$$

where σ_B and σ_C are, respectively, the standard deviation of shocks to marginal benefit and marginal cost; and ρ_{BC} is the correlation coefficient between them. According to this new rule, a positive (negative) correlation tends to favour the quantity (price) instruments and, theoretically, these effects can overturn Weitzman's relative-slopes instrument recommendation.

Because these analyses are of partial equilibrium, it is appropriate to question whether Weitzman's rule and revisions are applicable in the general equilibrium setting. Pizer (1997a, 1997b, 1999) presents a numerical general equilibrium framework to determine optimal climate change policy under uncertainty. He finds that a tax is preferred to tradable permits, due to the relative flatness of the marginal benefit schedule in reducing greenhouse gas emission and a negative correlation between control costs and benefit. His findings confirm Weitzman's rule. However, an analytical result has not been presented, therefore generality is yet to be developed.

This chapter attempts to analyse the environmental policy choice under uncertainty and Weitzman's rule in a general equilibrium setting. Even with a very simple model, it is found that the analytical result is very complicated and Weitzman's rule cannot be applied directly in the general equilibrium setting without certain assumptions. The rest of this chapter is organised as follows. The next section describes the analytical model and section 3.3 presents the results and discusses Weitzman's rule. A revised model is then introduced in section 3.4 to recapture Weitzman's rule and analyse the impact on policy choice under uncertainty of risk aversion of household and earmarking of pollution charges or auction revenues. The last section summarises the chapter.

3.2   THE MODEL

There are two agents in the economy: a household[3] and a firm. The household owns the firm and an environment endowment (V). It tries to maximise its utility, which is the objective of this economy. The utility function is $U = U(C,E)$, where C is the amount of consumption good, and E is the environmental quality. The utility function has the usual properties, specifically they are

$$U_C > 0,\ U_E > 0,\ U_{CC} < 0,\ U_{EE} < 0,\ U_{CE} = U_{EC} > 0.$$

To produce the consumption good, the firm uses the environmental factor (D) supplied by the household.[4] The unit of this factor can be carefully selected such that environmental quality can be represented by the difference between environmental endowment and the amount used in production: $E = V - D$. Production is subject to shocks due to various factors, such as weather and so on. The uncertainty about environmental quality will be introduced later. The production function is thus written as $Y = f(D, \varepsilon)$, where ε is the error term with zero mean and variance of δ^2. And the properties of this production function are

$$f_D > 0,\ f_{DD} < 0,\ f_\varepsilon > 0,\ f_{\varepsilon\varepsilon} \le 0,\ f_{D\varepsilon} = f_{\varepsilon D} > 0,$$
$$f_{DD}f_{\varepsilon\varepsilon} - f_{D\varepsilon}^2 \ge 0,\ f(0,\varepsilon) = 0,\ f_D(0,\varepsilon) = \infty.$$

3.3   THE POLICY OPTIONS

3.3.1   The First-Best Outcome

Before discussing policies, it is necessary to find the first-best outcomes.[5] From profit and utility maximisation and market clearing conditions, the following conditions can be derived:

$$P^* = f_D(D^*, \varepsilon), \tag{3.1}$$

$$P^* = \frac{U_E(C^*, V - D^*)}{U_C(C^*, V - D^*)}, \tag{3.2}$$

$$C^* = f(D^*, \varepsilon) = \pi^* + P^* D^*. \tag{3.3}$$

where P is the price of the environmental good relative to the consumption good, and π is the firm's profit after paying environmental cost. The above conditions lead to

$$P^* = P(V, \varepsilon) \text{ and } D^* = D(V, \varepsilon).$$

It is clear that, ideally, the price and quantity of environmental input vary across states. However, practically, the regulation of environmental management should be determined before the uncertainty is resolved, and the policy should remain long enough to be effective (Weitzman 1974). The popular approaches are either imposing a fixed price (pollution taxes) or setting a fixed quantity (emission permits, quotas and so on).[6] In the first-best solution, price and quantity are determined simultaneously by the economy, so they are equivalent. But this is not the case in the following discussion.

How to determine the price or quantity for future regulation? One approach is to use the price and quantity determined without uncertainty, that is,

$$\overline{P} = P(V, 0), \ \overline{D} = D(V, 0).$$

It may be called the deterministic approach. A more rigorous method is to find the price or quantity that maximises the expected utility, that is,

$$\overline{D} = \{D \mid \arg\max_D E[U(f(d, \varepsilon), V - D)]\}, \text{ or}$$
$$\overline{P} = \{P \mid \arg\max_P E[U(f(d, \varepsilon), V - D)] \text{ and } f_D(D, \varepsilon) = P\}.$$

This can be called the expected utility maximisation approach. However, two main reasons make this difficult in practice. Firstly, it needs additional information about the distribution of the random variable that is usually not known. Secondly, it is very complicated to estimate the results. By contrast, the deterministic approach is natural because it is known that the mean of errors is zero. It should also be pointed out that $\overline{P}$ and $\overline{Q}$ are equivalent when there is no uncertainty, while they are usually not when the price and quantity are determined by the expected utility maximisation approach, that is, a state cannot be found where the two approaches lead to the same result.

3.3.2 Shocks and Consequences

The case where there is a positive shock, that is, the shock increases the output level for given input level, is discussed first. The price control means that a price is set beforehand as a commitment that the household will sell as much environmental good as the firm demands; while the quantity control turns out that the equilibrium price should induce the firm demand at exactly the amount of preset quantity. Note that, at any time under price control, the firm should follow $f_D(D^P,\varepsilon) = \overline{P}\left(= f_D(\overline{D},0)\right)$, and because $f_{DD} < 0$, $f_{D\varepsilon} > 0$ and $\varepsilon > 0$, it should thus be the case that $D^P > \overline{D}$ for the above relationship to hold. So, if there is a positive shock, the quantity demanded under the price control mode is larger than that set in the quantity control mode.

Once the quantity demanded for the environmental factor is determined, the output, and thus the consumption, is determined. It turns out that the relative advantage of these control modes depends on the deviation of environmental supply from the first-best quantity D^*. This gives the following rule:

Result 3.1 *With a positive shock,*
if $D^* < \overline{D}$, the quantity control mode is better;
if $D^* > D^P$, the price control mode is better; and
if $\overline{D} < D^* < D^P$, further conditions are needed to determine which is the better mode.

The situation with negative shock is symmetric to that with positive shock, therefore, if there is a negative shock, the quantity demanded under the price control mode is smaller than that set in the quantity control mode, that is, $D^P < \overline{D}$. The corresponding rule to judge a policy option is given below.

Result 3.2 *With a negative shock,*
if $D^* > \overline{D}$, the quantity control mode is better;
if $D^* > D^P$, the price control mode is better; and
if $\overline{D} < D^* < D^P$, further conditions are needed to determine which is the

better mode.

To apply the above rules, it is necessary to find the change in the first-best outcomes. Taking the total differential of (3.1)–(3.2) and collecting terms leads to

$$\frac{\mathrm{d}D^*}{\mathrm{d}\varepsilon} = \frac{(U_C)^2 f_{D\varepsilon} - (U_{EC}U_C - U_{CC}U_E)f_\varepsilon}{(U_{EC}U_C - U_{CC}U_E)f_D + (U_{CE}U_E - U_{EE}U_C) - (U_C)^2 f_{DD}} \quad (3.4)$$

Note that the denominator in the above expression is positive because of the properties of production and utility functions. Therefore

$$\frac{\mathrm{d}D^*}{\mathrm{d}\varepsilon} \gtreqless 0 \ \text{ if } \ (U_C)^2 f_{D\varepsilon} \gtreqless (U_{EC}U_C - U_{CC}U_E)f_\varepsilon$$

$$\text{or } f_{D\varepsilon} \gtreqless \frac{U_{EC}U_C - U_{CC}U_E}{(U_C)^2} f_\varepsilon \ .$$

Note also that, $(U_{EC}U_C - U_{CC}U_E)/(U_C)^2 = \partial(U_E/U_C)/\partial C = \partial MRS/\partial C$, is the change in the marginal rate of substitution due to a change in consumption. The term $\partial MRS/\partial C \, f_\varepsilon$ is therefore the change in the marginal rate of substitution due to a change in consumption resulting from a change in the shock; while $f_{D\varepsilon}$ is the change in marginal product due to a change in the shock. In the first-best equilibrium, the marginal product should be equal to the marginal rate of substitution. This condition says that, if the change in *MRS* caused by the change in shock is greater than the change in *MP*, the first-best quantity of environmental supply will decrease.

Clearly this condition is related to the curvature of indifference curve and the production frontier. Loosely speaking, around the deterministic equilibrium, the steeper the indifference curve or the flatter the production frontier, the more favourable a quantity control policy.

Two problems arise with the application of this condition. First, it is only half way to determining which policy is better. If the sign of $\mathrm{d}D^*/\mathrm{d}\varepsilon$ is negative, it can be concluded that a quantity policy is better; however, if it is positive, it is not possible to tell which is better. Second, the sign will change during the course of shocks. That is, as the magnitude of shock changes, the direction of changes in the first-best quantity will vary.

However, if the shock is small enough, it may be assumed that the direction will not change. And because the *MP* and *MRS* are equal at certainty when $\overline{D}$ or $\overline{P}$ are set, if the shock is small, *MP* and *MRS* can be directly compared after the uncertainty is resolved.

If at the preset quantity, the marginal rate of substitution is greater than the marginal product after a positive shock, that is,

$$\frac{U_E(C^Q, V - \overline{D})}{U_C(C^Q, V - \overline{D})} > f_D(\overline{D}, \varepsilon),$$

where $C^Q = f(\overline{D}, \varepsilon)$, the optimal quantity will be smaller than the preset quantity, that is, $D^* < \overline{D}$. This is illustrated in Figure 3.1(a). Without uncertainty, the price control $\overline{P}$ and quantity control $\overline{D}$ are equivalent, and both achieve the equilibrium E^0. After a positive shock, the production frontier shifts above the old frontier. Under the price control scheme, the emissions will be D^P, to the right of the emissions under the quantity control

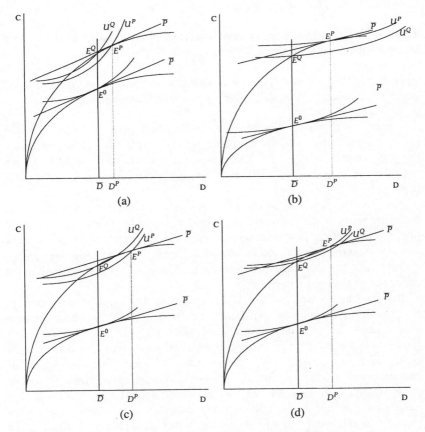

(a)   (b)

(c)   (d)

Figure 3.1   Price- and quantity-control after a positive shock

scheme $\overline{D}$. If the marginal rate of substitution is greater than the marginal product, the optimal quantity will lie somewhere to the left of $\overline{D}$. It turns out that the quantity control is better than the price control, which can be seen from the fact that the indifference curve U^P, which passes through the price control equilibrium E^P, lies below the indifference curve U^Q, which passes through the quantity control equilibrium E^Q. Symmetrically, if the marginal rate of substitution is smaller than the marginal product after a negative shock, the optimal quantity will be larger than the preset quantity, and the quantity control is better.

Applying equation (3.4), the change of first-best price along with a shock can be derived as

$$\frac{\mathrm{d}P^*}{\mathrm{d}\varepsilon} = \frac{(U_{EC}U_C - U_{CC}U_E)(f_D f_{D\varepsilon} - f_\varepsilon f_{DD}) + (U_{CE}U_E - U_{EE}U_C)f_{D\varepsilon}}{(U_{EC}U_C - U_{CC}U_E)f_D + (U_{CE}U_E - U_{EE}U_C) - (U_C)^2 f_{D\varepsilon}} \geq 0 .$$

That is, the first-best price cannot decrease after a positive shock, nor increase after a negative shock, which gives the following result:

Result 3.3 *The first-best quantity is less (larger) than quantity demanded under price control mode, D^P, after a positive (negative) shock.*

Figure 3.1(b) shows that because the first-best price is lower than the preset price $\overline{P}$, the first-best emissions will be larger than emissions under the price control scheme, D^P. Therefore the price control would be better than the quantity control. However, according to Result 3.3, this cannot happen.

Needless to say, the above rules are just sufficient conditions. The difficulty arises when the marginal product is larger (less) than the marginal rate of substitution at the preset quantity and the opposite at D^P after a positive (negative) shock. As illustrated in Figure 3.1(c) and (d), the optimal quantity falls between these two quantities, $\overline{D}$ and D^P, and it is possible for either one of the modes to be better.

It should be pointed out that assuming normality in utility function does not provide a clearer indication about the movement of the first-best outcome after a shock. Suppose there is a positive shock, the production frontier shifts above the old one. If the price of environmental good relative to consumption good were unchanged, the consumption, C, and the enjoyment of environmental quality, E, would increase under the assumption of normal utility, implying lower emissions, D. However, according to the discussion leading to Result 3.3, the relative price increases at the same time. This increase in relative price will decrease E, that is, increase D, for a given amount of wealth. These two opposing effects lead to uncertain prediction about the change in the first-best quantity.

3.3.3 Is Weitzman's Rule Valid in a General Equilibrium Setting?

The first difficulty in applying Weitzman's rule in general equilibrium is with the concept of marginal benefit and cost. Unlike in partial equilibrium, it is difficult to distinguish between benefit and cost. It is possible to argue that an increase in consumption due to an increase in the use of the environmental factor is a benefit while the fall in environmental quality caused by this use is a cost. However, it is equally valid to argue that the improvement of environmental quality through the reduction in the use of the environmental factor is a benefit, while the fall in consumption is a cost.

Weitzman (1974) indicates that the supply (demand) curve is equivalent to the marginal benefit (cost) function. Therefore an attempt can be made to find the supply and demand functions of environmental good in the general equilibrium. The demand for the environmental factor is derived from the profit maximisation, so, by taking the total differential of the first order condition (3.1), the slope of the demand function can be expressed as follows:

$$\frac{dP}{dD} = f_{DD} + f_{D\varepsilon}\frac{d\varepsilon}{dD}\ .$$

The household's provision of environmental good is based on utility maximisation. Using the first order condition of utility maximisation (3.2) and budget constraint (3.3), gives

$$U_C(\pi + PD^S, V - D^S)P = U_E(\pi + PD^S, V - D^S).$$

Taking the total differential of the above equation gives

$$\big(U_{CC}(d\pi + DdP + PdD) - U_{CE}dD\big)P + U_C dP$$
$$= U_{EC}(d\pi + DdP + PdD) - U_{EE}dD$$

A problem arises from $d\pi$, the change in profit. In the decentralised general equilibrium economy, the household takes the profit as given, although it is actually affected by the provision of environmental good. There are two ways to treat $d\pi$. First, differentiating it further gives the slope of supply function as follows:

$$\frac{dP}{dD} = \frac{(U_{CE} - U_{CC}f_D)P + (U_{EC}f_D - U_{EE})}{U_C} + \frac{(U_{EC} - PU_{CC})f_\varepsilon}{U_C}\frac{d\varepsilon}{dD}\ .$$

Alternatively, leaving $d\pi$ as it is, gives

$$\frac{dP}{dD} = \frac{(U_{CC}P - U_{CE})P - (U_{EC}P - U_{EE})}{U_{EC}D - U_{CC}PD - U_C} + \frac{U_{CC}P - U_{EC}}{U_{EC}D - U_{CC}PD - U_C}\frac{d\pi}{dD}.$$

It is clear that Weitzman's rule cannot be directly used because the shock to production leads to shifts in both the supply of and demand for environmental good. And also the shock is not additive. Even if the shock to marginal product is additive, the resulting shock to the supply curve is multiplicative (note P or f_D, which by assumption is affected by the shock, appears in the above expression).

Using Weitzman's (or Stavins') rule may lead to the wrong conclusion. As mentioned above, one conclusion in Weitzman's rule is that only the uncertainty in supply matters, that is, if there is uncertainty only in demand, the quantity and price controls are equivalent. This is misleading in the general equilibrium setting. Suppose there is no uncertainty in production, but there is uncertainty in utility. It turns out that there is no uncertainty in demand, but there is uncertainty in supply. According to Weitzman's rule, the two control modes will give different results unless the absolute slopes of demand and supply are the same. However, this prediction is wrong! From equation 3.1, it is clear that the price- and quantity-control are exactly the same – price and quantity have a unique relationship – if there is no uncertainty in production. The reason behind this is quite simple. In Weitzman's (1974) model, the behavioural function is given by the supply function – price is equal to marginal benefit – while, in the current case, the firm's behaviour is governed by $P = f_D$, which is actually the demand function for environmental good.

3.4   A REVISED MODEL

The revised model follows the popular assumption that the utility is separable in consumption and environmental quality. Still further, the enjoyment of environmental quality is represented by the disutility of pollution to avoid the measurement problem of environmental endowment. In sum, the household has a money metric utility function

$$U = C - g = f(D,\varepsilon) - g(D,\theta). \tag{3.5}$$

Note that C or $f(D,\varepsilon)$ is the national product, and $g(D,\theta)$ is the damage function caused by pollution, so $f(D,\varepsilon) - g(D,\theta)$ is the net product. This makes the assumption that the household is risk-neutral to its income or net income. In addition to the properties stated above, the damage function has the following properties:

$$g_D > 0, \ g_\theta > 0, \ g_{DD} \geq 0, \ g_{\theta\theta} \geq 0, \ g_{\theta D} = g_{D\theta} > 0, \ g(0,\theta) = 0.$$

Therefore, $dD^*/d\varepsilon > 0$ is guaranteed because $U_{EC} = U_{CE} = 0$.

3.4.1 Weitzman's Rule Revisited

With the separability and risk neutrality assumption, the relative advantage of price over quantity is approximated as

$$\Delta \cong -\frac{m+n}{2m^2}\sigma_f^2 + \frac{1}{m}\sigma_{fg}^2, \tag{3.6}$$

where m and n are, respectively, the slope of marginal product and marginal pollution damage function around the optimal (or deterministic) quantity; σ_f^2 is variance of shocks to marginal product; and σ_{fg}^2 is the covariance of uncertainties in marginal product and marginal damage. The derivation of (3.6) is given in Appendix 3.A.

The expression is similar to Weitzman's rule, except that the slope of marginal damage function is replaced by that of marginal product function; and the variance of shocks to marginal damage is replaced by that of marginal product. This is because in this case the household exercises the price control via the production process, while in Weitzman's original paper (1974), the behaviour function linking price and quantity is expressed by the equation that price is equal to the marginal cost. Therefore the shocks to marginal cost are important in his case, while the shocks to marginal product are relevant in this case.

The first term is the famous 'relative-slope' criterion. According to the properties of production and damage function, it is known that around the optimum, $m \leq 0$ and $n \geq 0$. Therefore this criterion says that, if around the optimum, the marginal product is steeper than the marginal damage, a price control is favourable. One extreme case will be the linear utility function where $n = 0$. If in addition there is no uncertainty to the damage, the marginal rate of substitution is a fixed ratio and independent of quantity and shocks, thus the household can plug the price at that ratio to achieve the first-best outcome in any states. On the other hand, if the marginal damage function is steeper, a quantity control policy is favourable.

The second term is the effect of correlated uncertainties of production and damage, as pointed out by Stavins (1996). A positive correlation tends to favour the quantity control mode, while a negative one tends to favour the price control mode.

3.4.2 Risk Aversion

It is clear that the revised model assumes that the household is risk-neutral to the net product (or income). How about risk aversion? The utility function may be rewritten as

$$U = U\big(C - g(D,\theta)\big) = U\big(f(d,\varepsilon) - g(D,\theta)\big),$$

where the utility function has the property $U' > 0$ and $U'' < 0$. Still further, because the uncertainty in production is crucial, it may be assumed there is only production uncertainty to simplify the derivation process. Specifically, the following utility function is assumed[7]

$$U = \ln\big(f(D,\varepsilon) - g(D)\big). \tag{3.7}$$

In this case, the relative advantage of price control over quantity control is

$$\Delta \cong -\frac{(m+n)(a-b)\sigma_f^2}{2m^2(a-b+(m-n)\rho/2)^2} - \frac{(m^2+n^2)\rho\sigma_f^2}{4m^2(a-b+(m-n)\rho/2)^2} + \ln\frac{a-b+(m-n)\rho/2}{a-b}.$$

The definition of parameters and the derivation process are given in Appendix 3.B. A couple of observations can be made from the above expression.

Note that $a > b$ by definition, so the first term is similar to the revised Weitzman's rule. It states that a steeper (flatter) marginal product curve tends to favour the price (quantity) control approach.

The last two terms are new. Note that $\rho > 0$ (see Appendix 3.B) and $m - n < 0$, therefore the last two terms are all negative. This means that a risk-averse household tends to favour the quantity control mode.

For the current case to be directly comparable with Weitzman's rule, the definition of relative advantage (3.B.3) can be replaced by (3.A.5), then the relative advantage becomes

$$\Delta \cong \frac{m+n}{2m^2}\sigma_f^2 + \frac{m-n}{2}\rho.$$

The first term in the above expression is exactly the same as the first one in (3.6). It is very clear that a quantity control mode is more likely desirable for the risk aversion utility than the risk neutral utility. Because a price control results in uncertainties in both production and damage while a quantity control leads to uncertainty only in the production side, it is natural for a risk-averse household to favour the quantity control, *ceteris paribus*. For appropriate parameters, this risk aversion effect may overwhelm the relative slope judgement.

In the above analysis, only one representative firm is considered. Therefore the quantity control and price control can be compared without considering the transaction costs involved to implement these policies. However, in a multi-firm economy, the preset quantity should be allocated via a tradable permit system if a quantity approach is implemented, while only one price is needed for the price approach. Therefore the price approach may incur less transaction cost than the quantity approach. The transaction cost may cause a quantity approach selected according to the relative-slope criterion to be unfavourable, or reinforce a price policy recommendation.

3.4.3 Environmental Investment

As discussed in the previous chapter, environmental investment or pollution cleansing activities cannot be omitted in the analysis. There are two ways to model a pollution cleansing activity. First, it can be expressed as a cleansing function separable to the damage function, that is,

$$U = f(D,\varepsilon) - S - g(D,\theta) + h(S,\mu),$$ (3.8)

where S is the spending on cleansing activities, μ is the uncertainty associated with the activities. The properties of the cleansing function are

$$h_S(S,\mu) > 0, \ h_{SS}(S,\mu) < 0, \ h_\mu(S,\mu) > 0, \ h_{\mu\mu}(S,\mu) \le 0, \ h_{S\mu}(S,\mu) \ge 0.$$

For the cleansing activities to be justified, $h_S > 1$ at least for some small value of S. And the budget constraint becomes

$$C + S \le f(D,\varepsilon),$$ (3.9)
$$S \le PD.$$ (3.10)

It can be postulated before detailed analysis that the inclusion of environmental investment is relevant to the policy choice of D or P, only if the constraint (3.10) is binding. As the condition for a fully earmarked scheme can be found in the previous chapter, and holding to the case that (3.10) is binding, (3.8) can be rewritten as

$$U = f(D,\varepsilon) - PD - g(D,\theta) + h(PD,\mu). \tag{3.11}$$

Alternatively, the spending can be used to directly reduce the pollution:

$$U = f(D,\varepsilon) - S - g(D - h(S,\mu),\theta).$$

This approach is more like the end-of-pipe treatment by firms. As argued previously, the environmental absorption capacity D is a production factor, and the treatment by firms is seen as a part of their production process. Therefore the former approach is more appropriate. After the messy derivation given in Appendix 3.C, the relative advantage of price control over quantity control is approximated as

$$\Delta \cong -\frac{(m+n)\sigma_f^2}{2m^2} + \frac{\sigma_{fg}^2}{m} + \frac{(c-d)\sigma_{fh}^2}{m(j-1)} + \frac{(m-n)\left(\sigma_{fh}^2\right)^2}{m(j-1)(2mj-m-n)}. \tag{3.12}$$

The first two terms in the above expression are revised Weitzman's rule as developed in (3.6), while the last two terms are new. Basically, they capture the effect of earmarking pollution-related revenues. Several observations can be made from this expression.

First, because the magnitude of cleansing activity is determined by the pollution charges or permit auction revenues which are, in turn, affected by the production, the covariance of uncertainties in cleansing and production enters into the relative advantage. If there is no uncertainty in cleansing activity, or the uncertainty is independent of that in the production process, the inclusion of cleansing activity in the model does not change the revised Weitzman's rule. However, it is highly possible they are correlated because the cleansing activity is just another kind of production activity.

Second, the relationship between uncertainties in damage and cleansing does not affect the relative advantage of price control over quantity control. This seems surprising. Although technically there is some relationship between damage and cleansing, they have separate effects in this model, and do not interact with each other. As mentioned in the previous paragraph, the cleansing activity is determined by the spending, while the damage is determined by the pollution (or environmental factor used).

Last, it is known that, for the pollution tax to be fully earmarked, the condition that $j \geq 1$ should be satisfied; and that $m < 0$, $n > 0$ and $c > d$ according to the properties of production and utility functions. It turns out that the last term is negative, and the sign of the third depends on the correlation between production and cleansing uncertainties. If they are positively (negatively) correlated, the sign is negative (positive). Therefore, if the pollution tax or permit auction revenue is used in environmental protection and the uncertainties in production and cleansing are positively correlated, it is more likely for a quantity control to be a better policy than in the case where earmarking is not considered. This effect reinforces that of correlation between uncertainties in production and damage, and may reverse the price control recommendation drawn from relative slopes. Even if the correlation is negative, it is still possible for a quantity control to be a better instrument. Because the relative advantage has a quadratic form in the covariance between production and cleansing uncertainties, σ_{fh}^2, and the coefficient of $(\sigma_{fh}^2)^2$ is negative, given other parameters, only a closed range of negative covariance can lead to a positive relative advantage. If the absolute value of the covariance is high enough, a quantity control is still desirable.

To see whether the effect of earmarking is likely to make a real difference, simple numerical exercises can be conducted. It is assumed that the production and damage uncertainties are independent in order to focus on the effect of earmarking. Expression (3.12) can be rearranged in terms of relative slope as

$$\Delta \cong \frac{1}{m}\left[-\frac{1}{2}\left(1+\frac{n}{m}\right)\sigma_f^2 + \frac{c-d}{j-1}\sigma_{fh}^2 + \frac{1-n/m}{(j-1)(2j-1-n/m)}(\sigma_{fh}^2)^2 \right], \qquad (3.13)$$

and assuming a unit value of σ_f^2, the right-hand side of (3.13) can be set equal to zero and solved for the 'threshold value' of covariance as follows:

$$\sigma_{fh}^2 = \frac{-(c-d)(2j-1-r) \pm \sqrt{(c-d)^2(2j-1-r)^2 + 2(j-1)(1-r^2)(2j-1-r)}}{2(1-r)},$$

where $r = n/m$ is the relative slope.

The numeric results are presented in Table 3.1. The high and low values in the table are threshold values of covariance between production and cleansing uncertainties that turn the policy recommendation from one mode to the other. Covariance falling between these two values justifies a price control mode, while covariance higher than the higher value or lower than the low value will make the price control unfavourable. The results confirm the above statement – a positive correlation between production and cleansing uncertainties tends to favour quantity control. For example, when the relative slope is the same, it would be the case of 'policy neutral' – both price and quantity controls lead to the same welfare, however a small positive correlation will make a quantity control policy desirable. If the marginal product is 10 times steeper than the marginal damage ($-1/r = -m/n = 10$), a

Table 3.1   Threshold value of covariance reversing policy choice

Relative	Threshold value of covariance*							
Slope	$j = 1.1$		$j = 1.5$		$j = 2.0$		$j = 2.5$	
$(-1/r)$	high	low	high	low	high	low	high	low
				$c - d = 1$				
0.1	n.a.	n.a.	n.a.	n.a.	n.a.	n.a.	n.a.	n.a.
0.2	-0.271	-0.762	n.a.	n.a.	n.a.	n.a.	n.a.	n.a.
0.5	-0.053	-1.014	-0.333	-1.000	n.a.	n.a.	n.a.	n.a.
1.0	0.000	-1.100	0.000	-1.500	0.000	-2.000	0.000	-2.500
2.0	0.025	-1.158	0.117	-1.784	0.228	-2.561	0.337	-3.337
5.0	0.039	-1.205	0.182	-2.015	0.353	-3.020	0.522	-4.022
10.0	0.043	-1.225	0.203	-2.112	0.397	-3.213	0.584	-4.311
				$c - d = 10$				
0.1	-0.045	-10.137	-0.230	-10.679	-0.469	-11.350	-0.715	-12.012
0.2	-0.020	-10.313	-0.101	-11.566	-0.203	-13.130	-0.306	-14.694
0.5	-0.005	-10.662	-0.025	-13.308	-0.050	-16.617	-0.075	-19.925
1.0	0.000	-11.000	0.000	-15.000	0.000	-20.000	0.000	-25.000
2.0	0.003	-11.336	0.0125	-16.679	0.025	-23.358	0.038	-30.038
5.0	0.004	-11.671	0.020	-18.353	0.040	-26.707	0.060	-35.060
10.0	0.005	-11.823	0.023	-19.113	0.045	-28.227	0.067	-37.340

Notes:
*   Covariance of production and cleansing uncertainties falling between the high and low values will justify a price control model. A covariance higher than the high value or lower than the low value will make the price control unfavourable.
n.a. Not applicable.

price control would be highly favourable according to the relative slope rule. However, when $j = 1.1$ and $c - d = 1$, a covariance as small as 0.043 will reverse the policy recommendation and make a quantity control policy favourable. But there is an asymmetry in the result. For example, if the marginal damage is 10 times steeper than the marginal product ($-1/r = 0.1$), it is impossible for a quantity control policy to become unfavourable for $c - d = 1$.

3.5   CONCLUDING REMARKS

Weitzman (1974) presents a simple rule to choose the policy options under uncertainty in a partial equilibrium model. The selection of policies is determined by the relative slopes of marginal benefit (demand) and cost (supply) functions. However, it is found that the selection of policy options is very complicated in a general equilibrium setting, so Weitzman's rule cannot be directly applied. The complication arises from the interaction between the production and consumption sides, and from the confusion of benefits and costs of the environmental factor. A revised rule similar to Weitzman's has been found under strong assumptions, namely, risk neutrality and separable utility. Introducing risk aversion and environmental spending in the model changes the relative advantages of one policy over the other. A quantity control policy is more likely to be favourable in these two situations.

There are several limitations in this analysis and further work is needed. First, the analysis is of the static general equilibrium type. It would be interesting to explore the idea in a dynamic setting. Second, more factors and more products could be included in the model. Third, the hybrid policy, which combines the quantity control and price control, could be compared to the two 'pure' policies discussed in this chapter.

APPENDIX

3.A   Derivation of Weitzman's Rule in General Equilibrium

With the new objective function (3.5), under a quantity control mode, the household selects a quantity level to maximise the expected value of (3.5):

$$\max_D\ E[f(D,\varepsilon) - g(D,\theta)].$$

The corresponding first order condition is

$$E[f_D(\overline{D},\varepsilon)] = E[g_D(\overline{D},\theta)],\qquad\qquad(3.A.1)$$

where $\overline{D}$ is used to denote a quantity control policy. When a price policy is announced, as mentioned above, the producer will adjust its production according to the following relationship

$$\overline{P} = f_D(D^P,\varepsilon),\qquad\qquad(3.A.2)$$

or $$D^P = D(\overline{P},\varepsilon).\qquad\qquad(3.A.3)$$

Knowing this relationship, the household selects a proper price to maximise the expected value of (3.5), that is,

$$\max_{\overline{P}}\ E[f(D^P(\overline{P},\varepsilon),\varepsilon) - g(D^P(\overline{P},\varepsilon),\theta)].$$

The first order condition is

$$E\left[f_D\big(D^P(\overline{P},\varepsilon),\varepsilon\big)\frac{\partial D^P}{\partial \overline{P}}\right] = E\left[g_D\big(D^P(\overline{P},\varepsilon),\theta\big)\frac{\partial D^P}{\partial \overline{P}}\right],$$

which gives

$$\overline{P} = \frac{E[g_D(D^P(\overline{P},\varepsilon),\theta)\partial D^P/\partial\overline{P}]}{E[\partial D^P/\partial\overline{P}]}, \tag{3.A.4}$$

The relative advantage of price over quantity can be defined as

$$\Delta = E[f(D^P,\varepsilon) - g(D^P,\theta)] - E[f(\overline{D},\varepsilon) - g(\overline{D},\theta)]. \tag{3.A.5}$$

Following Weitzman (1974), it is assumed that both functions are of the following quadratic form within an appropriate neighbourhood of $D = \hat{D}$:

$$f(D,\varepsilon) \cong a(\varepsilon) + (c + \alpha(\varepsilon))(D - \hat{D}) + \frac{m}{2}(D - \hat{D})^2, \tag{3.A.6}$$

$$g(D,\theta) \cong b(\theta) + (d + \beta(\theta))(D - \hat{D}) + \frac{n}{2}(D - \hat{D})^2, \tag{3.A.7}$$

where $a(\varepsilon)$, $\alpha(\varepsilon)$, $b(\theta)$ and $\beta(\theta)$ are stochastic functions and c, d, m and n are fixed coefficients. The following assumption has been made:

$$E[\alpha(\varepsilon)] = 0, \ E[(\alpha(\varepsilon))^2] = \sigma_f^2, \ E[\beta(\theta)] = 0, \ E[(\beta(\theta))^2] = \sigma_g^2, \tag{3.A.8}$$

and $$E[\alpha(\varepsilon)\beta(\theta)] = \sigma_{fg}^2. \tag{3.A.9}$$

Assuming zero mean of $\alpha(\varepsilon)$ and $\beta(\theta)$ does not lose generality. A non-zero mean is just like adding a constant number to the parameter c or d, but neither of them enters the final expression (3.A.20). If shocks to production and damage functions are independent, then the covariance in the above equation (3.A.9) would be zero.

The stochastic functions $a(\varepsilon) = f(\hat{D},\varepsilon)$ and $b(\theta) = f(\hat{D},\theta)$ translate different values of ε and θ into pure vertical shifts of the functions. Differentiating (3.A.6) and (3.A.7) with respect to D gives:

$$f_D(D,\varepsilon) \cong c + \alpha(\varepsilon) + m(D - \hat{D}), \tag{3.A.10}$$

$$g_D(D,\theta) \cong d + \beta(\theta) + n(D - \hat{D}). \tag{3.A.11}$$

Using the above equations and (3.A.8), the following relations are available for the fixed coefficients of (3.A.6) and (3.A.7):

$$E[f_D(\hat{D},\varepsilon)] \cong c, \ E[g_D(\hat{D},\theta)] \cong d, \ f_{DD}(D,\varepsilon) \cong m, \ g_{DD}(D,\theta) \cong n.$$

From (3.A.8) and $\overline{D} = \hat{D}$, it is derived that

$$c = d . \tag{3.A.12}$$

And from (3.A.8) and (3.A.10), the variance of marginal product is

$$E\left[\left(f_D(D,\varepsilon) - E[f_D(D,\varepsilon)]\right)^2\right] = E\left[\left(\alpha(\varepsilon) - E[\alpha(\varepsilon)]\right)^2\right] = \sigma_f^2 . \tag{3.A.13}$$

Similarly the variance of the marginal damage is

$$E\left[\left(g_D(D,\theta) - E[g_D(D,\theta)]\right)^2\right] = E\left[\left(\beta(\theta) - E[\beta(\theta)]\right)^2\right] = \sigma_g^2 .$$

Now consider the price control. From (3.A.10) and (3.A.2), we have

$$D^P \cong \hat{D} + \left(\overline{P} - c - \alpha(\varepsilon)\right)/m , \tag{3.A.14}$$

which implies

$$\partial D^P / \partial \overline{P} \cong 1/m . \tag{3.A.15}$$

Substituting (3.A.15) into (3.A.4) yields

$$\overline{P} \cong E[g_D(D^P(\overline{P},\varepsilon),\theta)] . \tag{3.A.16}$$

Replacing D in (3.A.11) by the expression for D^P from (3.A.14) and plugging into (3.A.16), the following equation is obtained after using (3.A.8)

$$\overline{P} \cong d + (\overline{P} - c)n/m . \tag{3.A.17}$$

From (3.A.12) and the condition $m \neq 0$ and $n \neq 0$, (3.A.17) implies

$$\overline{P} \cong d = c . \tag{3.A.18}$$

Combining (3.A.3), (3.A.14), and (3.A.18),

$$D^P \cong \hat{D} - \alpha(\varepsilon)/m . \tag{3.A.19}$$

Now alternately substitute $D = \hat{D} = \overline{D}$ and $D = D^P$ from (3.A.19) into (3.A.6) and (3.A.7). Then plugging the resulting values of (3.A.6) and (3.A.7) into (3.A.5), using (3.A.8) and (3.A.9), and collecting terms, gives

$$\Delta \cong -\frac{m+n}{2m^2}\sigma_f^2 + \frac{1}{m}\sigma_{fg}^2. \qquad (3.A.20)$$

3.B   Derivation of Policy Rule in General Equilibrium when Household is Risk-Averse

With the new objective function (3.7), under a quantity control mode, the household selects a quantity level to maximise the expected value of (3.7)

$$\max_D \; E[\ln(f(D,\varepsilon) - g(D))].$$

The corresponding first order condition is

$$E\left[\frac{f_D(\overline{D},\varepsilon) - g'(\overline{D})}{f(\overline{D},\varepsilon) - g(\overline{D})}\right] = 0, \qquad (3.B.1)$$

where $\overline{D}$ denotes the preset quantity control.   When a price policy is announced, the producer will adjust its production according to the relationship (3.A.2) or (3.A.3).   Knowing this relationship, the household selects a proper price to maximise the expected value of (3.7), that is,

$$\max_{\overline{P}} \; E[\ln(f(D^P(\overline{P},\varepsilon),\varepsilon) - g(D^P(\overline{P},\varepsilon)))].$$

The first order condition is

$$E\left[\frac{f_D(D^P(D,\varepsilon),\varepsilon) - g'(D^P(\overline{P},\varepsilon))}{f(D^P,\varepsilon) - g(D^P)}\frac{\partial D^P}{\partial \overline{P}}\right] = 0. \qquad (3.B.2)$$

The relative advantage of price over quantity can be defined as

$$\Delta \cong E[\ln(f(D^P,\varepsilon) - g(D^P))] - E[\ln(f(\overline{D},\varepsilon) - g(\overline{D}))]. \qquad (3.B.3)$$

It is assumed that both production and damage functions are of the following quadratic form within an appropriate neighbourhood of $D = \hat{D}$:

$$f(D,\varepsilon) \cong a + (c + \alpha(\varepsilon))(D - \hat{D}) + \frac{m}{2}(D - \hat{D})^2, \qquad (3.B.4)$$

$$g(D) \cong b + d(D - \hat{D}) + \frac{n}{2}(D - \hat{D})^2 ,$$ (3.B.5)

where a, b, c, d, m and n are fixed coefficients, and $\alpha(\varepsilon)$ is a stochastic function which is characterised as:

$$E[\alpha(\varepsilon)] = 0, \ E[(\alpha(\varepsilon))^2] = \sigma_f^2 .$$ (3.B.6)

Differentiating (3.B.4) and (3.B.5) with respect to D gives (3.A.10) and:

$$g'(D) \cong d + n(D - \hat{D}) .$$ (3.B.7)

Using (3.B.6), (3.B.7) and (3.A.10), the following relations are available for the fixed coefficients of (3.B.4) and (3.B.5):

$$f(\hat{D}, \varepsilon) \cong a, \ g(\hat{D}) \cong b, \ E[f_D(\hat{D}, \varepsilon)] \cong c,$$
$$g'(\hat{D}) \cong d, \ f_{DD}(D, \varepsilon) \cong m, \ g_{DD}(D) \cong n.$$

From (3.B.1), using $\overline{D} = \hat{D}$ gives

$$c = d .$$ (3.B.8)

Now consider the price control. Following the previous procedure, from (3.A.10) and (3.A.2), gives (3.A.14), which implies (3.A.15). Substituting from (3.A.15) into (3.B.2) yields

$$E\left[\frac{\overline{P} - g'(D^P(\overline{P}, \varepsilon))}{f(D^P, \varepsilon) - g(D^P)} \right] \cong 0 .$$ (3.B.9)

To proceed, it is necessary to use the following approximation of expectation

$$E[x(\alpha)] \cong x(0) + x'(0)E[\alpha] + \frac{x''(0)}{2} E[\alpha^2] .$$ (3.B.10)

Replacing D in (3.B.4), (3.B.5) and (3.B.7) by the expression for D^P from (3.A.14) and plugging into (3.B.9), the following equation is obtained after using (3.B.10) and (3.B.6):

$$\overline{P} \cong c + m\rho^{1/2} ,$$ (3.B.11)

where
$$\rho = \frac{-B \pm \sqrt{B^2 - 4AC}}{2A};$$

and
$$A = \frac{1}{2}m^2(m-n)^3,$$

$$B = \frac{1}{2}\sigma_f^2(m-n)(m^2+n^2) + 2m^2(m-n)^2(a-b),$$

$$C = (a-b)\left(\sigma_f^2(m^2 - 3n^2) + 2m^2(m-n)(a-b)\right).$$

Combining (3.A.3), (3.A.14), and (3.B.11), gives

$$D^P \cong \hat{D} + \rho^{1/2} - \alpha(\varepsilon)/m. \tag{3.B.12}$$

Now alternately substitute $D = \hat{D} = \overline{D}$ and $D = D^P$ from (3.B12) into (3.B.4) and (3.B.5). Then plugging the resulting values of (3.B.4) and (3.B.5) into (3.B.3), using (3.B.10) and (3.B.6), and collecting terms,

$$\Delta \cong -\frac{\left(2(m+n)(a-b) + (m^2+n^2)\rho\right)\sigma_f^2}{4m^2(a-b+(m-n)\rho/2)^2} + \ln\frac{a-b+(m-n)\rho/2}{a-b}. \tag{3.B.13}$$

If the definition of relative advantage (3.B.3) is replaced by (3.A.5) for the current case to be directly comparable with Weitzman's rule, the procedure giving (3.B.13) leads to the following result

$$\Delta \cong -\frac{m+n}{2m^2}\sigma_f^2 + \frac{m-n}{2}\rho. \tag{3.B.14}$$

3.C   Derivation of Policy Rule in General Equilibrium when Environmental Spending is Considered

With the new objective function (3.11), under a quantity control mode, the household selects a quantity level to maximise the expected value of (3.11)

$$\max_D \ E[f(D,\varepsilon) - PD - g(D,\theta) + h(PD,\mu)],$$

and the price of the environmental factor is determined by (3.A.2). The corresponding first order condition is

$$E[\overline{D}f_{DD}(\overline{D},\varepsilon)(h_S(P\overline{D},\mu)-1) + h_S(P\overline{D},\mu)f_D(\overline{D},\varepsilon)] = E[g_D(\overline{D},\theta)], \tag{3.C.1}$$

where $\overline{D}$ is used to denote it is a quantity control policy, and h_S denotes the partial derivative of $h(S, \mu)$ with respect to its first argument $S (= PD)$.

As mentioned above, when a price policy is announced, the producer will adjust its production according to the relationship (3.A.2) or (3.A.3). Knowing this relationship, the household selects a proper price to maximise the expected value of (3.11), that is,

$$\max_{\overline{P}} \ E[f(D^P(\overline{P}, \varepsilon), \varepsilon) - \overline{P}D^P - g(D^P(\overline{P}, \varepsilon), \theta) + h(\overline{P}D^P, \mu)].$$

The first order condition is

$$E\left[-D^P - g_D(D^P(\overline{P}, \varepsilon), \theta)\frac{\partial D^P}{\partial \overline{P}} + h_S(\overline{P}D^P, \mu)\left(D^P + \overline{P}\frac{\partial D^P}{\partial \overline{P}} \right) \right] = 0,$$

which gives

$$\overline{P} = \frac{E[g_D(D^P(\overline{P}, \varepsilon), \theta)\partial D^P/\partial \overline{P} + (1 - h_S(\overline{P}D^P, \mu))D^P]}{E[h_S(\overline{P}D^P, \mu)\partial D^P/\partial \overline{P}]}. \qquad (3.C.2)$$

The relative advantage of price over quantity can be written as

$$\Delta \cong E[f(D^P, \varepsilon) - \overline{P}D^P - g(D^P, \theta) + h(\overline{P}D^P, \mu)]$$
$$- E[f(\overline{D}, \varepsilon) - P\overline{D} - g(\overline{D}, \theta) + h(P\overline{D}, \mu)]. \qquad (3.C.3)$$

It is assumed that both the production and damage functions are of the quadratic form within an appropriate neighbourhood of $D = \hat{D}$, expressed as (3.A.6) and (3.A.7). However, for simplicity, it is assumed that the cleansing function has a linear form of spending:

$$h(S, \mu) \cong (j + \gamma(\mu))S = (j + \gamma(\mu))PD, \qquad (3.C.4)$$

where $\gamma(\mu)$ is a stochastic function and j a fixed coefficient. The mean and variance of the stochastic terms are assumed as expressed in (3.A.8) and (3.A.9), and

$$E[\gamma(\mu)] = 0, \ E[(\gamma(\mu))^2] = \sigma_h^2,$$
$$E[\alpha(\varepsilon)\gamma(\mu)] = \sigma_{fh}^2, \ E[\beta(\theta)\gamma(\mu)] = \sigma_{gh}^2. \qquad (3.C.5)$$

Implicitly, the cleansing function has a quadratic form in D too. Differentiating (3.A.6) and (3.A.7) with respect to D gives (3.A.10) and

(3.A.11), and differentiating (3.C.4) with respect to S gives

$$h_S(S,\mu) \cong j + \gamma(\mu).$$ (3.C.6)

Using equations (3.A.8)–(3.A.10) and (3.C.5)–(3.C.6), the following relations are available

$$f_{DD}(D,\varepsilon) \cong m,\ E[h_S(S,\mu)] \cong j,$$
$$E[\hat{D}f_{DD}(\hat{D},\varepsilon)(h_S(S,\mu)-1)] \cong m(j-1)\hat{D},$$
$$E[h_S(S,\mu)f_D(\hat{D},\varepsilon)] \cong jc + \sigma_{fh}^2,\ E[g_D(\hat{D},\theta)] \cong d.$$

From (3.C.1),

$$d = m(j-1)\hat{D} + jc + \sigma_{fh}^2.$$ (3.C.7)

Now consider the price control. From (3.A.10), (3.A.11), (3.A.2) and (3.A.14), (3.A.15) is obtained, and

$$E\left[g_D(D^P,\theta)\frac{\partial D^P}{\partial \overline{P}}\right] \cong \frac{1}{m}\left(d + \frac{n}{m}(\overline{P}-c)\right),$$ (3.C.8)

$$E[D^P] \cong \hat{D} + \frac{\overline{P}-c}{m},$$ (3.C.9)

$$E[h_S(\overline{P}D^P,\mu)D^P] \cong j\hat{D} + \frac{j(\overline{P}-c)}{m} - \frac{1}{m}\sigma_{fh}^2,$$ (3.C.10)

$$E\left[h_S(\overline{P}D^P,\mu)\frac{\partial D^P}{\partial \overline{P}}\right] \cong \frac{j}{m}.$$ (3.C.11)

Substituting from (3.C.8)–(3.C.11) into (3.C.2), and using (3.C.7) yields

$$\overline{P} \cong c + \frac{2m\sigma_{fh}^2}{2mj - m - n}.$$ (3.C.12)

Combining (3.A.14) and (3.C.12) gives

$$D^P \cong \hat{D} - \frac{\alpha(\varepsilon)}{m} + \frac{2\sigma_{fh}^2}{2mj - m - n}.$$ (3.C.13)

Now alternately substitute $D = \hat{D} = \overline{D}$ and $D = D^P$ from (3.C.13) into (3.A.6), (3.A.7) and (3.C.4). Then plugging the resulting values of (3.A.6), (3.A.7) and (3.B.4) into (3.A.5); using (3.A.8), (3.A.9) and (3.C.5); and collecting terms,

$$\Delta \cong -\frac{m+n}{2m^2}\sigma_f^2 + \frac{1}{m}\sigma_{fg}^2 + \frac{(c-d)\sigma_{fh}^2}{m(j-1)} + \frac{(m-n)(\sigma_{fh}^2)^2}{m(j-1)(2mj-m-n)}. \qquad (3.C.14)$$

NOTES

1. A hybrid policy, such as that proposed by Roberts and Spence (1976), Weitzman (1978) and McKibbin and Wilcoxen (1997), is a combination of these two policy options.

   As discussed in Chapter 2, as price instrument (tax) can generate revenues to the government, while quantity instrument (grandfathered permit system) cannot, they are not equivalent even with complete knowledge and perfect certainty. Moreover, as will be shown in Chapters 5 and 8, they are different because permit trading can generate income transfers across borders while an emission tax may not.

2. Similar results can be found in Fishelson (1976).

3. Here the household also exerts the function of government. As there is no tax on the household's income by government and no environmental spending in the current discussion, it is equivalent to a more decentralised three agent firm–household–government model. For details see the appendix to Chapter 2.

4. For simplicity and without losing generality, this one-factor production process is assumed. Introducing other factors will significantly complicate the analysis.

5. Throughout this chapter, the first-best refers to the *ex post* optimum, while the policies are set at best to achieve the *ex ante* optimum.

6. In this one-firm economy, it does not matter how the quantity is allocated. However, it is important in a multi-firm economy to have the quantity or permit allocated efficiently. This means that the quantity approach should be a tradable permit system for it to be comparable with the price control approach.

7. The selection of this functional form is purely for simplicity. However, it can be shown that other functional forms representing risk aversion will lead to similar results.

4. Effectiveness and Efficiency: An Assessment of China's Environmental Protection Policy[*]

Opinions about China's pollution control policies have been controversial. Critics argue that the policies have failed to succeed as China's environmental quality tends to worsen, while supporters claim China has achieved much in environmental protection.[1] However, those discussions are mainly qualitative or based on particular case studies. Moreover, both arguments do not necessarily contradict each other as they are often made against different criteria. A policy can be evaluated using two criteria. The first, which may be termed the 'effectiveness' criterion, is to investigate whether the policy helps to achieve the specified objectives. In the case of an environmental policy, the effectiveness refers to whether the policy induces firms and/or consumers to change their behaviour and reduce the emissions below the level that would have existed if the policy had not been implemented. The second, which may be termed the 'efficiency' criterion, is to ask whether the objectives are set at a level to achieve the welfare maximum.

This chapter attempts to examine the effectiveness and efficiency of China's pollution control policies in a quantitative way. It is organised as follows. The next section gives a brief introduction to policies, with the emphasis on the pollution levy system. Section 4.2 gives a simple description of the data used for this analysis. Then the changes in China's pollutant discharges are decomposed in section 4.3 to identify the factors contributing to these changes. The theory of equilibrium pollution is introduced in section 4.4 to set up a mechanism for efficiency testing, and the estimation functions of environmental supply and demand are specified in section 4.5. The estimation results are presented and discussed in section 4.6, followed by some concluding remarks.

4.1 CHINA'S POLLUTION CONTROL POLICIES

One important environmental policy in China is 'prevention first'. The official view has been the slogan of 'harmonised development of the economy and the environment'. It was argued that the pattern of 'control after pollution' is only a phenomenon in the capitalist world, whilst economic growth could be achieved with an improvement in environmental quality in socialist China. However, this view is challenged by the real situation, and the guidelines for environmental protection have gradually become more pragmatic. The change can first be found in the inaugural speech to the inter-ministerial National Committee of Environmental Protection by the then State Counciller Song Jian when he took the office of Committee Chairman in September 1988. He pointed out, 'our current task is ... to prevent the environmental quality from further deterioration along with the economic development. ... When the economy develops to a certain level and we have enough economic resources later, we will improve the environmental quality eventually' (Song 1988).

Another policy, which is more operational, is 'whoever causes pollution is responsible for its elimination', or 'polluter pays'. It is argued that, if the industries, enterprises and institutions that discharge pollutants shifted responsibility for pollution control onto the government and the society, it would be difficult to raise the funds to control pollution (Qu 1991). As will be seen, the requirement that enterprises meet discharge standards, the pollution levy system, and the 'three-synchronisation' system are all based on this policy.

As the funds for constructing waste treatment and new 'clean' production facilities are not available in the short term, the Chinese government has adopted the policy of strengthening environmental management as a realistic and active way to control pollution (Qu 1992). The term 'environmental management' includes a broad range of activities, from monitoring and enforcement by environmental protection authorities to good housekeeping practices at factories.

A set of instruments has been developed to carry out these policies in China. They are environmental impact assessment (EIA), pollution levy system, three-synchronisation policy, pollution report and discharge permit system, environmental responsibility system, centralised pollution control, limited time treatment, assessment of urban environmental quality, and so on. Most of them fall into the category of command and control regulation.

4.1.1 Pollution Levy System

China's pollution levy system dates from the late 1970s. A brief introduction to the history and implementation of this system was given in section 1.3 of this book.

This system has received heavy criticism. For example, the standard was set on the concentration only, and firms could simply dilute their emissions to meet the standard. Now quantity control has also been introduced. It is also argued that the levy rate is too low to create an incentive for firms to comply with the environmental regulation. Thus, from some critics' point of view, the levy is merely a local financing mechanism and is ineffective as a regulation instrument. Moreover, the strictness of enforcement is believed to vary widely, so that factories in different regions face very different penalties for polluting (Qu 1991, NEPA 1994, Shibli and Markandya 1995, Wang and Lu 1997).[2]

However, a series of papers by World Bank staff show that the pollution levy system has played an important role in preventing China's water environment from further deterioration. Using firm level data, Dasgupta et al. (1996) find that the current pollution levy system provides an economic incentive to abate. However, their results also suggest that changing to a full emissions charge system would greatly reduce overall abatement cost. Based on the equilibrium pollution theory, an econometric analysis by Wang and Wheeler (1996) finds that the water pollution levy system is neither arbitrary nor ineffective. Across provinces, and over time, variations in the effective levy rate are well explained by proxies for local valuation of environmental damage and community capacity to enforce local norms. But their findings cannot be extended to air pollution control without further analysis. Moreover, as the environmental supplies are concurrently determined for all elements, consideration of only wastewater may bias the results.

4.1.2 Environmental Impact Assessment

Clause 6 of the 1979 Provisional Environmental Protection Law states:

> All enterprises and institutions shall pay adequate attention to the prevention of pollution and damage to the environment during site selection, design, construction, and operation. Project design cannot be started until the report on the potential environmental effects has been reviewed and approved by the responsible environmental protection department and other relevant administrative departments ...

Formal implementation of EIA was followed by an administrative order from the National Environmental Protection Commission in 1981. New projects are required to fill in a simple environmental impact assessment form or carry out a formal EIA procedure according to the nature and size of the proposed project, which also determines the jurisdiction of evaluating and approving the EIA report among environmental protection authorities at different levels. Similar to the practice in other countries, an EIA for a proposed project involves assessing the existing environmental quality of the project site, predicting the effect on environmental quality of the project and raising some recommendations on how to mitigate any adverse effects. However, the public in China has little chance of participating in the EIA process. The practice of EIA in China is often criticised as 'merely following the procedure and making a gesture to give the impression of doing something' because the proposed projects are usually backed by the government and it is hard to reject them merely on the basis of environmental concerns.

4.1.3 Three-Synchronisation Policy

The three-synchronisation policy, or 'three simultaneous steps' policy, requires that the design, construction and operation of a new production facility be synchronised with the design, construction and operation of appropriate waste treatment facilities. A production facility cannot be put into operation without passing the evaluation of this three-synchronisation requirement by environmental protection and industrial administrative authorities.

This policy has also been criticised as 'purely making a gesture' because firms can just shut down the waste treatment facilities after passing the evaluation. Actually this has been a common practice for firms, especially township and village enterprises. This not only contributes nothing to environmental protection, but also wastes resources in building treatment facilities which may never be used.

4.1.4 Other Policy Instruments

Limited time treatment. Every year, environmental protection authorities identify some heavily polluting factories in their jurisdictions and set deadlines for these firms to treat their pollution to meet the standard. If the requirement is not met in time, the firm will be ordered to temporarily halt production, or even be closed or relocated.

The pollution report and discharge permit system requires polluting factories to report their pollution discharge to local environmental authorities. A discharge permit is then issued after assessing the situation. Although implemented for several years, this system is still at the preliminary stage, because it is difficult and costly to determine the appropriate number of permits. To date, only a few regional markets have emerged for permit trading at an experimental stage.

Centralised pollution control. In newly established industrial parks, individual firms are encouraged to pipe their emissions into a centralised treatment facility. This practice has been promoted because it may provide economies of scale and may be cost-efficient.

The environmental responsibility system is usually taken to refer to the environmental protection contract signed by government leaders at different levels. This system is mainly designed as a tool to draw more attention to environmental protection from government leaders.

An assessment of urban environmental quality is conducted annually and the results are reported in the media. This creates public pressure on local government to improve environmental quality.

A taxation exemption or deduction is granted to firms using or recycling wastes. However, this instrument is outside the control of local environmental authorities.

4.2   THE DATA

Five-year (1992–96) environmental and economic data for 28 provinces, autonomous regions and municipalities directly under the central government in mainland China (Chongqing is included in Sichuan and Tibet and Hainan are excluded due to missing data) are mainly taken from various China Environmental Yearbooks (Editorial Committee of China Environmental Yearbook 1993–98) and China Statistical Yearbooks (SSB 1990–98).

However, the pollution emission data in China Environmental Yearbooks include only 'polluting firms owned by governments at and/or above county level'. In order to get the whole picture of emissions, the total emissions are estimated using two assumptions: (1) other firms owned by governments at and/or above county level are pollution-free, otherwise they would be included in the statistics by requirement (and definition); and (2) firms owned by township and village governments and private firms have the same pollution emission ratio.[3] Therefore, the total emissions of one pollutant are calculated as follows:

$$e_t = \frac{e_c}{Y_c} \times Y_t,$$

where e_t and Y_t are, respectively, total emission amount and total industrial output value; e_c and Y_c are, respectively, the emission and output value of firms owned by governments at and/or above county level.

There are no data available for waste gas and solid waste emissions violating the standard. However, the treated amount of waste gas emissions is identified in the statistics. It is assumed that those treated discharges meet the emission standard, that is, the excess waste gas emissions[4] are calculated as the difference between total emissions and treated volume.

The environmental regulation indices are calculated as the enforcement rates of environmental impact assessment, three synchronisation, pollution permit and limited time treatment, and the staff numbers in environmental protection authorities. The enforcement rate of the pollution permit system is measured in the ratio of the number of firms reporting their emissions to the total number of firms in each region. The enforcement rate of the pollution control within deadline (limited time treatment) is measured in the ratio of the number of pollution control projects actually completed in the year to the number of projects that should be completed. Staff is measured in number per 10 000 RMB yuan of industrial output and normalised across regions and over time.

Because the producer price index is not available for every province, the price index of firms' capital investment is used to deflate the output value. The consumer price index is used to calculate real per capita income.

4.2.1 A First Look at the Data

The data show that there are tremendous variations in effective levy rates across regions. For example, in 1996 the effective levy rate varies from 0.221 (Shanghai) to 0.024 yuan/ton (Hubei) for excess wastewater; from 0.292 (Beijing) to 0.026 yuan/kg (Shandong) for chemical oxygen demand (COD); from 6.458 (Tianjin) to 0.536 yuan/10 000m^3 (Ningxia) for excess waste gas; from 0.637 (Xingjiang) to 0.066 yuan/10 000m^3 (Shandong) for waste gas; from 0.063 (Heilongjiang) to 0.005 yuan/kg (Shaanxi) for SO$_2$; from 0.152 (Guangdong) to 0.009 yuan/kg (Shaanxi) for smoke dust; from 0.194 (Tianjin) to 0.015 yuan/kg (Shaaxi) for powder dust; and from 9.295 (Shandong) to 0.020 yuan/ton (Qinghai) for solid wastes (see Table 4.1 and Figure 4.1). Moreover, the difference in effective levy rate across regions has tended to increase over time (see Table 4.1 and Figure 4.2). This supports the criticism that the stringency of enforcement varies widely across regions. However, this disparity in effective rates may reflect the differences in conditions across regions, and it may be desirable in order to achieve cost-efficiency. Without further study, a judgement cannot be made based only on this observation.

The second observation from the data is that effective levy rates in real terms remain at similar levels, or even decline over time (see Figure 4.2). For example, the mean of effective rates for excess wastewater was, respectively, 0.0709 yuan/ton in 1992 and 0.0714 yuan/ton in 1996, while the mean rate for COD declined from 0.1174 to 0.1054 yuan/kg over the same period. A similar result is found for other pollutants. Given this trend, the relationship between the effective rate and pollution intensity is quite complicated. The difference across regions suggests a negative relationship, while the change over time gives the reverse answer since the intensity has declined over time.

Table 4.1   Selected statistics for effective levy rates

Pollutants	Year	Max	Min	Mean	Median	Variance	Coeff. variation
Excess	1992	0.155	0.028	0.071	0.064	0.001	45.485
wastewater	1993	0.165	0.024	0.058	0.050	0.001	50.607
(yuan/ton)	1994	0.140	0.022	0.057	0.047	0.001	51.115
	1995	0.222	0.014	0.066	0.051	0.002	71.213
	1996	0.221	0.024	0.071	0.043	0.003	76.168
COD	1992	0.292	0.035	0.117	0.113	0.003	47.014
(yuan/kg)	1993	0.249	0.041	0.106	0.080	0.003	54.037
	1994	0.219	0.013	0.098	0.090	0.003	54.799
	1995	0.309	0.025	0.100	0.073	0.006	77.503
	1996	0.292	0.026	0.105	0.070	0.006	75.479
Excess	1992	3.671	0.341	1.845	1.883	0.500	38.323
waste gas	1993	3.573	0.655	1.591	1.641	0.383	38.862
(yuan/	1994	3.527	0.722	1.625	1.425	0.506	43.781
10 000m^3)	1995	5.732	0.434	1.657	1.448	1.297	68.724
	1996	6.458	0.536	1.812	1.463	1.718	72.346
Waste gas	1992	0.834	0.057	0.377	0.363	0.024	40.626
(yuan/	1993	0.547	0.118	0.304	0.275	0.012	36.334
10 000m^3)	1994	0.488	0.102	0.278	0.233	0.012	40.216
	1995	0.660	0.087	0.267	0.229	0.022	55.564
	1996	0.637	0.066	0.258	0.198	0.022	57.709
SO$_2$	1992	0.143	0.004	0.035	0.029	0.001	88.439
(yuan/kg)	1993	0.081	0.008	0.027	0.023	0.000	67.406
	1994	0.070	0.005	0.024	0.019	0.000	64.481
	1995	0.063	0.005	0.023	0.018	0.000	70.964
	1996	0.063	0.005	0.024	0.018	0.000	70.600
Smoke dust	1992	0.085	0.008	0.043	0.040	0.000	49.834
(yuan/kg)	1993	0.090	0.010	0.037	0.034	0.000	54.278
	1994	0.093	0.008	0.036	0.033	0.000	52.845
	1995	0.157	0.008	0.039	0.030	0.001	82.229
	1996	0.152	0.009	0.041	0.032	0.001	75.469
Powder	1992	0.174	0.016	0.061	0.049	0.001	54.360
dust	1993	0.178	0.019	0.053	0.037	0.001	65.385
(yuan/kg)	1994	0.165	0.014	0.051	0.040	0.001	62.235
	1995	0.241	0.013	0.053	0.038	0.002	90.537
	1996	0.193	0.015	0.056	0.039	0.002	71.677
Solid	1992	12.774	0.000	1.824	0.987	8.015	155.210
wastes	1993	7.075	0.001	1.335	0.692	2.487	118.105
(yuan/ton)	1994	5.826	0.000	1.409	0.900	1.804	95.321
	1995	15.755	0.010	2.944	1.304	17.223	140.954
	1996	9.295	0.020	1.683	0.885	4.343	123.829

Source: Author's calculation based on data from Editorial Committee of China Environmental Yearbook (1993–98).

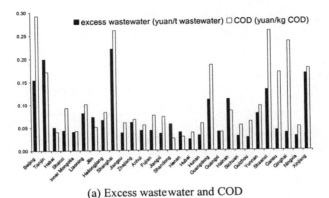

(a) Excess wastewater and COD

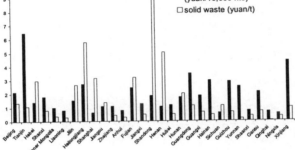

(b) Excess waste gas and solid wastes

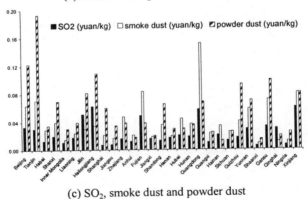

(c) SO₂, smoke dust and powder dust

Source: Author's construction based on data from Editorial Committee of China Environmental Yearbook (1993–98).

Figure 4.1   Effective pollution levy rates, 1996

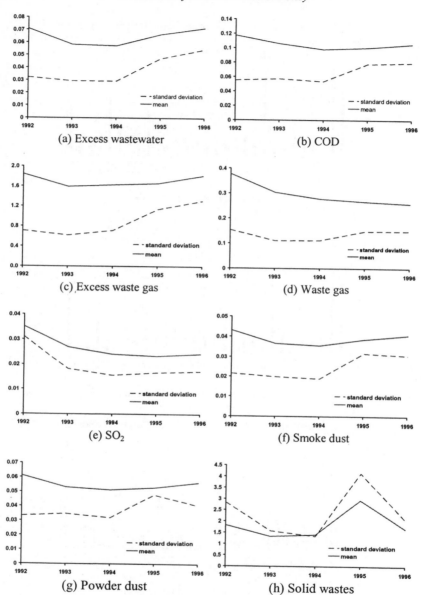

Source: Author's construction based on data from Editorial Committee of China Environmental Yearbook (1993–98).

Figure 4.2 Average and variance of effective levy rates

In contrast to the levy system, other regulation indices vary across regions to a much smaller degree, and the variation seems to decrease over time (see Table 4.2). Except for the permit system, other systems have a much smaller coefficient of variation. This is because these systems have been implemented for quite a long time. In contrast, the pollution report and permit system is at the preliminary stage of implementation and the related data may not be reliable. Therefore the index for the permit system is dropped in the following work.

The pollution intensities decrease steadily over time. This shows that China has made a significant achievement in preventing further environmental deterioration along with economic development. This will be discussed in detail in the following section. The variance of pollution intensities across regions is slightly higher than that of effective levy rates, but in contrast to the

Table 4.2   Selected statistics for regulation indices

	Year	Max	Min	Mean	Median	Variance	Coeff. variation
EIA	1992	100.00	1.46	64.93	70.69	641.53	39.01
	1993	100.00	1.66	66.67	70.94	581.42	36.17
	1994	100.00	14.25	71.36	79.71	546.80	32.77
	1995	100.00	23.35	81.25	87.01	314.22	21.82
	1996	100.00	43.90	84.47	92.45	232.69	18.06
Three	1992	100.00	43.36	86.72	89.97	144.13	13.84
synchro-	1993	98.53	53.54	84.37	88.55	131.04	13.57
nisations	1994	99.27	69.72	86.64	86.59	57.50	8.75
	1995	96.99	31.62	85.10	88.21	151.10	14.44
	1996	99.80	77.65	89.60	90.00	36.03	6.70
Limited	1992	143.36	66.28	88.74	89.11	241.58	17.51
time	1993	107.26	66.67	85.89	85.00	66.45	9.49
treatment	1994	106.27	26.32	83.02	85.04	198.34	16.96
	1995	125.68	8.06	79.53	82.88	393.23	24.94
	1996	112.00	26.32	78.27	82.28	381.86	24.96
Staff in	1992	8.88	0.86	3.07	3.05	3.16	57.85
environ-	1993	7.55	0.83	2.95	2.82	2.81	56.87
mental	1994	7.18	0.73	2.60	2.23	2.52	61.02
authority	1995	7.67	0.55	2.44	2.04	2.39	63.41
	1996	7.56	0.56	2.45	2.30	2.34	62.50
Permit	1992	32.34	0.00	1.66	0.32	35.25	357.66
	1993	32.32	0.01	1.63	0.44	35.15	364.65
	1994	30.21	0.00	2.55	0.41	55.26	290.97
	1995	48.97	0.00	2.35	0.49	81.24	382.91
	1996	41.47	0.00	3.65	0.71	70.89	230.89

Source: Author's calculation based on data from Editorial Committee of China Environmental Yearbook (1993–98).

trend of levy rates, the variance of intensities tends to dampen over time (see Table 4.3 and Figure 4.3).

Finally, plotting the effective levy rate against the intensity for each pollutant clearly shows there is a negative relation between them (see Figure 4.4). This implies that there may exist a well-behaved demand function for pollution or environmental absorption capacity.

4.3   FACTORS CONTRIBUTING TO THE FALL IN POLLUTION INTENSITY

Let Q_{it} and Q_t denote the real output level of sector i and the total output level, respectively, in time t; E_{it} the pollution emission of sector i in time t; e_{it} the emission coefficient of sector i in time t (pollution emission per unit of real output value); s_{it} the output share of sector i in time t. The difference in pollution emission between two points of time can be decomposed into:

$$
\begin{aligned}
E_2 - E_1 &= \Sigma_i Q_{i2} e_{i2} - \Sigma_i Q_{i1} e_{i1} \\
&= \Sigma_i Q_{i2} e_{i2} - \Sigma_i Q_{i2} e_{i1} + \Sigma_i Q_{i2} e_{i1} - \Sigma_i Q_{i1} e_{i1} \\
&= \Sigma_i Q_{i2} (e_{i2} - e_{i1}) + \Sigma_i (Q_{i2} - Q_{i1}) e_{i1} \\
\Sigma_i (Q_{i2} - Q_{i1}) e_{i1} &= \Sigma_i (Q_2 s_{i2} - Q_1 s_{i1}) e_{i1} \\
&= \Sigma_i (Q_2 s_{i2} - Q_2 s_{i1} + Q_2 s_{i1} - Q_1 s_{i1}) e_{i1} \\
&= \Sigma_i [Q_2 (s_{i2} - s_{i1}) + (Q_2 - Q_1) s_{i1}] e_{i1} \\
&= Q_2 \Sigma_i (s_{i2} - s_{i1}) e_{i1} + (Q_2 - Q_1) \Sigma_i s_{i1} e_{i1}
\end{aligned}
$$

Therefore, the decrease or increase in emissions consists of three effects: the efficiency effect, which is the change in emission coefficient for a given amount of output resulting from the economical use of input materials, the structural effect, and the growth effect:

$$
E_2 - E_1 = \Sigma_i Q_{i2} (e_{i2} - e_{i1}) + Q_2 \Sigma_i (s_{i2} - s_{i1}) e_{i1} + (Q_2 - Q_1) \Sigma_i s_{i1} e_{i1} .
$$

It should be pointed out that selecting different levels of output, sectoral shares and emission coefficients results in different decompositions. In addition to the above decomposition, there are three more decompositions:

$$
\begin{aligned}
E_2 - E_1 &= \Sigma_i Q_{i2} (e_{i2} - e_{i1}) + Q_1 \Sigma_i (s_{i2} - s_{i1}) e_{i1} + (Q_2 - Q_1) \Sigma_i s_{i2} e_{i1} , \\
E_2 - E_1 &= \Sigma_i Q_{i1} (e_{i2} - e_{i1}) + Q_1 \Sigma_i (s_{i2} - s_{i1}) e_{i2} + (Q_2 - Q_1) \Sigma_i s_{i2} e_{i2} , \\
E_2 - E_1 &= \Sigma_i Q_{i1} (e_{i2} - e_{i1}) + Q_2 \Sigma_i (s_{i2} - s_{i1}) e_{i2} + (Q_2 - Q_1) \Sigma_i s_{i1} e_{i2} .
\end{aligned}
$$

Table 4.3   Selected statistics for pollution intensities

Pollutant	Year	Max	Min	Mean	Median	Variance	Coeff. variation
Excess	1992	123.778	14.748	57.061	51.404	868.271	51.640
wastewater	1993	104.845	9.799	48.642	43.995	589.205	49.903
(ton/10 000	1994	91.493	9.164	40.943	34.051	473.644	53.156
yuan)	1995	89.938	5.926	38.156	30.648	506.166	58.963
	1996	93.493	5.669	35.832	28.377	450.826	59.256
COD	1992	102.291	10.583	35.574	32.715	443.222	59.181
(kg/10 000	1993	111.826	4.942	28.866	26.360	394.373	68.797
yuan)	1994	188.916	6.363	30.308	20.697	1280.385	118.063
	1995	121.001	4.284	28.964	20.756	570.506	82.466
	1996	94.469	4.056	26.162	23.523	328.905	69.321
Excess	1992	2.733	0.323	1.053	0.894	0.402	60.172
waste gas	1993	2.994	0.242	1.017	0.826	0.495	69.191
(m³/yuan)	1994	2.789	0.196	0.821	0.674	0.334	70.444
	1995	2.337	0.125	0.819	0.679	0.320	69.124
	1996	2.157	0.101	0.782	0.611	0.238	62.394
Waste gas	1992	10.806	1.927	4.867	4.300	5.021	46.037
(m³/yuan)	1993	10.137	1.582	4.818	4.241	5.508	48.706
	1994	9.280	1.758	4.365	3.874	4.590	49.076
	1995	8.770	1.683	4.244	3.952	3.785	45.837
	1996	9.676	1.646	4.796	4.371	5.138	47.258
SO_2	1992	439.133	19.233	82.910	51.612	7695.435	105.806
(kg/10 000	1993	254.386	19.320	71.407	49.715	3120.368	78.228
yuan)	1994	255.456	16.601	66.973	46.484	3091.762	83.024
	1995	212.278	13.900	61.182	43.887	2236.278	77.292
	1996	225.722	14.122	64.403	47.015	2696.252	80.626
Smoke	1992	332.043	7.997	57.328	45.719	3822.622	107.849
dust	1993	130.019	8.018	49.783	44.696	1088.934	66.285
(kg/10 000	1994	102.265	6.449	41.161	37.939	773.715	67.578
yuan)	1995	93.455	5.134	38.672	34.842	692.803	68.062
	1996	105.766	5.368	38.357	34.501	746.195	71.217
Powder	1992	79.762	3.676	33.417	30.712	313.399	52.976
dust	1993	70.523	3.564	32.657	29.979	300.381	53.071
(kg/10 000	1994	64.138	2.823	28.017	26.510	251.375	56.591
yuan)	1995	76.838	2.422	27.790	26.182	286.178	60.874
	1996	51.483	2.413	25.750	23.816	192.571	53.892
Solid	1992	1 331.739	6.387	247.801	68.193	123 691.742	141.928
Wastes	1993	954.771	5.496	192.202	60.501	57 974.905	125.274
(kg/10 000	1994	836.640	1.855	150.283	48.222	41 082.631	134.872
yuan)	1995	842.621	1.155	152.604	53.641	57 013.677	156.467
	1996	764.081	1.379	109.845	50.467	25 644.420	145.786

Sources: Author's calculation based on data from Editorial Committee of China Environmental Yearbook (1993–98) and SSB (1990–98).

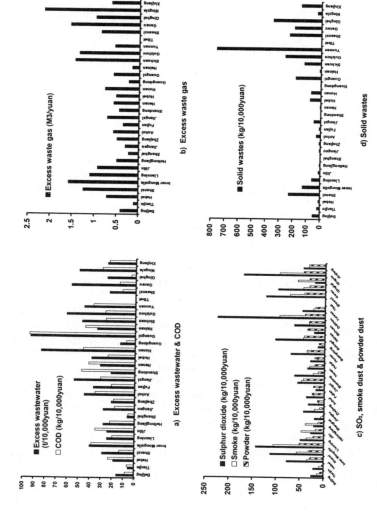

Note: Author's construction based on data from Editorial Committee of China Environmental Year Book (1993–98).

Figure 4.3 Pollution intensities, 1996

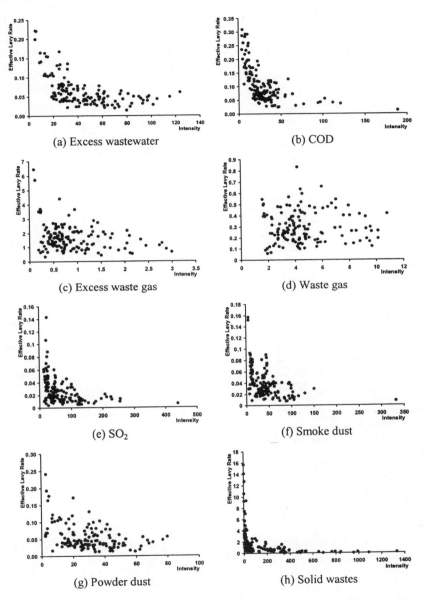

(a) Excess wastewater

(b) COD

(c) Excess waste gas

(d) Waste gas

(e) SO$_2$

(f) Smoke dust

(g) Powder dust

(h) Solid wastes

Source: Author's construction based on data from Editorial Committee of China Environmental Yearbook (1993–98).

Figure 4.4   Pollution intensities versus effective levy rates

Table 4.4   Decomposition of change in emissions: three effects

Effect	1992–93	1993–94	1994–95	1995–96	1992–96
Wastewater (billion ton)					
Efficiency	-5.36	-11.63	3.95	-22.66	-35.70
Structural	-0.73	-0.21	-0.60	1.82	0.28
Growth	6.28	13.57	5.78	9.74	35.36
Total	0.19	1.73	9.13	-11.11	-0.06
Mercury (ton)					
Efficiency	-8.84	-15.52	3.28	-12.08	-33.16
Structural	-3.24	1.54	0.15	0.68	-0.87
Growth	5.77	9.79	3.26	5.84	24.66
Total	-6.32	-4.19	6.69	-5.55	-9.37
Cadmium (ton)					
Efficiency	5.09	-71.25	85.06	-166.42	-147.53
Structural	-31.67	61.82	9.71	-37.38	2.48
Growth	35.57	80.17	44.26	90.03	250.04
Total	8.99	70.74	139.04	-113.77	104.99
Chromium (ton)					
Efficiency	-170.31	-277.08	45.27	-505.11	-907.22
Structural	89.63	9.47	-0.49	-8.8	89.81
Growth	115.82	263.46	105.88	174.81	659.96
Total	35.14	-4.15	150.66	-339.11	-157.46
Lead (ton)					
Efficiency	81.26	-551.29	189.15	-666.68	-947.56
Structural	-103.68	163.44	-62.22	-126.79	-129.25
Growth	249.03	628.9	294.7	487.06	1659.69
Total	226.61	241.04	421.62	-306.41	582.87
Arsenic (ton)					
Efficiency	-51.46	-303.33	-54.71	-406.32	-815.82
Structural	-87.56	61.39	54.91	50.97	79.70
Growth	228.23	527.42	261.08	406.46	1423.19
Total	89.21	285.47	261.27	51.11	687.07
Volatile phenol (1000 ton)					
Efficiency	-2.45	-2.10	1.97	-5.81	-8.37
Structural	-0.56	0.20	-0.52	1.09	0.21
Growth	1.70	3.12	1.47	2.61	8.90
Total	-1.30	1.22	2.93	-2.10	0.74
Cyanide (1000 ton)					
Efficiency	-1.94	-1.15	0.14	-1.24	-4.19
Structural	-0.07	0.03	-0.36	0.13	-0.28
Growth	0.87	1.40	0.61	0.91	3.79
Total	-1.13	0.28	0.39	-0.21	-0.68
Oil (1000 ton)					
Efficiency	-1.87	-61.91	16.53	-48.40	-95.66
Structural	-1.61	1.56	-2.93	2.82	-0.16
Growth	17.40	43.16	14.58	25.73	100.88
Total	13.92	-17.19	28.19	-19.84	5.06

Effect	1992–93	1993–94	1994–95	1995–96	1992–96
Sulphide (1000 ton)					
Efficiency	-35.48	-23.14	2.59	-53.62	-109.65
Structural	-0.77	-3.29	1.14	6.58	3.67
Growth	16.58	27.52	11.31	18.44	73.86
Total	-19.67	1.09	15.05	-28.60	-32.13
Chemical oxygen demand (COD) (million ton)					
Efficiency	-2.17	-1.74	2.58	-8.92	-10.25
Structural	-0.23	-0.62	-0.49	2.22	0.88
Growth	2.03	4.21	2.01	3.59	11.84
Total	-0.37	1.84	4.10	-3.11	2.46
Suspending substances (million ton)					
Efficiency	-4.89	-4.31	3.16	-7.36	-13.40
Structural	-0.50	0.28	0.07	0.73	0.59
Growth	2.51	4.20	1.73	3.41	11.85
Total	-2.88	0.17	4.96	-3.22	-0.97
Waste gas (1000 billion m3)					
Efficiency	-0.48	-5.93	1.41	-5.75	-10.75
Structural	-0.72	1.84	0.72	-0.92	0.92
Growth	2.39	5.63	2.54	4.42	14.99
Total	1.19	1.54	4.67	-2.25	5.15
SO_2 (million ton)					
Efficiency	-1.77	-7.26	-1.54	-8.52	-19.09
Structural	-1.32	1.32	2.27	-0.82	1.45
Growth	3.39	7.40	3.24	5.21	19.24
Total	0.30	1.47	3.97	-4.14	1.60
Smoke dust (million ton)					
Efficiency	-0.63	-6.77	-1.04	-6.28	-14.73
Structural	-0.80	0.76	1.45	-0.45	0.97
Growth	2.24	5.15	1.94	3.11	12.43
Total	0.81	-0.86	2.34	-3.62	-1.33
Powder dust (million ton)					
Efficiency	0.29	-10.01	5.94	-11.19	-14.96
Structural	-0.49	5.45	-0.82	-1.67	2.47
Growth	2.21	5.59	2.43	4.93	15.16
Total	2.01	1.03	7.55	-7.93	2.67
Solid wastes (million ton)					
Efficiency	-8.67	-18.05	4.44	-20.66	-42.94
Structural	-2.89	4.03	1.59	-1.93	0.81
Growth	6.80	12.65	4.89	8.96	33.29
Total	-4.76	-1.37	10.92	-13.64	-8.84

Source: Author's calculation based on data from Editorial Committee of China Environmental Yearbook (1993–98).

These results are different in general. The result of the first decomposition approach for China pollution data is reported in Table 4.4. It can be found that the decline in China's pollution intensity mainly results from the efficiency effect.[5] For example, actual wastewater discharge fell by 58.2 million tons over the period between 1992 and 1996. If the emission rate and industrial structure had remained stable, the discharge would have increased by 35.36 billion tons over the same period. The structural effect puts another 275.4 million tons on the top of that, which implies that China's economy is moving to a more polluting structure.[6] Thus the only driving force for reducing that discharge to its actual level is the efficiency effect. Most other water pollutants, air pollutants and solid wastes show a similar pattern.

The fact that structural change had a minor or even negative effect on the decrease in pollutant discharge is not as surprising as it first seems. Although the government is dedicated to encouraging the development of 'low-polluting' or 'pollution-free' industries, it cannot resist the strong demand for goods produced by 'high-polluting' industries. As the inverted U-shape theory suggests, at the initial stage of development, a country's environmental quality will worsen along with the development.[7]

However, the above decomposition reveals that actual pollution is well below the *laissez-faire* case. The government's goal, to 'prevent the environmental quality from further deterioration along with the economic development', has been achieved in this sense. In turn this means that the action taken in China has been effective in reducing pollution. However, many factors may be related to the favourable efficiency effect. In addition to tighter and effective environmental regulation, the opening of the economy and increasing competition lead to efficient resource allocation and usage, and this may reduce emission intensity due to less wasteful use of raw materials. Therefore further study is needed to identify the underlining factors. A simple approach which further decomposes the efficiency effect is presented below.

Let g_{it} denote the pollutant generation coefficient of sector i in time t (amount of pollutant generated from the production of each unit of real output value); and d_{it} the pollutant treatment rate of sector i in time t. So, $e_{it} = g_{it}(1 - d_{it})$. The efficiency effect can be decomposed:

$$\Sigma_i Q_{i2}(e_{i2} - e_{i1}) = \Sigma_i Q_{i2}[g_{i2}(1 - d_{i2}) - g_{i1}(1 - d_{i1})]$$
$$= \Sigma_i Q_{i2}[g_{i2}(1 - d_{i2}) - g_{i2}(1 - d_{i1}) + g_{i2}(1 - d_{i1}) - g_{i1}(1 - d_{i1})]$$
$$= \Sigma_i Q_{i2}g_{i2}(d_{i1} - d_{i2}) + \Sigma_i Q_{i2}(g_{i2} - g_{i1})(1 - d_{i1})$$

The first component in the above equation is the effect on pollution discharge of the change in treatment rate, which can be termed as treatment effect. The second component is the effect of the change in the generation coefficient. As the generation coefficient measures the amount of pollutant generated from the production process, a decline in the coefficient reflects the improvement in the utilisation efficiency of resources, therefore it may be termed the productivity effect. The productivity effect is mainly affected by economic policies, whilst the treatment effect is mainly, if not solely, the result of environmental policies. Therefore the change in pollutant discharge can be decomposed into four parts:

$$E_2 - E_1 = \Sigma_i Q_{i2} g_{i2} (d_{i1} - d_{i2}) + \Sigma_i Q_{i2} (g_{i2} - g_{i1})(1 - d_{i1})$$
$$+ Q_2 \Sigma_i (s_{i2} - s_{i1}) g_{i1} (1 - d_{i1}) + (Q_2 - Q_1) \Sigma_i s_{i1} g_{i1} (1 - d_{i1})$$

It is clear that the above decomposition is not the only approach. Selecting different levels of output, sectoral shares and emission coefficients results in different decomposition approaches. The detailed results are presented in Table 4.5. These results are different in general. If it is acknowledged that the output level increases while the pollutant generation coefficient decreases over time, $\Sigma_i Q_{i2} g_{i1} (d_{i1} - d_{i2})$ is the highest estimate, while $\Sigma_i Q_{i1} g_{i2} (d_{i1} - d_{i2})$ is the lowest estimate of the treatment effect.

Due to data limitation, the exercise was carried out only for SO_2, smoke dust, powder dust and solid wastes, and the results reported in Table 4.6 are quite encouraging. Except in the case of SO_2, the treatment effect accounts for about 34–46 percent of total efficiency gains. Considering that environmental policies may also contribute to the productivity effect, it may be concluded that nearly half the pollution reduction comes from environmental policies. Of course, this approach is very simple and the conclusion cannot be extended to other pollutants without further work. At most, this exercise indicates that the pollution control policies in China are effective, but does not allow judgements about whether the action taken is enough and whether it is efficient. These issues are discussed in the following sections.

4.4   THEORY OF EQUILIBRIUM POLLUTION

To set a framework for the econometric analysis of China's environmental policy, this section introduces the theory of equilibrium pollution, which has been discussed in the previous chapters. According to the theory, pollution or environmental absorption capacity can be viewed as a special good which is supplied by the government on behalf of households and demanded by firms. The realised level of pollution is jointly determined by the demand and supply.

Table 4.5 Decomposition methods of emission changes

| | Efficiency effect | | Structure effect | Growth effect |
	Treatment effect	Productivity effect		
1.	$\Sigma_i Q_{i2} g_{i2}(d_{i1} - d_{i2})$	$\Sigma_i Q_{i2}(g_{i2} - g_{i1})(1 - d_{i1})$	$Q_2 \Sigma_i (s_{i2} - s_{i1}) g_{i1}(1 - d_{i1})$	$(Q_2 - Q_1)\Sigma_i s_{i1} g_{i1}(1 - d_{i1})$
2.	$\Sigma_i Q_{i2} g_{i1}(d_{i1} - d_{i2})$	$\Sigma_i Q_{i2}(g_{i2} - g_{i1})(1 - d_{i2})$	$Q_2 \Sigma_i (s_{i2} - s_{i1}) g_{i1}(1 - d_{i1})$	$(Q_2 - Q_1)\Sigma_i s_{i1} g_{i1}(1 - d_{i1})$
3.	$\Sigma_i Q_{i2} g_{i2}(d_{i1} - d_{i2})$	$\Sigma_i Q_{i2}(g_{i2} - g_{i1})(1 - d_{i1})$	$Q_1 \Sigma_i (s_{i2} - s_{i1}) g_{i1}(1 - d_{i1})$	$(Q_2 - Q_1)\Sigma_i s_{i2} g_{i1}(1 - d_{i1})$
4.	$\Sigma_i Q_{i2} g_{i1}(d_{i1} - d_{i2})$	$\Sigma_i Q_{i2}(g_{i2} - g_{i1})(1 - d_{i2})$	$Q_1 \Sigma_i (s_{i2} - s_{i1}) g_{i1}(1 - d_{i1})$	$(Q_2 - Q_1)\Sigma_i s_{i2} g_{i1}(1 - d_{i1})$
5.	$\Sigma_i Q_{i1} g_{i1}(d_{i1} - d_{i2})$	$\Sigma_i Q_{i1}(g_{i2} - g_{i1})(1 - d_{i2})$	$Q_2 \Sigma_i (s_{i2} - s_{i1}) g_{i2}(1 - d_{i2})$	$(Q_2 - Q_1)\Sigma_i s_{i1} g_{i2}(1 - d_{i2})$
6.	$\Sigma_i Q_{i1} g_{i2}(d_{i1} - d_{i2})$	$\Sigma_i Q_{i1}(g_{i2} - g_{i1})(1 - d_{i1})$	$Q_2 \Sigma_i (s_{i2} - s_{i1}) g_{i2}(1 - d_{i2})$	$(Q_2 - Q_1)\Sigma_i s_{i1} g_{i2}(1 - d_{i2})$
7.	$\Sigma_i Q_{i1} g_{i1}(d_{i1} - d_{i2})$	$\Sigma_i Q_{i1}(g_{i2} - g_{i1})(1 - d_{i2})$	$Q_1 \Sigma_i (s_{i2} - s_{i1}) g_{i2}(1 - d_{i2})$	$(Q_2 - Q_1)\Sigma_i s_{i2} g_{i2}(1 - d_{i2})$
8.	$\Sigma_i Q_{i1} g_{i2}(d_{i1} - d_{i2})$	$\Sigma_i Q_{i1}(g_{i2} - g_{i1})(1 - d_{i1})$	$Q_1 \Sigma_i (s_{i2} - s_{i1}) g_{i2}(1 - d_{i2})$	$(Q_2 - Q_1)\Sigma_i s_{i2} g_{i2}(1 - d_{i2})$

Table 4.6   Decomposition of changes in emissions: four effects

Effect	1992–93	1993–94	1994–95	1995–96	1992–96
SO$_2$ (million ton)					
Treatment	0.03	-0.07	-0.94	-1.06	-2.03
Productivity	-1.79	-7.18	-0.61	-7.47	-17.05
Structural	-1.32	1.32	2.27	-0.82	1.45
Growth	3.39	7.40	3.24	5.21	19.24
Total	0.30	1.47	3.97	-4.14	1.60
Smoke dust (million ton)					
Treatment	-0.12	-2.45	-1.11	-2.53	-6.22
Productivity	-0.50	-4.32	0.07	-3.75	-8.51
Structural	-0.80	0.76	1.45	-0.45	0.97
Growth	2.24	5.15	1.94	3.11	12.43
Total	0.81	-0.86	2.34	-3.62	-1.33
Powder dust (million ton)					
Treatment	-0.14	-0.68	0.47	-6.57	-6.93
Productivity	0.44	-9.33	5.47	-4.61	-8.04
Structural	-0.49	5.45	-0.82	-1.67	2.47
Growth	2.21	5.59	2.43	4.93	15.16
Total	2.01	1.03	7.55	-7.93	2.67
Solid wastes (million ton)					
Treatment	-5.50	-2.95	4.57	-10.71	-14.59
Productivity	-3.16	-15.10	-0.13	-9.96	-28.36
Structural	-2.89	4.03	1.59	-1.93	0.81
Growth	6.80	12.65	4.89	8.96	33.29
Total	-4.76	-1.37	10.92	-13.64	-8.84

4.4.1 The Environmental Demand

A representative firm is assumed to maximise its profit. The firm employs capital, labour and environmental absorption capacity to produce its product:

$$Q = f(K, L, D),\qquad(4.1)$$

where Q is the product amount, K is the capital input, L is labour input, and D is a set of environmental inputs (pollutant emissions). Normalising by the product price, the firm's problem is:

$$\max_{K,L,D} \; f(K,L,D) - (rK + wL + \tau D)$$
$$\text{s.t.} \qquad D \le D_S \qquad(4.2)$$

where r, w, τ are, respectively, cost of capital, wage rate and the effective pollution emission levy rate.

This approach is different from the usual one in the treatment of pollution abatement cost. Most literature assumes an objective function of minimising abatement cost and pollution levy or tax (for example, Wang and Wheeler 1996; Xie 1996). However, it is often difficult to distinguish between 'normal' production activities and pollution abatement activities even from an engineer's viewpoint. The abatement activity employs capital and labour too, therefore it could be included in the 'normal' production process as in equation (4.1). Assuming pollution abatement cost and levy/tax minimisation may omit the possibility of substitution between production activities and abatement activities. Moreover, this kind of treatment reduces the data requirement. The usual approach needs disaggregated cost accounts and more technical data like influent and effluent concentrations and amounts, which are not available in most cases.[8]

Another distinguishing feature of problem (4.2) is the constraint on pollution emissions. This constraint, although not explicitly set in the real world, comes from regulation requirements. It is understandable that firms face stringent environmental requirements in regions where the regulations are strict and the government authorities put serious effort into implementing these regulations. Thus this feature leaves room for embodying regulation variables in the pollution demand function.

Assuming concavity of $f(\cdot)$, the inverse pollution demand function can be derived from problem (4.2):[9]

$$\tau = -\lambda + f_D, \tag{4.3}$$

where λ is the Lagrangian multiplier of environmental requirement for which the regulation strictness may be set as a proxy; f_D is the partial derivative of the production function with respect to pollution emission. It is noteworthy to point out that the above expression is actually a system of equations because there are many pollutants. However, it is difficult to determine whether it is appropriate to estimate them simultaneously at the aggregate level. Because an individual firm may discharge only some of the pollutants, it is hard to say whether pollution emissions are jointly or separately decided by the representative firm at the regional aggregation.

There are considerable concerns about the assumption of profit maximisation. Chinese firms, especially state-owned enterprises (SOEs), have various objectives set by government, which often contradict the goal of profit maximisation. For example, local governments want to provide social welfare, maintain high employment and keep economic parity between firms (Ma 1997). However, the profit maximisation assumption can be justified on two grounds. First, the share of SOEs in total output has been declining over time, and firms with other ownership assumed to be more market-oriented (collectively owned and private firms) are playing a more and more important role in the economy. Secondly, economic reform has been encouraging SOEs to maximise profits.

4.4.2 The Environmental Supply

A representative household in the region earns a certain amount of income Y, which can be spent on a consumption good C (the price of consumption good is normalised to be one) to meet its various living demands, and owns a certain environmental endowment $\overline{E}$. Part of the income is from earnings in the industrial activities determined by the output price and factor prices P.[10] The household could enjoy the environment, and/or also supply it to the firm at the ongoing effective rate and use the proceeds for consumption. Therefore the household's problem is to maximise its utility:

$$\max_{D_S} \ U(C,\overline{E} - D_S)$$
$$s.t. \quad C \leq Y(P) + \tau D_S \tag{4.4}$$

It may be argued that environmental quality constraint $\overline{E} - D_S \geq 0$ should be imposed to construct the problem. However, it is difficult to determine these environmental quality constraints and it seems that these constraints, if any, are usually not bounded, because there is no evidence that environmental degradation is so severe that a whole region like a province is no longer suitable for habitation. Also the built-in care about the environment in utility function makes these constraints redundant.

The inverse environmental supply function can be derived by solving the above utility maximisation problem:

$$\tau = U_E/U_C \,, \tag{4.5}$$

where U_E and U_C are, respectively, partial derivatives of the utility function with respect to environmental quality and consumption.

The environmental supply function (4.5) is also a system of equations, but, unlike the demand function, this supply system definitely needs to be estimated simultaneously, because all environmental elements are virtually owned by the representative household.

System (4.3) and (4.5) jointly determine the *equilibrium pollution*. Obviously this approach is similar to the determination of labour supply and wage. It may be argued that the environment is a public good and there is open access to it. The firm is a leader in the process, setting the pollution level according to its own problem, and the household a follower with no control over pollution emission and therefore the problem (4.4) is misspecified. However, after careful consideration, it may be concluded that this is not the case. First, since the state has assumed the rights to the environment within its boundaries and controls access to, for example, water and air, it should be referred to as state property rights. Therefore the open access regime to which no property rights have been assigned is no longer valid in the legal sense (Bromley 1991). Second, state property rights enable the representative household to actively participate in the game: it can raise the effective levy rate, through either more strict regulation or more effective regulation enforcement, if it feels environment is more valuable. Of course, institutional concerns are still related, whether or not public interests are well represented and realised by the government, especially for a country like China.

This kind of equilibrium pollution approach is a partial equilibrium analysis for environmental goods. It derives environmental demand from profit maximisation of firms, environmental supply from utility maximisation of households and assumes market clearing of environmental goods. But it is far too simple to have general equilibrium for all factors and products.

Although it is not necessarily true in the general equilibrium case, the equilibrium pollution in this setting is a Walrasian equilibrium, because it satisfies both profit and utility maximisation and clears the market. It turns out that this can be used as an instrument to test the efficiency of pollution control policies. If well-behaved demand and supply functions can be recovered from the realised pollution and prices following the theory, it may be concluded that the realised quantity and price are Walrasian equilibria – optimal quantity and price – and that the underlying policies are desirable.

4.5   SPECIFICATION OF FUNCTIONS

4.5.1 Environmental Demand Function

Assuming Cobb–Douglas technology, that is, for the *l*th sector, the production function is:

$$Q_l = A_l K_l^{\alpha_{1l}} L_l^{\alpha_{2l}} \Pi_j D_{lj}^{\alpha_{3lj}} , \qquad (4.6)$$

then equation (4.3) becomes

$$\tau_j + \lambda_j = \frac{\alpha_{3lj}}{D_{lj}} .$$

As argued above, λ_j is affected by the regulation. Thus the above expression can be rearranged as:

$$\frac{D_{lj}}{Q_l} = \frac{\alpha_{3lj}}{\tau_j + g^j(R)},$$

where R is an index for regulations other than the pollution levy. Therefore the pollution intensity can be written as:

$$\frac{D_j}{Q} = \frac{\Sigma_j D_{lj}}{Q} = \sum_l \frac{\alpha_{3lj}}{\tau_j + g^j(R)} \frac{Q_l}{Q} = \sum_l \frac{s_l \alpha_{3lj}}{\tau_j + g^j(R)},$$

that is, the pollution intensity is affected not only by the pollution levy and regulation, but also by sectoral output shares, s_j, which makes sense. First, different sectors employ different levels of technology, therefore, they have different production functions. Second, the discharge standards, and thus pollution levy rates, are different across sectors. In this study, industry is divided into two sectors: heavy and light industries. Due to data limitation, it is impossible to estimate a different production function for each region, and therefore, the share of heavy industry in total industrial output (*HEAVY*) is used as one explanatory variable. Alternatively, industry can also be divided according to the size and ownership of firms because these factors may also affect firms' behaviour. Therefore the share of large firms (*LARGE*) and the share of SOEs (*STATE*) also are included in the explanatory variables. However, because these three variables are highly correlated, 0.73 between *HEAVY* and *LARGE*, 0.80 between *HEAVY* and *STATE*, 0.76 between *LARGE* and *STATE*, including all in one equation may cause a collinearity problem. Therefore only one is included in each estimation.

To sum up, the environmental demand function for *j*th pollutant in *i*th region could be specified as:[11]

$$\log e_{ji} = \beta_{oj} + \beta_{1j} \log S_i + \beta_{2j} \log \tau_{ji} + \beta_{3j} \log R_i + \varepsilon_{ji}, \qquad (4.7)$$

where $e_i = (e_{1i}, e_{2i}, \cdots, e_{ji}, \cdots)$ is a set of pollution intensities measured in pollutant discharges (excess wastewater, COD, waste gas and solid wastes) per unit of industrial output; S_i is one of the three share variables ($HEAVY_i$, $LARGE_i$ and $STATE_i$); τ_{ji} is the effective pollution levy rate per unit of pollutant discharge; R_i is a set of regulation indices measured in the implementation ratio of specific environmental regulation; ε_i is the error term.

In the above specification, a positive sign of β_{1j} is expected when the variable $HEAVY_i$ is used, because heavy industrial firms are usually heavy polluters, or when the variable $STATE_i$ is used and if the soft budget hypothesis of state-owned enterprises holds. When the variable $LARGE_i$ is used, a negative sign of β_{1j} will be expected if economies of scale for pollution abatement exist. Negative signs of β_{2j} and β_{3j} are expected if the pollution levy system and other regulations play their roles.

4.5.2 Environmental Supply Function

The inverse environmental supply system (4.5) implies that the environmental supply is determined by income, environmental endowment and effective pollution levy rate, that is, the reduced form is:

$$D_j = D_j(INC, \overline{E}, \tau) \qquad (4.8)$$

where j denotes the pollutants – wastewater (or COD), waste gas (or representative air pollutant) and solid waste.

Note that $\overline{E}$ and τ are vectors; supply of one environmental element is affected not only by its own endowment and price but also by endowment and prices of other elements. However, it is difficult to measure endowment for various elements. One appropriate method is to choose land area as a proxy because nearly all of the environmental elements are virtually related to land. Also note that equation (4.4) is derived from the representative household's utility maximisation problem, so E_j, INC and ED are in absolute values. In order to avoid the measurement problem and to coincide with the variable in demand function, it is natural to scale it down by population, that is, in per capita terms,

$$E_j = \frac{emission_j}{population} = \frac{emissions_j}{output} \frac{output}{population} = e_j IND .$$

The estimating supply equation for jth environmental element in ith region is therefore specified as follows:

$$\log e_{ji} + \log IND_i = \omega_0 + \omega_{1j} \log INC_i + \omega_{2j} \log LAND_i + \Sigma_k \omega_{3kj} \log \tau_{kj} + \mu_{ji} \quad (4.9)$$

where e_{ji} and τ_{kj} are defined as the same as above; INC_i is per capita income; $LAND_i$ is per capita land area (reciprocal of population density); IND_i is per capita industrial output; μ_{ji} is error term.

This specification is similar to that in Wang and Wheeler (1996), but it does not include education. Of course education affects people's willingness to supply environmental good, but education itself is not an independent variable which is actually affected by the income level, and vice versa. The estimation shows that including an education variable does not improve the result as the coefficient of education variables is insignificant in almost all equations (see Table 4.14 below).

One problem with (4.9) is that the dependent variable is actually the per capita emission, which is not compatible with that in the demand function. However, putting the term $\log IND_i$ in the right-hand side of the equation may face another problem: multicollinearity between *IND* and *INC* (actually the correlation is 0.9). Therefore it is appropriate to drop the per capita industrial output when estimating the supply equation. It is partly justified by the fact that the per capita industrial output enters into equation (4.9) mainly for a transformational rather than behavioural reason.

According to the utility theory, as income rises, the demand for leisure and recreation will rise, that is, the supply of environmental goods will decrease. Therefore a negative sign of ω_{1j} is expected. By contrast, a larger endowment will lead to a larger environmental supply, that is, the sign ω_{2j} would be positive. As the price of a good rises, the supply for that good will increase, therefore a positive sign of ω_{3j} will be expected.

4.6   ECONOMETRIC RESULTS

The estimation has been undertaken in several ways. First, the demand and supply functions are estimated for each of the three types of pollutants (water, air and solid wastes) to serve as a reference. Secondly, all the demand and supply equations for the three types of pollutants are jointly estimated as one system of equations. Thirdly, because the levy collected from solid wastes is only a minor part of the total amount collected, and there are some missing observations in this series, the system is estimated including only equations for water and air pollutants. A reduced form function is also estimated by putting all independent variables in one equation. During each stage of estimation, both pooled and fixed-effect models are used. In addition, different types of specification are also tested in the process. Some estimation results are reported in Tables 4.7–4.14.[12]

4.6.1   Water Pollution

The demand of and supply for excess wastewater looks well-behaved when the system is estimated independently of other pollutants. For example, when the inverse supply function is specified (lower part of Table 4.7), the coefficients of *LIWW* and *LPWW* have expected signs and are significant at

Table 4.7   Demand and supply: excess wastewater

	Demand function			Supply function	
	Coefficient	t-ratio		Coefficient	t-ratio
Dependent variable: LPWW			Dependent variable: LIWW		
LHEAVY	0.7420	4.76***	LINCOME	-0.9889	-3.63***
LEIA	0.1004	2.80***	LLAND	4.2184	2.91***
LTHREE	0.1598	1.25	LPWW	0.2602	1.03
LDDLINE	0.0399	0.56	LPXGAS	-0.0449	-0.78
LIWW	-0.3198	-2.14**	LPSOLID	-0.0060	-0.27
D-W=	1.4189		D-W=	2.4280	
Dependent variable: LIWW			Dependent variable: LPWW		
LHEAVY	1.3640	4.32***	LINCOME	1.6416	1.69*
LEIA	0.0583	0.72	LLAND	-11.6050	-3.17***
LTHREE	0.2841	1.61	LIWW	2.0496	2.43**
LDDLINE	0.1457	1.50			
LPWW	-1.3142	-2.24**			
D-W=	1.1263		D-W=	2.3772	

Notes: *** significant at 1 percent; ** significant at 5 percent; * significant at 10 percent.

the 5 percent level. The price elasticity of demand is −1.3142, implying the effective wastewater levy rate has a strong influence on the demand for wastewater. When the inverse demand function is specified and other effective levy rates are added into the supply function (upper part of Table 4.7), the relevant coefficients also have the expected sign, but the coefficient of *LPWW* in supply function become insignificant. The situation worsens when the system is estimated jointly with the demand and supply of excess waste gas and solid wastes (Tables 4.10–4.13). A well-behaved demand and supply function of excess wastewater can rarely be found in these specifications. This suggests the levy system may be efficient in the single market for wastewater, but is not efficient in the whole environmental market, or it may suggest a specification problem in the waste gas part of the model.

The fact that the pollution levy system is efficient in the single market for wastewater may be due to the nature of water pollution. Because water pollution tends to be more local than air pollution, local residents are more sensitive to the problem of water pollution and push harder for the government to act. Consequently, the government deals with the water pollution problem more actively, for example, heightening the emission standards and/or strengthening the monitoring effort to improve enforcement. In other words, households' preferences are more likely to be consulted when formulating water pollution control policies.

Even if it is acknowledged that the wastewater market is efficient, there is still room for policy improvement. Referring to Figure 4.4, the equilibrium

Table 4.8   Demand and supply: excess waste gas

	Demand function			Supply function	
	Coefficient	t-ratio		Coefficient	t-ratio
Dependent variable: LIXGAS			Dependent variable: LPXGAS		
LHEAVY	0.5664	5.95***	LINCOME	-0.6803	-1.80*
LEIA	-0.1256	-3.39***	LLAND	5.6023	2.81***
LTHREE	0.4245	3.44***	LPWW	0.4610	4.16***
LDDLINE	0.2654	4.08***	LIXGAS	-1.0344	-3.20***
LPXGAS	0.0237	0.24	LSOLID	0.0543	1.81*
D-W=	2.0193		D-W=	1.8844	
Dependent variable: LPXGAS			Dependent variable: LIXGAS		
LHEAVY	0.2318	0.64	LINCOME	-0.6729	-4.23***
LEIA	0.2222	2.31**	LLAND	3.8943	4.20***
LTHREE	-0.5031	-1.51	LPWW	0.1459	1.89*
LDDLINE	0.0607	-0.32	LPXGAS	-0.3520	-3.49***
LIXGAS	0.1514	0.28	LSOLID	0.0023	0.13
D-W=	2.1966		D-W=	1.8005	

Notes: *** significant at 1 percent; ** significant at 5 percent; * significant at 10 percent.

intensities and prices are quite diverse across regions. These outcomes are optimal only when each region is isolated from each other; there must exist some barrier restricting the integration of the pollution market. This 'autarky' state leads to unequal levy rates, therefore an 'opening up' policy may help to get a Pareto improvement. For example, industrial relocation may reduce the enforcement cost in the regions with higher pollution levy rates, and increase revenue in the regions with lower rates. Unfortunately, the current environmental policy may enhance the barrier to open up, in addition to other natural and economic considerations. One guideline of environmental protection in China is 'prohibiting firms from shifting polluting workshops or production processes into other regions'. According to the results presented here, this guideline needs to be reviewed.

When excess wastewater is replaced by chemical oxygen demand (COD) as the representative water pollutant, in most cases the estimated coefficients are not significant. This might be the result of a measurement problem. The levy is collected from excess wastewater, which violates the discharge standards, but COD is calculated from all wastewater discharges. Moreover, COD is only one of many water pollutants, and other water pollutants may also contribute to the excess wastewater levy.

4.6.2 Air Pollution

The demand for and supply of excess waste gas and other air pollutants is not

Table 4.9   Demand and supply: solid wastes

	Demand function			Supply function	
	Coefficient	t-ratio		Coefficient	t-ratio
Dependent variable: LISOLID			Dependent variable: LPSOLID		
LHEAVY	1.4848	6.50***	LINCOME	1.7170	0.76
LEIA	-0.1264	-1.38	LLAND	1.0620	0.18
LTHREE	0.2983	0.99	LPWW	0.9778	2.65***
LDDLINE	0.1911	1.17	LPXGAS	0.3759	2.08**
LPSOLID	-0.2755	-2.06*	LISOLID	-0.0325	-0.04
D-W=	1.4753		D-W=	1.6415	
Dependent variable: LPSOLID			Dependent variable: LISOLID		
LHEAVY	0.5178	0.86	LINCOME	-2.2846	-2.74***
LEIA	0.2071	1.40	LLAND	3.6157	1.35
LTHREE	-0.4307	-0.85	LPWW	-0.1481	-0.35
LDDLINE	-0.0345	-0.12	LPXGAS	0.0944	0.44
LISOLID	-0.4932	-1.61	LPSOLID	-0.2112	-0.50
D-W=	1.5508		D-W=	1.6274	

Notes: *** significant at 1 percent; ** significant at 5 percent; * significant at 10 percent.

well behaved according to the estimation (Tables 4.8, 4.10–4.13). In some cases, the coefficients are significant, but have the 'wrong' sign. This is partly due to the measurement problem, as they are calculated from total emissions no matter whether they violate the emission standards, but the levy is only collected for excess emissions. However, the main reason is probably that the market for air pollutant may not be efficient. More specifically, this is because the price on the supply side is set arbitrarily by the environmental authority, and most likely does not take into account utility maximisation. This argument can be justified by looking at Figure 4.4, where the plotting shows a nice demand curve. A reduced form function of this system is also estimated separately for each pollutant. It is found that the coefficients of own price are significant and have the 'right' sign, and the equations fit the data well (Table 4.B). Another piece of evidence is that other coefficients in the system are usually significant and have the right sign, implying that the specification is correct.

4.6.3 Solid Wastes

Similar phenomena for solid wastes (Tables 4.9, 4.10, 4.12 and 4.13) are observed as for air pollutants. Besides data problems, this suggests that the levy system does not work well for solid wastes. The government does not pay much attention to the solid wastes, which could be evidenced by facts that

Table 4.10   Demand and supply: excess wastewater, excess waste gas and solid wastes (including LHEAVY)

	Demand Function				Supply Function		
	LIWW	LIXGAS	LISOLID		LPWW	LPXGAS	LPSOLID
LHEAVY	1.276	0.303	1.330	LINCOME	-3.440	-2.032	2.354
	(4.09***)	(1.59)	(3.30***)		(-1.31)	(-1.88*)	(0.96)
LEIA	0.014	-0.288	0.168	LLAND	5.675	3.274	-7.486
	(0.165)	(-3.26***)	(0.55)		(0.64)	(0.66)	(-0.67)
LTHREE	0.253	0.790	0.163	LIWW	-0.689		
	(1.36)	(3.16***)	(0.23)		(-0.36)		
LDDLINE	0.107	0.272	0.136	LIXGAS		-0.316	
	(1.04)	(2.35***)	(0.54)			(-0.42)	
LPWW	-1.010			LISOLID			0.574
	(-1.76*)						(0.44)
LPXGAS		0.791		LPWW		-0.780	0.234
		(2.41***)				(-1.66*)	(0.25)
LPSOLID			-0.965	LPXGAS	-1.648		0.839
			(-1.25)		(-2.05**)		(2.30**)
				LPSOLID	1.921	1.166	
					(2.28**)	(2.76***)	
D-W=	1.047	2.333	1.368	D-W=	1.660	1.637	1.733

Notes: Numbers in parentheses are t-ratios; *** significant at 1 percent level, ** significant at 5 percent level, * significant at 10 percent level.

revenues of solid wastes levy are very small, accounting for about 1 percent of the total levy revenues in recent years (Table 1.4), and statistics about solid wastes are often incomplete.

4.6.4   Other Regulations

EIA has a significant negative effect on the demand for pollution in some cases, whilst three-synchronisation and limited time treatment have insignificant effects, and, in some cases even have significant positive effects: a higher enforcement rate of these two systems leads to higher pollution intensity! There are several explanations for this result. First, as noted above, these regulation indices are of similar values across regions, therefore it is natural to have an insignificant coefficient in the regression. However, this does not mean they are not effective. Secondly, recall the origin of these indices (equation 4.3). They serve as a proxy of the Lagrangian multiplier of environmental supply constraints as these regulations put restrictions on the use of environmental goods. Therefore there is a mutual causality between these indices and environmental demand (in this estimation it is the realised

Table 4.11   Demand and supply: excess wastewater and waste gas

| | Demand function | | | Supply function | |
	LPWW	LPXGAS		LIWW	LIXGAS
LHEAVY	0.670	-0.146	LINCOME	-0.966	-0.506
	(4.29***)	(-0.35)		(-3.38***)	(-1.81*)
LEIA	0.104	0.317	LLAND	4.353	5.015
	(2.74***)	(2.87***)		(2.90***)	(3.43***)
LTHREE	0.202	-0.729	LPWW	0.262	0.528
	(1.62)	(-1.88*)		(0.93)	(1.99**)
LDDLINE	0.083	-0.186	LPXGAS	0.042	-0.405
	(1.30)	(-0.88)		(0.31)	(-3.19***)
LIWW	-0.253		LPSOLID	0.0006	0.014
	(-1.66*)			(0.22)	(0.50)
LIXGAS		0.807			
		(1.27)			
D-W=	1.478	2.316	D-W=	2.442	1.873

Notes: Numbers in parentheses are t-ratios; *** significant at 1 percent level, ** significant at 5 percent level, * significant at 10 percent level.

intensity or levy rate).   It is true that higher regulation enforcement is expected to help reduce the demand for environmental goods, but the higher indices may well be the reaction to the higher pollution intensity. This may explain why they sometimes have significant positive coefficients. One way around this would be to endogenise these regulation indices in the system. This is left for the general equilibrium analysis in future work. Finally, of course, this may also be due to the weak mechanism of these regulations. For example, as pointed out above, the three-synchronisation system may be in effect in only one specific time: when the firm is waiting for approval of operation. After the approval, the pollution control facilities may be shut down and have no effect on pollution control. In this sense, a high index does not necessarily represent high or tight enforcement.

4.6.5 Economic Structure

The share of heavy industry has a significant positive effect on the demand for pollution (Tables 4.7–4.11). This is straightforward and needs no further explanation.

The share of state owned enterprises (SOEs) in industrial output also has a significant positive coefficient (Table 4.12). This positive relationship may be due to two factors. As noted above, SOEs are more likely to be heavy industrial firms which need more pollutants for operation. The other factor is the so-called 'soft-budget hypothysis'. As the enterprises are owned by the

Table 4.12 *Demand and supply: excess wastewater, excess waste gas and solid wastes (including LSTATE)*

	Demand function			Supply function	
	Coefficient	t-ratio		Coefficient	t-ratio
Dependent variable: LIWW			Dependent variable: LPWW		
LSTATE	0.9234	9.60***	LINCOME	-0.6130	-0.49
LEIA	-0.0489	-1.36	LLAND	-5.3543	-1.40
LTHREE	0.2036	2.27**	LIWW	0.3656	0.50
LDDLINE	0.1125	2.22**	LPXGAS	0.0784	0.18
LPWW	-0.2456	-1.08	LPSOLID	0.0987	0.22
D-W=	1.8188		D-W=	1.9016	
Dependent variable: LIXGAS			Dependent variable: LPXGAS		
LSTATE	0.5506	5.19***	LINCOME	-2.6886	-1.50
LEIA	-0.1396	-2.59***	LLAND	-2.9472	-0.28
LTHREE	0.5447	3.19***	LPWW	-1.8571	-1.00
LDDLINE	0.2299	2.68***	LIXGAS	-0.2372	-0.24
LPSOLID	0.1521	0.89	LPSOLID	1.1599	2.28**
D-W=	2.1330		D-W=	1.6781	
Dependent variable: LISOLID			Dependent variable: LPSOLID		
LSTATE	1.2823	2.93***	LINCOME	2.7848	0.85
LEIA	0.2416	0.65	LLAND	6.2042	0.27
LTHREE	0.0160	0.02	LPWW	2.3535	0.92
LDDLINE	0.1818	0.55	LPXGAS	0.5957	1.39
LPSOLID	-1.0424	-1.07	LISOLID	-0.0265	-0.01
D-W=	1.5067		D-W=	1.6883	

Notes: *** significant at 1 percent level, ** significant at 5 percent level, * significant at 10 percent level.

government, SOEs lack the incentive to maximise their profits and are less efficient, thus producing more pollutants due to more wasteful use of resources.

The coefficient of the share of large enterprises is insignificant (Table 4.13). It is also quite understandable. Large enterprises are more likely to be heavy industrial firms and SOEs, and therefore tend to demand more pollutants. On the other hand, large enterprises are well-equipped and have economies of scale for pollution controls, and are also closely monitored. These opposing effects cause its coefficient to be insignificant.

4.6.6 Other Factors

The per capita income and the environmental endowment proxy (per capita land area or reciprocal of population density) are crucial for determining the supply of environmental goods. In most cases, as expected, their coefficients

Table 4.13 Demand and supply: excess wastewater, excess waste gas and solid wastes (including LLARGE)

	Demand function			Supply function	
	Coefficient	t-ratio		Coefficient	t-ratio
Dependent variable: LIWW			Dependent variable: LPWW		
LLARGE	-0.4901	-1.25	LINCOME	-3.1946	-0.22
LEIA	-0.2211	-3.03***	LLAND	40.7430	1.30
LTHREE	0.0672	-0.27	LIWW	-3.1407	-0.45
LDDLINE	0.2220	1.63	LPXGAS	3.6384	0.16
LPWW	1.0845	2.29**	LPSOLID	-0.4987	0.03
D-W=	1.9192		D-W=	1.9756	
Dependent variable: LIXGAS			Dependent variable: LPXGAS		
LLARGE	-0.3812	-0.92	LINCOME	-1.4986	-1.65*
LEIA	-0.2507	-2.37**	LLAND	6.1438	1.65*
LTHREE	0.6040	1.75*	LPWW	-0.3001	-0.90
LDDLINE	0.2801	1.71*	LIXGAS	-0.0167	-0.14
LPSOLID	0.6240	1.49	LPSOLID	1.2412	3.50***
D-W=	2.2001		D-W=	1.6409	
Dependent variable: LISOLID			Dependent variable: LPSOLID		
LLARGE	1.0688	0.64	LINCOME	1.4010	1.58
LEIA	1.2923	1.78*	LLAND	-5.5738	-1.43
LTHREE	-1.4323	-1.04	LPWW	0.3286	0.88
LDDLINE	-0.2969	-0.67	LPXGAS	0.7433	1.90*
LPSOLID	-4.2586	-2.04**	LISOLID	0.0688	0.97
D-W=	1.6567		D-W=	1.6427	

Notes: *** significant at 1 percent level, ** significant at 5 percent level, * significant at 10 percent level.

are significant and have the right sign (even in the case where the pollution levy rate or intensity is not significant). The higher the per capita income level, the less willing the household to supply the environment; the more environmental endowment, the greater the supply. This is especially clear when the supply equation is estimated as the normal form (Tables 4.7–4.9 and 4.11). This may enhance the argument that the specification is correct and the failure to estimate a well-behaved environmental supply function is mainly due to the fact that the levy rate is arbitrarily set by a central policy body.

To compare the result in this chapter with those in other studies, for example, Wang and Wheeler (1996), the system including an education factor in the supply functions is re-estimated. Education is measured as the percentage of people in the total population who received high school and higher education. It turns out that the parameters of education variable in all the estimations are insignificant except one where the parameter is positively significant with 10 percent confidence (see Table 4.14). As pointed out

Table 4.14   Testing the significance of the education variable

Dependent variable	Education variable Coefficient	*p*-value	Note
LIWW	-0.3832	0.226	Corresponding to the upper part of Table 4.7
LPWW	-0.1745	0.796	Corresponding to the lower part of Table 4.7
LPXGAS	0.8802	0.096	Corresponding to the upper part of Table 4.8
LIXGAS	-0.3614	0.151	Corresponding to the lower part of Table 4.8
LPSOLID	0.2738	0.821	Corresponding to the upper part of Table 4.9
LISOLID	-0.3338	0.621	Corresponding to the lower part of Table 4.9
LPWW	-0.2564	0.879	Corresponding to Table 4.10
LPXAS	0.3206	0.784	
LPSOLID	-0.2479	0.815	
LIWW	-0.5285	0.148	Corresponding to Table 4.11
LIXGAS	-0.2655	0.458	

earlier, education might be correlated with income level. The result supports the argument that the education variable need not be included in the supply function.

4.7   CONCLUSION

This study has shown that China's pollution control policies are effective in the sense that China's pollution intensity has decreased significantly over time and nearly half of the reduction in the discharge of some pollutants is traced from these policies. In addition, the well-behaved demand function for pollution justifies that firms have responded well to the levy rates.

However, because well-behaved supply functions could not be estimated, very little can be said about the efficiency of environmental regulation in China. This may be due to data problems, thus, it was not possible to identify supply functions even though they exist. On the other hand, it could be the case that the government sets environmental controls without reference to the preferences of households. Despite this disappointing aspect of the results, what can be said is that the differential effective levy rates across regions in China imply that the enforcement cost could be reduced and overall welfare raised by withdrawing some restrictions.

The estimation shows that there are well-behaved supply and demand functions for wastewater, which implies that the pollution levy system works better for water pollution than for other pollutants. This might be due to the nature of water pollution: it is a more local problem than other pollution, therefore policy-makers are more likely to set the policy along with local residents.

APPENDIX

Table 4.A   Variable definition

Variable	Definition
IWW	Excess wastewater intensity, measured as the amount of wastewater discharge, which violates the standard, per unit of industrial output (ton/10 000yuan)
LIWW	Log of IWW
PWW	Effective levy rate for excess wastewater, obtained by dividing total levy collected from excess wastewater discharge by the amount of excess wastewater discharge (yuan/ton)
LPWW	Log of PWW
IXGAS	Excess waste gas intensity, measured as the volume of waste gas emission which is not treated per unit of industrial output (m^3/yuan)
LIXGAS	Log of IXGAS
PXGAS	Effective levy rate for excess waste gas, obtained by dividing total levy collected from excess waste gas emission by the volume of excess waste gas emission (yuan/10 000m^3)
LPXGAS	Log of PXGAS
ISOLID	Solid waste intensity, measured as the discharge amount of solid waste per unit of industrial output (kg/10 000yuan)
LISOLID	Log of ISOLID
PSOLID	Effective levy rate for solid waste, obtained by dividing total levy collected from solid waste discharge by the discharge amount of solid waste (yuan/ton)
LPSOLID	Log of PSOLID
ICOD	Chemical oxygen demand (COD) intensity, measured as the amount of COD in wastewater per unit of industrial output (kg/yuan)
LICOD	Log of ICOD
PCOD	Effective levy rate for COD, obtained by dividing total levy collected from excess wastewater discharge by the amount of COD in wastewater (yuan/kg)
LPCOD	Log of PCOD
ISO2	Sulphur dioxide (SO_2) intensity, measured as the amount of SO_2 in waste gas per unit of industrial output (kg/10 000yuan)
LISO2	Log of ISO2
PSO2	Effective levy rate for SO_2, obtained by dividing total levy collected from excess waste gas discharge by the amount of SO_2 in waste gas (yuan/kg)
LPSO2	Log of PSO2
ISMK	Industrial smoke dust intensity, measured as the volume of smoke dust per unit of industrial output (kg/10 000yuan)
LISMK	Log of ISMK
PSMK	Effective levy rate for industrial smoke dust, obtained by dividing total levy collected from excess waste gas by the amount of industrial smoke dust (yuan/kg)

Variable	Definition
LPSMK	Log of PSMK
IPWD	Industrial powder dust intensity, measured as the amount of powder dust per unit of industrial output (kg/10 000yuan)
LIPWD	Log of IPWD
PPWD	Effective levy rate for industrial powder dust, obtained by dividing the total levy collected from excess waste gas by the amount of powder dust (yuan/kg)
LPPWD	Log of PPWD
IDUST	Industrial dust intensity, measured as the total volume of industrial smoke and powder dust per unit of industrial output (kg/10 000yuan)
LIDUST	Log of IDUST
PDUST	Effective levy rate for industrial dust, obtained by dividing total levy collected from excess waste gas discharge by the amount of smoke and powder dust in waste gas (yuan/kg)
LPDUST	Log of PDUST
HEAVY	Share of heavy industry in total industrial output (%)
LHEAVY	Log of HEAVY
STATE	Share of state-owned enterprises in total industrial output (%)
LSTATE	Log of STATE
LARGE	Share of large enterprises in total industrial output (%)
LLARGE	Log of LARGE
EIA	Enforcement rate of environmental impact assessment (EIA) system, measured as the ratio of the number of projects that pass the EIA procedure in one year to the number of projects which need EIA in that year (%)
LEIA	Log of EIA
THREE	Enforcement rate of three-synchronisation system, measured as the ratio of the number of projects that pass the evaluation of this system to the total number of projects in that year (%)
LTHREE	Log of THREE
DDLINE	Enforcement rate of limited time treatment – pollution control within deadline – measured as the ratio of the number of pollution control projects that are actually completed in the year to the total number of projects that should be completed in that year (%)
LDDLINE	Log of DDLINE
STAFF	Staff number in local environmental protection authorities per unit of industrial output (head/10 000yuan)
PERMIT	Enforcement rate of permit system, measured as the ratio of the number of firms reporting their emissions to the government agencies to the total number of firms (%)
INCOME	Per capita income (yuan)
LINCOME	Log of INCOME
LAND	Per capita land area (m^2)
LLAND	Log of LAND
IND	Per capita industrial output (yuan)
LIND	Log of IND

Economics of Pollution Control Policy

Table 4.B   *Estimation of reduced form functions*

	Coeff.	t-ratio	Coeff.	t-ratio	Coeff.	t-ratio
	LIWW		LIXGAS		LISOLID	
LHEAVY	0.29	2.82	0.24	2.33	0.48	1.46
LEIA	0.07	2.26	0.04	1.13	0.09	0.90
LTHREE	0.09	1.02	0.22	2.37	0.23	0.80
LDDLINE	0.06	1.26	0.19	3.73	0.05	0.32
LINCOME	-0.93	-5.05	-0.42	-2.25	-1.60	-2.72
LLAND	3.74	3.88	3.91	3.94	5.85	1.89
LPWW	-0.21	-3.72	0.08	1.35	-0.10	-0.56
LPXGAS	-0.03	-0.87	-0.31	-8.68	0.15	1.33
LPSOLID	0.00	0.02	0.00	0.06	-0.25	-5.58
R-square		0.71		0.67		0.52
adjusted		0.69		0.65		0.49
	LIWW		LISO2		LISOLID	
LHEAVY	0.29	2.89	0.12	1.28	0.45	1.37
LEIA	0.06	1.96	0.08	2.97	0.11	1.13
LTHREE	0.11	1.25	-0.03	-0.41	0.17	0.59
LDDLINE	0.06	1.19	-0.06	-1.22	0.01	0.08
LINCOME	-0.93	-5.04	-0.32	-1.91	-1.58	-2.68
LLAND	3.44	3.56	3.56	4.01	6.14	1.97
LPWW	-0.24	-4.08	0.06	1.13	-0.08	-0.44
LPSO2	0.01	0.36	-0.20	-5.59	0.11	0.91
LPSOLID	0.00	-0.14	0.01	0.90	-0.25	-5.49
R-square		0.71		0.42		0.51
adjusted		0.69		0.38		0.48
	LIWW		LISMK		LISOLID	
LHEAVY	0.29	2.89	0.17	1.63	0.46	1.40
LEIA	0.06	2.03	0.12	3.98	0.11	1.17
LTHREE	0.11	1.24	-0.04	-0.47	0.17	0.60
LDDLINE	0.06	1.26	0.05	0.92	0.02	0.15
LINCOME	-0.93	-5.05	-0.55	-2.85	-1.62	-2.74
LLAND	3.50	3.66	4.79	4.77	6.17	2.01
LPWW	-0.23	-4.02	0.08	1.26	-0.09	-0.50
LPSMK	0.01	0.16	-0.24	-5.90	0.14	1.10
LPSOLID	0.00	-0.13	0.01	0.47	-0.25	-5.53
R-square		0.71		0.59		0.52
adjusted		0.69		0.56		0.49

	Coeff.	t-ratio	Coeff.	t-ratio	Coeff.	t-ratio
	LIWW		LIPWD		LISOLID	
LHEAVY	0.29	2.89	0.14	1.51	0.45	1.36
LEIA	0.06	1.91	0.02	0.87	0.12	1.18
LTHREE	0.11	1.26	0.22	2.73	0.17	0.59
LDDLINE	0.06	1.27	0.09	1.92	0.04	0.24
LINCOME	-0.93	-5.05	-0.78	-4.70	-1.61	-2.71
LLAND	3.44	3.47	1.74	1.94	6.46	2.02
LPWW	-0.23	-4.04	0.04	0.80	-0.05	-0.28
LPPWD	0.01	0.26	-0.19	-5.43	0.05	0.38
LPSOLID	0.00	-0.14	0.01	0.82	-0.25	-5.42
R-square		0.71		0.61		0.51
adjusted		0.69		0.59		0.48
	LIWW		LIDUST		LISOLID	
LHEAVY	0.30	2.90	0.17	1.82	0.45	1.39
LEIA	0.06	1.95	0.08	2.94	0.11	1.15
LTHREE	0.11	1.27	0.08	1.03	0.18	0.63
LDDLINE	0.06	1.25	0.05	1.10	0.03	0.19
LINCOME	-0.93	-5.06	-0.65	-3.85	-1.62	-2.74
LLAND	3.43	3.54	3.29	3.73	6.18	1.98
LPWW	-0.24	-4.07	0.04	0.71	-0.08	-0.42
LPDUST	0.01	0.37	-0.17	-4.60	0.11	0.82
LPSOLID	0.00	-0.15	0.01	0.72	-0.25	-5.48
R-square		0.71		0.60		0.51
adjusted		0.69		0.58		0.48
	LICOD		LIXGAS		LISOLID	
LHEAVY	0.51	3.64	0.25	2.45	0.41	1.29
LEIA	0.04	0.97	0.03	0.96	0.09	0.88
LTHREE	0.26	2.04	0.23	2.53	0.20	0.69
LDDLINE	0.05	0.70	0.19	3.71	0.05	0.32
LINCOME	-1.01	-3.90	-0.40	-2.12	-1.52	-2.57
LLAND	1.21	0.91	3.78	3.93	6.43	2.14
LPCOD	-0.71	-12.96	0.07	1.73	0.04	0.31
LPXGAS	0.04	0.88	-0.31	-8.86	0.12	1.08
LPSOLID	0.06	3.22	0.01	0.69	-0.26	-5.74
R-square		0.67		0.68		0.52
adjusted		0.65		0.66		0.49

Economics of Pollution Control Policy

	Coeff.	t-ratio	Coeff.	t-ratio	Coeff.	t-ratio
	LICOD		LISO2		LISOLID	
LHEAVY	0.50	3.59	0.10	1.08	0.39	1.22
LEIA	0.03	0.78	0.07	2.62	0.10	1.06
LTHREE	0.25	2.03	-0.03	-0.36	0.15	0.53
LDDLINE	0.02	0.24	-0.05	-1.24	0.02	0.14
LINCOME	-1.00	-3.89	-0.24	-1.51	-1.50	-2.53
LLAND	0.85	0.65	3.67	4.45	6.68	2.21
LPCOD	-0.72	-13.63	0.13	3.77	0.06	0.48
LPSO2	0.12	2.26	-0.21	-6.41	0.08	0.70
LPSOLID	0.06	3.06	0.02	1.81	-0.25	-5.66
R-square		0.68		0.47		0.51
adjusted		0.66		0.44		0.48
	LICOD		LISMK		LISOLID	
LHEAVY	0.51	3.64	0.16	1.57	0.40	1.24
LEIA	0.04	0.97	0.11	3.69	0.10	1.09
LTHREE	0.24	2.00	-0.03	-0.39	0.15	0.53
LDDLINE	0.03	0.48	0.05	0.93	0.03	0.19
LINCOME	-1.03	-4.00	-0.49	-2.57	-1.53	-2.58
LLAND	1.05	0.81	4.78	5.02	6.71	2.24
LPCOD	-0.72	-13.49	0.11	2.90	0.05	0.42
LPSMK	0.10	1.98	-0.25	-6.44	0.11	0.88
LPSOLID	0.06	3.04	0.02	1.25	-0.25	-5.69
R-square		0.68		0.61		0.51
adjusted		0.66		0.58		0.49
	LICOD		LIPWD		LISOLID	
LHEAVY	0.50	3.61	0.12	1.38	0.40	1.23
LEIA	0.03	0.63	0.02	0.63	0.11	1.13
LTHREE	0.28	2.26	0.22	2.83	0.15	0.52
LDDLINE	0.04	0.56	0.09	1.97	0.04	0.26
LINCOME	-1.06	-4.12	-0.72	-4.41	-1.52	-2.54
LLAND	0.64	0.48	1.86	2.19	6.98	2.26
LPCOD	-0.73	-13.51	0.09	2.60	0.07	0.57
LPPWD	0.11	2.07	-0.20	-6.05	0.02	0.15
LPSOLID	0.06	3.05	0.02	1.46	-0.25	-5.51
R-square		0.68		0.63		0.51
adjusted		0.66		0.61		0.48

	Coeff.	t-ratio	Coeff.	t-ratio	Coeff.	t-ratio
	LICOD		LIDUST		LISOLID	
LHEAVY	0.51	3.64	0.14	1.63	0.40	1.23
LEIA	0.03	0.79	0.07	2.66	0.11	1.08
LTHREE	0.26	2.15	0.08	1.07	0.16	0.56
LDDLINE	0.03	0.47	0.05	1.15	0.03	0.22
LINCOME	-1.05	-4.08	-0.58	-3.52	-1.53	-2.57
LLAND	0.81	0.62	3.43	4.13	6.73	2.22
LPCOD	-0.73	-13.60	0.10	2.92	0.06	0.48
LPDUST	0.12	2.26	-0.18	-5.31	0.07	0.59
LPSOLID	0.06	3.01	0.02	1.38	-0.25	-5.62
R-square		0.68		0.62		0.51
adjusted		0.66		0.60		0.48

NOTES

* This chapter draws heavily from Jiang and McKibbin (2002), 'Assessment of China's Pollution Levy System: An Equilibrium Pollution Approach'. Permission to use the material by Cambridge University Press is acknowledged.

1. A comprehensive discussion of the problems and difficulties in China's environmental protection can be found in Sims (1999).

2. Responding to these critiques, NEPA has been reforming the system in four directions: from a pollution levy only for excess emissions to a levy for total emissions; from charging the 'worst case' pollutant to charging multiple-pollutants; from a pollution levy based on only concentration standard to both concentration and volume standards; adjusting levy rates according to inflation.

3. Because large state-owned enterprises (SOEs) have more advanced technology and are more closely monitored by government agencies than the township and village enterprises (TVEs) and private firms, TVEs and private firms tend to discharge more pollutants per unit of output. Therefore this assumption may make the estimated emissions conservative. However, this conservativeness may be corrected or perhaps overcorrected by the fact that large SOEs may have a high proportion of heavily polluting sectors.

4. The term *excess pollutant* refers to the amount of the pollutant discharged in wastewater or waste gas where the concentration exceeds the limit set by the standard, that is, violating the standard.

5. This result is similar to the findings of Zhang (1998b, 2000b) and Garbaccio et al. (1999b) about energy efficiency improvement in China.

6. A similar result is reported by Garbaccio et al. (1999b) who find that structural change actually increased the use of energy in China between 1978 and 1995.

7. For the discussion and empirical work about this theory, see Grossman and Krueger (1993, 1995), Selden and Song (1994), Shafik (1994), de Bruyn et al. (1998), Kaufmann et al. (1998), Rothman (1998), Suri and Chapman (1998), Torras and Boyce (1998), Unruh and Moomaw (1998), Agras and Chapman (1999), and Dinda et al. (2000). Most authors report an inverted U-shaped curve between environmental quality indicators and development. The turning point reported in the literature is between US$1375 and US$10 000 of per capita income. China's income level, about US$800 per capita, is well below that point. Dinda et al. (2000) show that the environmental Kuznets curves are downward sloping for suspended particulate matter and SO_2 in a broad range of per capita income – from zero to more than US$8000. However, a closer observation of the lower end of per capita income, probably less than US$1000, where China lies, may still reveal a positive relationship between pollution and income (Dinda et al. 2000, Figure 1).

8. From minimising abatement cost and pollution levy, Wang and Wheeler (1996) derive the pollution intensity as a function of wastewater amount, output level, influent concentration, concentration standard and effective levy rate. But they discard the influent concentration and standard variables when specifying the pollution demand function. Therefore their specified function is rather more ad hoc than the previously assumed firm's cost minimisation behaviour.

9. Throughout this chapter, it is assumed, unless specified, that the usual properties of production and utility functions hold and interior solutions exist.

10. When specifying and estimating the model, the per capita income is treated as an exogenous variable for the following reason. In this partial equilibrium setting, income is only weakly linked to the price as some income is earned out of the system. Endogenising income provides no better estimation of the system, as many coefficients turn out to be insignificant.

11. This specification is similar to that in Wang and Wheeler (1996). However, a profound theoretical ground has been provided here for this specification.

12. Some test statistics are included in these tables. It can be seen that they are moderately satisfactory. However, these statistics should be interpreted with caution, as they might be invalid when estimating equation systems (White et al. 1997, pp. 319).

PART II

Economic Instruments of Carbon Dioxide
Emissions Control

5.   Policy Choices of International Carbon Dioxide Emissions Control[*]

5.1   INTRODUCTION

Since the First World Climate Conference was held in 1979, and especially during the 1990s, the possibility of climate change has attracted growing attention because of its ubiquitous impact on the environment and the global economy. There have been some important developments since then. For example, although not a binding international agreement, the United Nations Framework Convention on Climate Change (UNFCCC), established at the 1992 United Nations Conference on Environment and Development held in Rio de Janeiro, Brazil, stated that advanced industrialised countries (Annex I countries[1]) must reduce their emissions to 1990 levels by 2000. In the following Conferences of Parties (COP), countries began to negotiate legally binding targets and timetables and feasible mechanisms to limit emissions in Annex I countries. Most notably, the COP3, held in Kyoto, Japan, reached the 1997 Kyoto Protocol of the Framework Convention. The Kyoto Protocol states that the industrialised countries (now Annex B countries[2]) agree to a legally binding reduction in net greenhouse gas (GHG) emissions that would, on average, be 5.2 percent below 1990 levels by 2008–12. The Protocol also includes several flexibility mechanisms to allow nations to meet targets and timetables in a least-cost way. These mechanisms, including joint implementation (JI), and the clean development mechanism (CDM), fall into the broad category of emission trading.

Nevertheless, intense debate about the proposed mechanisms and reliable implementation of the Protocol emerged following Kyoto, so not enough actual effort has been made to implement it. The Protocol will enter into force only after it is ratified by 55 countries accounting for at least 55 percent of developed country carbon emissions (Article 25). In 1997, only three years from the date when the Annex I countries were meant to stabilise their GHG emissions to 1990 levels as specified in UNFCCC, most, apart from East Europe and the former Soviet Union countries, had higher emissions than in 1990 (see Table 5.1). The COP6, held in The Hague in November 2000, failed to achieve agreement on the mechanisms of implementing the

Table 5.1 Greenhouse gas emissions, tg of CO$_2$-equivalent

	CO$_2$			CH$_4$			N$_2$O			Total		
	1990	1997	±%	1990	1997	±%	1990	1997	±%	1990	1997	±%
Australia	275.3			112.2			23.2			410.8		
Austria	62.0	66.1	6.48	9.7	9.2	-4.33	2.0	2.3	11.97	73.7	77.6	5.21
Belgium	116.1			13.3			9.5			138.9		
Bulgaria	84.4	59.1	-29.92	29.8	18.7	-37.16	9.2	6.6	-28.62	123.4	84.5	-31.57
Canada	461.3	519.3	12.58	73.5	90.3	22.86	55.8	65.1	16.67	590.6	674.7	14.25
Czech Rep.	165.5	137.1	-17.14	16.3	11.8	-27.78	8.0	8.9	11.07	189.8	157.8	-16.87
Denmark	52.3	64.3	23.04	8.8	8.9	0.58	10.5	10.3	-2.38	71.7	83.5	16.53
Estonia	37.8	20.7	-45.19	2.2	2.2	-2.04	0.7	0.2	-69.57	40.7	23.1	-43.28
Finland	59.2	64.6	9.12	7.5	5.7	-23.87	5.8	5.9	1.61	72.5	76.2	5.10
France	395.5	402.2	1.70	63.5	55.0	-13.36	94.6	93.1	-1.57	553.6	550.3	-0.58
Germany	1 014.5	894.0	-11.88	117.0	74.8	-36.03	69.6	67.0	-3.83	1 201.1	1 035.8	-13.76
Greece	85.3			9.2			9.3			103.8		
Hungary	71.7			11.4			3.5			86.6		
Iceland	2.1			0.3			0.1			2.6		
Ireland	30.7			17.0			9.1			56.9		
Italy	432.6			49.3			51.0			532.9		
Japan	1 124.5	1 230.8	9.45	32.4	29.2	-10.00	18.1	20.4	12.63	1 175.0	1 280.4	8.97
Latvia	24.8	12.8	-48.16	3.9	1.9	-50.32	7.0	1.2	-83.22	35.7	16.0	-55.26
Liechtenstein	0.2			0.0			0.0			0.3		
Lithuania	39.5	16.2	-59.02	7.9	6.3	-20.10	4.1			51.5	22.5	-56.27
Monaco	0.1	0.1	32.41	0.0	0.0	0.00	0.0	0.0	200.00	0.1	0.1	32.43
Netherlands	161.4			27.1			19.8			208.3		
New Zealand	25.2	30.3	19.98	35.1	33.5	-4.73	11.5	11.6	1.04	71.9	75.4	4.87

Norway	35.2	41.4	17.69	6.7	7.4	10.41	5.3	5.0	-5.88	47.1	53.7	14.03
Poland	380.7	361.6	-5.01	58.8	47.9	-18.65	19.5	16.7	-14.27	459.0	426.2	-7.15
Portugal	47.1			17.0			4.3			68.4		
Romania	172.5			41.5			15.1			229.1		
Russia	2 372.3			556.5			70.0			2 998.8		
Slovakia	60.0			8.6			3.9			72.5		
Slovenia	13.9			3.7			1.6			19.2		
Spain	226.4			45.8			29.2			301.4		
Sweden	55.4	56.4	1.78	6.0	5.5	-8.45	8.1	7.4	-7.69	69.5	69.3	-0.20
Switzerland	45.1	43.4	-3.77	5.1	4.7	-8.02	3.6	3.6	1.74	53.7	51.7	-3.81
Ukraine	703.8	322.9	-54.12	197.4	138.7	-29.74	18.0	4.8	-73.10	919.2	466.5	-49.25
U.K.	584.2	540.6	-7.45	76.4	57.3	-25.03	66.1	59.5	-9.93	726.6	657.4	-9.52
U.S.	4 928.9	5 455.6	10.69	622.9	658.5	5.72	351.2	399.8	13.84	5 903.0	6 513.9	10.35
Total	14 347.7			2 294.1			1 018.3			17 660.1		
Sub-total*	8 843.4	9 409.2	6.40	1 064.5	1 039.9	-2.31	702.2	751.0	6.95	10 610.1	11 200.1	5.56
China	1 769.6			25.4			0.19			2 361.6		
				~33.9			~0.53			~2 624.5		

Note: *excluding East Europe and former Soviet Union nations and those without data in 1997.

Sources: UNFCCC; China data from ADB et al. (1998, Table 1-1).

Kyoto Protocol. It was then resumed in Bonn in July 2001. Taking note of the Bush Administration's announcement in March 2001 that the US would not proceed to ratify the Kyoto Protocol, the delegates proceeded without the US and reached the Bonn Agreements on the Implementation of the Buenos Aires Plan of Action. The Bonn Agreements significantly relaxed the stringency of the Kyoto Protocol by granting countries forestry and land use sinks allowances totalling 54.5 million metric tons (mmt) of carbon. It was also decided that the international flexibility mechanisms are not subject to quantitative restrictions. The Kyoto Protocol emissions targets were further relaxed in the Marrakesh Accord adopted in COP7 held in Marrakesh in October and November 2001 by increasing Russia's sink allowances from 17.63 mmt to 33 mmt. As a result, the emissions targets may not be binding during the 2008–12 budget period without the US participation (McKibbin and Wilcoxen 2002).

The long and difficult process of international negotiation reflects the developed countries' concern about the effects of a climate agreement on their economies and reluctance to solely bear the cost. Consequently, the developing countries are pressed to show their 'meaningful participation'. For example, as negotiations proceeded toward the 1997 Kyoto Protocol, the US Senate passed the Byrd–Hagel resolution by a vote of 95 to 0. This resolution stated that the United States should not accept a climate agreement that did not demand comparable sacrifices from all participants (Shogren and Toman 2000).

Another reason is that the required extent of GHG abatement cannot be achieved without the participation of the developing countries. Developing countries' GHG emissions have been increasing proportionally more than the world average, so that their share in world emissions has been steadily increasing (see Figure 5.1). China is often taken as an example. China is

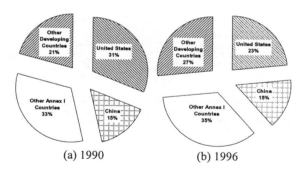

(a) 1990   (b) 1996

Source: World Bank (2000, Table 3.8), IEDB.

Figure 5.1   Composition of world carbon dioxide emissions

second only to the United States as the largest greenhouse gas emitter in the world. In 1996, China emitted 3363.5 million metric tons of carbon dioxide, accounting for 14.8 percent of world emissions (World Bank 2000). Projections show that, if the current trend of economic development continues, China will become the largest GHG emitter around 2020 (World Bank 1994; and some scenarios presented in Chapter 7 of this book).

However, global warming is determined by the stock of GHG, that is, the accumulation of past GHG emissions net of absorption. Developed countries have contributed a major part of this stock. In contrast, developing countries have a very low level of per capita GDP and per capita GHG emissions (Figure 5.2 and Table 5.2). From the point of view of developing countries, developed nations have the greater responsibility for the solution of global environmental problems – especially because they have been, or still are, the greatest polluters – and should therefore support the developing countries (Vermeer 1998; Zhang 1998b). Moreover, like other developing countries, China's priority is to eliminate poverty and enhance economic development. At present, there are about 80 million people in China who do not have enough food to eat or clothes to wear (Wu et al. 1998). Even in the field of environmental protection, control of greenhouse gas emissions is not a priority task. Other more local environmental problems like acid rain, water and air quality and desertification are more urgent for China to deal with. Therefore China sets its framework for environmental protection and international cooperation in this field as follows (Wu et al. 1998):

- Environmental protection will be integrated with the needs of economic development.
- Developed countries have the main responsibility for environmental deterioration.
- The right of developing countries to develop will be completely recognised.
- A new and fair international economic order will be established which supports the sustainable development of all countries, especially developing ones.
- International cooperation in the field of environmental protection will be based on the principle of the sovereign equality of all countries.
- Developed countries will provide enough new and additional funds to developing countries, thus creating the necessary conditions for global environmental protection.

These principles have been termed 'common but differentiated responsibilities' and are reflected in the Rio Declaration on Environment and Development (United Nations 1992, Principle 7):

In view of the different contributions to global environmental degradation, States have common but differentiated responsibilities. The developed countries acknowledge the responsibility that they bear in the international pursuit of sustainable development in view of the pressures their societies place on the global environment and of the technologies and resources they command.

The UNFCCC adopted this principle and stated that 'the developed country Parties should take the lead in combating climate change and the adverse effects thereof' (Article 3.1), while the commitment of developing countries is made in Article 4.7 conditional on the performance of developed countries:

> The extent to which developing country Parties will effectively implement their commitments under the Convention will depend on the effective implementation by developed country Parties of their commitments under the Convention related to financial resources and transfer of technology and will take fully into account that economic and social development and poverty eradication are the first and overriding priorities of the developing country Parties.

In sum, developed countries tend to plan their control over GHG emissions conditional on participation of developing countries, while the latter insist the former should demonstrate their real effort in the first instance. Many authors try to solve this dilemma by promoting developing countries' participation. For example, McKibbin and Wilcoxen (2000) propose a coordinated but

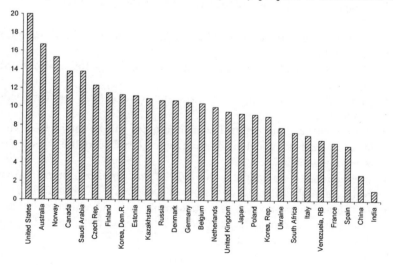

Source: Author's construction based on data from World Bank (2000, Table 3.8).

Figure 5.2   Per capita carbon dioxide emissions, 1996 (metric tons)

Table 5.2   *Carbon dioxide emissions and energy efficiency*

	Carbon dioxide emissions						Energy efficiency	
	Total (million ton)		Per capita (ton)		kg per PPP$ GDP		PPP$ per kg oil equivalent	
	1980	1996	1980	1996	1980	1996	1980	1997
China	1 476.8	3 363.5	1.5	2.8	3.6	1.0	0.7	3.3
US	4 575.4	5 301.0	20.1	20.0	1.6	0.7	1.6	3.6
Russia	n.a.	1 579.5	n.a.	10.7	n.a.	1.5	n.a.	1.7
Japan	920.4	1 167.7	7.9	9.3	0.9	0.4	3.0	6.0
India	347.3	997.4	0.5	1.1	0.8	0.5	1.8	4.2
Germany	n.a.	861.2	n.a.	10.5	n.a.	0.5	n.a.	5.2
UK	583.8	557.0	10.4	9.5	1.2	0.5	2.4	5.3
Canada	420.9	409.4	17.1	13.8	1.5	0.6	1.4	3.0
Korea, Rep.	125.2	408.1	3.3	9.0	1.2	0.6	2.5	3.9
Italy	371.9	403.2	6.6	7.0	0.7	0.3	3.7	7.3
Ukraine	n.a.	397.3	n.a.	7.8	n.a.	2.3	n.a.	1.1
France	482.1	361.8	9.0	6.2	0.9	0.3	2.7	5.0
Poland	456.2	356.8	12.8	9.2	3.7	1.3	1.0	2.7
Mexico	251.6	348.1	3.7	3.8	0.9	0.5	2.9	5.1
Australia	202.8	306.6	13.8	16.7	1.4	0.8	2.0	4.0
South Africa	211.3	292.7	7.7	7.3	1.3	0.8	2.5	3.3
Brazil	183.4	273.4	1.5	1.7	0.4	0.3	4.4	6.5
Saudi Arabia	130.7	267.8	14.0	13.8	1.3	1.3	2.8	2.1
Iran	116.1	266.7	3.0	4.4	1.1	0.9	2.7	3.0
Korea, Dem.Rep.	124.9	254.3	7.1	11.3	n.a.	n.a.	n.a.	n.a.
Indonesia	94.6	245.1	0.6	1.2	0.8	0.4	2.0	4.5
Spain	200.0	232.5	5.3	5.9	0.8	0.4	3.5	5.9
Thailand	40.0	205.4	0.9	3.4	0.6	0.5	2.9	4.7
Turkey	76.3	178.3	1.7	2.9	0.7	0.5	3.3	5.7
Kazakhstan	n.a.	173.8	n.a.	10.9	n.a.	2.5	n.a.	1.8
Netherlands	152.6	155.2	10.8	10.0	1.1	0.5	2.1	4.6
Venezuela, RB	89.6	144.5	5.9	6.5	1.5	1.1	1.7	2.4
Argentina	107.5	129.9	3.8	3.7	0.6	0.3	4.3	6.9
Czech Rep.	n.a.	126.7	n.a.	12.3	n.a.	0.9	n.a.	3.3
Romania	191.8	119.3	8.6	5.3	2.1	0.8	1.4	3.2
Malaysia	28.0	119.1	2.0	5.6	0.8	0.6	3.2	4.0
Belgium	127.2	106.0	12.9	10.4	1.3	0.5	2.2	4.1

Source: World Bank (2000, Table 3.8).

decentralised system of national permit trading systems with a fixed internationally negotiated decentralised price for permits. A permanent endowment of emission right is allocated to each country; beyond the endowment, the government of each country could sell an annual emission permit to firms at the negotiated price. The endowment for developing countries could be set far higher than the current amount they emit. Therefore firms in developing countries would not need to buy additional permits in the short or medium run. However, at present the endowment has a positive price, because the holders of the endowment foresee that as long as the countries keep growing, the endowment will eventually become a binding constraint. This gives incentives for carbon abatement in developing countries through price signals without imposing short- or medium-term costs in these economies.

Manne (1996) looks at two cases of GHG abatement. In one, the benefits of abatement enter directly into the utility functions of the individual regions. In the other, the benefits enter into their production functions. He shows that the abatement efforts and global welfare depend on the region's share of abatement costs in the first case. However, it is possible to separate the issue of equity from those of economic efficiency in the second case.

Peck and Teisberg (1999) analyse the incentives for participation in international CO$_2$ control agreements using tradable emission permits. Their analysis involves two aggregate regions: Annex-I and Non-Annex-I. They define a bargaining range as the range of permit allocation that leaves each region's welfare at least as high as it would be in a no control solution. From the simulation generated by the CETA-M model,[3] they find that the bargaining range for Non-Annex-I is 70–115 percent of its optimal emissions. They argue that a bargaining range must be fairly close to each region's optimal emissions so that interregional income transfers from the emission permit trade could not become large enough to cause one of the regions to drop out of the agreement. The asymmetric distribution around optimal emissions for Non-Annex-I contradicts the usual perspective that Annex-I could shift more permits to Non-Annex-I. They argue this is because Non-Annex-I grows faster than Annex-I in both income and population, and its future damage is higher. They also find that the Kyoto Protocol produces a large wealth transfer from Annex-I to Non-Annex-I, but fails to achieve efficiency. Chao and Peck (2000) characterise general conditions under which the Pareto-optimal environmental control will depend on the distribution of the cost burden among nations and provide a sufficient condition under which a Pareto optimum can be implemented by a market mechanism with tradable emission permits.[4]

Caplan et al. (1999) analyse several institutional arrangements in a world of one winner and one loser due to global warming. They show that only in the cases of full decentralisation and full altruism will the allocation be efficient. Although they doubt the prospect of international policy agreements on the GHG stock level, they suggest that agreements taking the current GHG stock as given are more likely to be successful than agreements that attempt to change the stock. Ulph (2000) analyses the environmental policy (emission permit) assuming that environmental damage costs are known only by state governments. He shows that asymmetric information narrows the difference in environmental policies across states, relative to full information, but does not justify harmonisation – identical environmental policy across states. However, as he assumes pollution does not cross state boundaries, his findings are not directly applicable in greenhouse gas emission control. Using game theoretical tools within a computable general equilibrium framework, Babiker (2001) shows that the international CO_2 abatement falls into the prisoner's dilemma class. In the absence of side payments, international cooperation may be achieved by suitably designed trade instruments such as imposing a tariff on energy-intensive imports from those non-cooperative countries.

It is often argued that emission trade and tax systems are identical with perfect information (Weitzman 1974). However, it is not guaranteed in a multi-country system. It might be true that both instruments will achieve the cost-efficiency to meet certain targets of GHG emission control. But the impact of the two instruments on economic growth and welfare might be different. In spite of implementability, the difference arises from the implicit restrictions on income transfer across boundaries.

This chapter discusses the interaction between China and the rest of the world (ROW) in a setting similar to that of Chao and Peck (2000). In addition to analysing the bargaining power and set, the focus is on the comparison of emission tax and permit trading schemes, in particular, whether a decentralised or differentiated emission tax scheme improves global welfare. The rest of the chapter is organised as follows. The next section sets up a theoretical model to formally discuss possible policy arrangements. Then a stylised numerical analysis is carried out on a hypothetical two region model (China and ROW). The final section concludes and discusses possible extensions.

5.2   THE THEORETICAL MODEL

Following Chao and Peck (2000), the model is structured as follows. Suppose there are N nations in the world. The social welfare function of nation i could be written as

$$U^i = P_i U^i(C_i, Q),$$

where P_i and C_i are, respectively, the population and per capita consumption of nation i; and Q is the environmental quality measured by the change in temperature. $U^i(C_i, Q)$ is thus per capita utility of nation i. As the focus of this chapter is on the interaction among different nations, it is assumed that all individuals within one nation have the same preferences.

The amount of domestic capital goods owned by each nation is denoted by $\overline{K}_i$. The technology for each nation is represented by a convex and twice-differentiable multi-factor production function. For simplicity, it is assumed that the production function, $F^i(K_i, E_i, Q)$, has two factor inputs, capital (environmentally benign), K_i, and energy (causing global climate change), E_i.[5] Capital is internationally mobile, and energy can be obtained at a price of c for all nations.[6] Global climate change enters into both utility and production functions because climate change may cause damages that can be valued in a market, for example, crop losses, and damages that do not have established market values such as species loss (Chao and Peck 2000). It is further assumed that both utility and production functions have usual properties.

5.2.1 Competitive Equilibrium Prior to Environmental Control

Because an individual country cannot control Q, and because the utility or social welfare function is an increasing function of consumption, the objective of each country is simply to achieve the highest possible net output. As the direct marginal (extraction) cost of energy is c, the net output for nation i, Y_i, can be expressed as:

$$Y_i = F^i(K_i, E_i, Q) - cE_i. \tag{5.1}$$

The following conditions are satisfied in a competitive equilibrium prior to environmental control:[7]

$$F_K^i(K_i, E_i, Q) = r, \tag{5.2}$$

$$F_E^i(K_i, E_i, Q) = c, \tag{5.3}$$

$$\sum_{i=1}^{N} K_i = \sum_{i=1}^{N} \overline{K}_i, \tag{5.4}$$

$$P_i C_i = Y_i + r(\overline{K}_i - K_i), \tag{5.5}$$

$$Q = G\left(\sum_{i=1}^{N} E_i\right). \tag{5.6}$$

System (5.1)–(5.6) has $4N+2$ variables in $4N+2$ equations, therefore the system can be solved to get the pre-environmental-control equilibrium values: $\hat{E}_i$, $\hat{K}_i$, $\hat{C}_i$, $\hat{Y}_i$, $\hat{Q}_i$ and $\hat{r}_i$. Consequently, the nation i's social welfare prior to environmental control is $\hat{V}_i = P_i U^i(\hat{C}_i, \hat{Q})$.

It is clear that this decentralised competitive equilibrium is not the first-best outcome (welfare optimum) because the external cost of using energy is not considered by any nation.

5.2.2 Welfare Optimum

Let λ_i denote the utility weight for nation i. The global social welfare maximisation problem can be stated as follows:

$$\max_{C_i,K_i,E_i,Q} \quad U = \sum_{i=1}^{N} \lambda_i P_i U^i(C_i,Q), \tag{5.7}$$

subject to (5.4), (5.6), and

$$\sum_{i=1}^{N} P_i C_i = \sum_{i=1}^{N} [F^i(K_i,E_i,Q) - cE_i]. \tag{5.8}$$

Let π_k, π_e and π_c be the shadow prices associated with above constraints respectively. Then the first order condition can be written as

$$\lambda_i U_C^i(C_i,Q) = \pi_c, \tag{5.9}$$

$$\pi_c[F_E^i(K_i,E_i,Q) - c] = \pi_e G'\left(\sum_i E_i\right), \tag{5.10}$$

$$\pi_c F_K^i(K_i,E_i,Q) = \pi_k, \tag{5.11}$$

$$\pi_e = -\sum_i \lambda_i P_i U_Q^i(C_i,Q) - \pi_c \sum_i F_Q^i(K_i,E_i,Q). \tag{5.12}$$

The last condition (5.12) shows that the shadow price of climate change consists of two parts: the values derived from the marginal utility and the marginal product of climate change. Condition (5.10) shows that the marginal product of energy reflects both the marginal extraction cost and the marginal external cost.

Equations (5.4), (5.6) and (5.8)–(5.12) form a system of $3N+4$ equations with $3N+4$ variables. Therefore they can be solved to get the optimal values of E_i^*, K_i^*, C_i^*, Q_i^*, π_c^*, π_e^*, π_k^*; and the corresponding global welfare is

$$V^* = \sum_{i=1}^{N} \lambda_i P_i U^i(C_i^*,Q^*). $$

5.2.3 Instruments to Achieve Welfare Optimum in a Decentralised Economy

The above global social welfare maximisation problem is constructed in a centralised pattern. However, the real world is a decentralised one. Moreover, national sovereignty makes the scheme more complicated. For example, the emission tax and/or permit trade may require a huge amount of income transfers across borders. Therefore two questions need to be answered. How to achieve welfare optimum in a decentralised economy? Are the approaches realistic to achieve the welfare optimum?

Emission tax

It seems straightforward to achieve the welfare optimum in a decentralised economy by imposing an emission tax. From equation (5.10), it is known that for a welfare optimum,

$$F_E^i(K_i, E_i, Q) = c + \frac{\pi_e}{\pi_c} G'\left(\Sigma_i E_i\right).$$

Therefore the tax rate can be set as:

$$
\begin{aligned}
t^* &= \frac{\pi_e^*}{\pi_c^*} G'\left(\Sigma_i E_i^*\right) \\
&= -\left[\frac{\Sigma_i \lambda_i P_i U_Q^i(C_i^*, Q^*)}{\lambda_i U_C^i(C_i^*, Q^*)} + \Sigma_i F_Q^i(K_i^*, E_i^*, Q^*) \right] G'\left(\Sigma_i E_i^*\right).
\end{aligned}
\tag{5.13}
$$

Note that the tax rate expressed in (5.13) captures the adverse effects of global warming on both utility and production. Clearly the optimal tax rate is affected by the welfare weight (λ_i) assigned to each nation. This result is in line with the finding of Manne (1996).

This tax rate may induce firms in each country to use energy at the optimal level E_i^* in a partial equilibrium setting. However, it cannot guarantee that each country has the optimal consumption C_i^*, because the welfare optimum for each country is achieved with the global income constraint (5.8) rather than individual income constraint (5.5). This means that in addition to the emission tax, it is necessary to allow income transfers across country borders.

From (5.11) it can be derived that the real interest rate for capital is $r^* = \pi_k^*/\pi_c^*$. For nation i, the spending on consumption is $P_i C_i^*$, while total disposable income is $F^i(K_i^*, E_i^*, Q^*) - cE_i^* + r^*(\overline{K}_i - K_i^*)$. It is obvious that only in very rare cases will these two terms be equal, although in aggregate they are equal according to equation (5.8).[8] Therefore, if they are not equal, income transfer is necessary to obtain the welfare optimum. Specifically, if $P_i C_i^* > F^i(K_i^*, E_i^*, Q^*) - cE_i^* + r^*(\overline{K}_i - K_i^*)$, nation i should receive net income support from the other countries.

It can be derived that a country should be a recipient of such a transfer if it has a small capital stock, low productivity and energy efficiency, and therefore low product, but a high consumption propensity. It can be seen that developing countries fall into this category.

However, this income transfer issue extends beyond the discussion of global warming policy, because if there were no global warming externality, it would still require income transfers to achieve welfare optimum as long as countries are not identical. Therefore it might be better to isolate a global warming policy from the general issue of income distribution. This can be done by replacing constraint (5.8) in the global welfare maximisation problem with condition (5.5), that is, each country should satisfy its own budget constraint. But these new constraints make the possibility set smaller, so the solution is of the second-best property, which will be discussed in more detail in subsection 5.2.4.

Tradable permit

Now consider a global tradable permit scheme. Two issues should be dealt with when such a scheme is designed. First, to determine the optimal number of permits $(\overline{E})$, which in turn determines the environmental quality through $Q = G(\overline{E})$. Second, to decide how to allocate these permits. Now the global social welfare maximisation problem can be written as follows:

$$\max_{C_i, K_i, E_i, \overline{E}} U = \sum_{i=1}^{N} \lambda_i P_i U^i\big(C_i, G(\overline{E})\big), \qquad (5.14)$$

subject to (5.4), (5.8), and

$$\sum_{i=1}^{N} E_i = \overline{E} . \qquad (5.15)$$

Let π_k, π_c and π_e be the shadow prices associated with the above constraints respectively. Then, in addition to (5.9) and (5.11), the first order condition can be written as[9]

$$\pi_c[F_E^i(K_i, E_i, Q) - c] = \pi_e , \qquad (5.16)$$

$$\pi_e = -G'(\overline{E})[\Sigma_i \lambda_i P_i U_Q^i(C_i, Q) + \pi_c \Sigma_i F_Q^i(K_i, E_i, Q)] . \qquad (5.17)$$

The above conditions are exactly the same as those given by (5.4), (5.6), (5.8)–(5.12), except that $\pi_e G'(\Sigma_i E_i)$ in (5.10) and (5.12) is equal to π_e in (5.16) and (5.17). It can be drawn from these conditions that the initial allocation of permits does not affect the optimal value of capital and energy use and consumption as long as the number of permits $(\overline{E})$ is set optimally.[10] It can also be seen that the allocation of permits may serve as a tool of income transfer to achieve the first-best outcome, which is problematic with the emission tax scheme. As in the case of the emission tax, the permit price and interest rate are set as follows:

$$p_e^* = \pi_e^*/\pi_c^*, \ r^* = \pi_k^*/\pi_c^*.$$

Country i's income other than permit sales is $F^i(K_i^*, E_i^*, G(\overline{E}^*)) - cE_i^*$ $+ r^*(\overline{K}_i - K_i^*)$; while total consumption is $P_i C_i^*$. Therefore the initial number of permits ($\overline{E}_i$) can be carefully selected such that

$$p_e^*(\overline{E}_i - E_i^*) = P_i C_i^* - [F^i(K_i^*, E_i^*, G(\overline{E}^*)) - cE_i^* + r^*(\overline{K}_i - K_i^*)].$$

However, it is quite possible that, for some nation i, the value of the right-hand side of the above equation is too high and $\overline{E}_i > \overline{E}^*$ is needed to equate both sides. Therefore, while a tradable emission permit scheme may help to achieve the first-best outcome, it does not guarantee it.

Chao and Peck (2000) claim that the welfare optimum can be achieved in an emission trading system if the initial permits are carefully allocated. However, what they dealt with is not what is discussed here. In contrast to condition (5.9) in this chapter, equation (24) in their paper states that each country should satisfy its own budget constraint, and no income transfer other than emission trading is allowed. This means that what they get is actually a second-best outcome.

In sum, the following statement can be made:

Result 5.1 *A pure emission (or energy use) tax can not achieve the first-best outcome – maximising global welfare, not just emission targets, and an emission (or energy use) permit trading scheme may achieve, but does not guarantee, the first-best outcome.*

5.2.4 The Second-Best Policy

Now suppose that the individual country meets its own budget constraint. It is necessary to discuss the emission (or in this case actually energy) tax scheme in a more decentralised way, because the interest rate appears in the constraint (5.5). In this decentralised world, it is necessary to distinguish producer and consumer (and social planner). The producer chooses capital and energy use to maximise profit given the interest rate, energy price and environmental regulation. The resultant first order conditions are (5.15) and

$$F_E^i(K_i, E_i, Q) = c + t_i. \tag{5.18}$$

At the same time, the global social planner chooses energy supply, consumption and environmental quality to maximise global social welfare (5.7) subject to constraints (5.5) and (5.6). Let π_c^i and π_e denote the shadow prices associated with the constraints (5.5) and (5.6). Then the first order condition can be written as:

$$\lambda_i U_C^i(C_i,Q) = \pi_c^i,\tag{5.19}$$

$$\pi_c^i[F_E^i(K_i,E_i,Q) - c] = \pi_e G'(\Sigma_i E_i),\tag{5.20}$$

$$\pi_e = -\Sigma_i \lambda_i P_i U_Q^i(C_i,Q) - \Sigma_i \pi_c^i F_Q^i(K_i,E_i,Q).\tag{5.21}$$

Condition (5.20), which determines the tax rate of energy use, is equivalent to condition (5.15). One important result can be found by comparing condition (5.19) with (5.9). Now the weighted marginal utility of consumption differs across countries. This verifies that the results are not the first-best outcome. One more important finding is that the tax rates are different across countries! This seems to contradict the usual wisdom that equal emission tax leads to least costs. However, a second thought reveals that it is not the case. As individuals in different countries face a common environmental quality, that is, global warming, by definition the marginal utility from that environmental quality is the same for them. On the other hand, because individuals in different countries face different budget constraints, that is, their available consumption differs, their marginal utility from consumption differs accordingly. As a result, the marginal rate of substitution of consumption for environment differs for individuals in different countries, leading to different prices of environmental quality, or emission taxes. From (5.20), the tax rate should be set as

$$\frac{\pi_e}{\pi_c^i} G'(\Sigma_i E_i).$$

As π_c^i differs across countries, the whole term differs as well. If a uniform tax rate is set, then using (5.15), (5.20) can be rewritten as:

$$\pi_c^i t = \pi_e G'(\Sigma_i E_i).\tag{5.22}$$

This in turn implies that π_c^i should be identical for all i. As the usual optimisation requires different multipliers for different constraints, this restriction causes the result to deteriorate further. In sum, the following result is found regarding the emission tax scheme if income transfer is not allowed, as in the real world situation.

Result 5.2 *If each country meets its own budget constraint and an emission tax scheme is considered, a differentiated tax scheme is better than a uniform tax scheme.*

Now moving to the tradable permit system, the problem can be set as follows. The global social planner chooses initial permit allocation, capital, energy, and consumption to maximise the global social welfare function (5.14) subject to (5.4) and

$$\Sigma_i E_i = \Sigma_i \overline{E}_i , \tag{5.23}$$

$$P_i C_i = F^i\left(K_i, E_i, G(\Sigma_i \overline{E}_i)\right) - cE_i + p_e(\overline{E}_i - E_i) + r(\overline{K}_i - K_i) . \tag{5.24}$$

Let π_k, π_e and π_c^i be the shadow prices associated with the above constraints, respectively. Then, in addition to (5.19), the first order condition can be written as

$$\pi_c^i[F_E^i(K_i, E_i, Q) - c - p_e] = \pi_e , \tag{5.25}$$

$$\pi_c^i[F_K^i(K_i, E_i, Q) - r] = \pi_k , \tag{5.26}$$

$$\pi_e + \pi_c^i p_e + G'(\overline{E})\Sigma_i\left(\lambda_i P_i U_Q^i(C_i, Q) + \pi_c^i F_Q^i(K_i, E_i, Q)\right) = 0 , \tag{5.27}$$

$$F_E^i(K_i, E_i, Q) - c - p_e = 0 , \tag{5.28}$$

$$F_K^i(K_i, E_i, Q) - r = 0 . \tag{5.29}$$

The last two are the first conditions of the profit maximisation problem, which imply that $\pi_e = \pi_k = 0$ in (5.25) and (5.26). And (5.27) implies that π_c^i is identical for all i. Thus these conditions are exactly the conditions given in (5.9), (5.11), (5.16), and (5.17). At first glance, it seems that, as argued by many authors (for example Chao and Peck 2000), the first-best outcome can be achieved by carefully choosing the initial allocation of permits. However, this is not guaranteed. The 'optimal' allocation for some countries could be well above the total optimal number of permits. As will be seen, this is exactly the case implied by a numerical model. If non-negative restrictions are imposed on allocations, it turns out that a corner solution is reached – some countries are not allocated any permits. Therefore the tradable permit scheme should be designed in a different way.

An alternative method would be to fix the total amount of permits, rather than endogenise it. Again, it is possible to get the spurious initial allocation. Another way would be to set up certain rules of allocating permits and then to find the optimal number of permits. No doubt, there are numerous rules to allocate permits, with pro rata population and pro rata current emissions as two important scenarios.

Before moving into numerical analysis, the following statement is presented to summarise the above theoretical analysis.

Result 5.3 *Even with perfect information, international emission tax and emission trading schemes are not identical because the latter allows income transfers across borders. Emission trading could achieve a better outcome than a differentiated tax scheme.*

5.3 NUMERICAL SIMULATION

In this section, a simple numerical model is presented.[11] There are two regions in the model: China and rest of the world (ROW). In order to illustrate the idea developed in the previous sections, the values of parameters for ROW are chosen in such a way that they represent a more developed world, which is somehow counterfactual.

5.3.1 The Climate Model

Following Oglesby and Saltzman (1990) and Chao (1995), the relationship between average global climate change (T) and global energy consumption (E) can be written as follows:

$$T = T_0 \log_2\left(1 + \gamma E / X_0\right),$$

where $T_0 (= 3°C)$ is the increase from the pre-industrial average global temperature as a result of doubling the carbon dioxide concentration in the atmosphere; X_0 is the pre-industrial level of carbon dioxide concentration in the atmosphere, which is about 280 ppm; and $\gamma (= 0.30$ ppm/exajoules/year) is a transfer coefficient which is chosen so that at the rate of emission of about 250 exajoules (energy equivalent), the equilibrium carbon concentration will remain at about 335 ppm, therefore γE is the carbon dioxide concentration in the atmosphere (Chao and Peck 2000).

5.3.2 The Utility Function

Following Chao and Peck (2000), the utility function for each region is assumed to be of the Cobb–Douglas form as follows:

$$U^i(C_i, T) = [C_i^{\theta_i} (\overline{T_i} - T)^{1-\theta_i}]^{1/2}.$$

The parameter $\overline{T_i}$ is the catastrophic level of average global temperature increase, as perceived by nation i, that is, at that level, the utility becomes zero, which is as bad as when consumption drops to zero. The values of parameters, $\overline{T}_i$ and θ_i, are highly uncertain and subjective. But one reasonable conjecture is that they are higher for China than for developed countries, because China has lower per capita consumption and thus cares about consumption more than about the environment. Specifically, the values are determined in such a way that the utility reduction from a 3°C rise in average global temperature is 2 percent for China and 4 percent for ROW, and the utility losses increase in a cubic order as the average global temperature increases (Chao and Peck 2000; Nordhaus 1994a):

$$(1.00)^{\theta_1}(\overline{T}_1)^{1-\theta_1} = (1.02)^{\theta_1}(\overline{T}_1 - 3)^{1-\theta_1} = (1.16)^{\theta_1}(\overline{T}_1 - 6)^{1-\theta_1},$$
$$(1.00)^{\theta_2}(\overline{T}_2)^{1-\theta_2} = (1.04)^{\theta_2}(\overline{T}_2 - 3)^{1-\theta_2} = (1.32)^{\theta_2}(\overline{T}_2 - 6)^{1-\theta_2}.$$

The resulting values are listed in Table 5.3.

Table 5.3   Numerical assumptions (before environmental control)

Parameter	China	ROW
θ_i	0.9720	0.9489
$\overline{T}_i$	6.03494	6.04728
Production shifter, A_i	4.08	29.93
Capital value share, α_i	0.20	0.15
Energy value share, β_i	0.06	0.05
GDP (US$ trillion)	12.00	100.00
Population (billion)	1.78	8.23
Capital stock, $\overline{K}_i$ (US$ trillion)	48.00	300.00
Energy consumption, E_i, (exajoules)	160.00	1,111.11
Marginal cost of energy, c, (US$/gigajoules)	4.50	4.50
Interest rate	0.05	0.05

5.3.3   The Production Function

The estimates of the impact of climate change on production are both diverse and controversial.[12] For example, the impact on agricultural yield varies from -100 percent to 180 percent (see Table 6.5). Therefore, it is assumed that the production is not affected by global warming[13] and the functional form is Cobb–Douglas as well:

$$F^i(K_i, E_i, Q) = A_i K_i^{\alpha_i} E_i^{\beta_i}.$$

The technologies employed by the two regions are different in the sense that China has a higher marginal product of capital and higher energy intensity. The assumption of Chao and Peck (2000) is followed about the capital and energy value shares and marginal cost of energy of ROW. However, a different assumption is made about the parameters of China. China has a capital/GDP ratio of about 3.0,[14] which implies the capital share is about 0.20. The energy/GDP ratio is about 13.33 megajoule/USD, implying the energy share is about 0.06.[15]

China's GDP growth rate was 10.1 percent per annum between 1980 and 1990, and 11.2 percent per annum between 1990 and 1998 (World Bank 2000). It is assumed that China will have moderate 5 percent growth in the next half century, which indicates a GDP in 2050 of about US$12.1 trillion. The world GDP growth rate was 3.2 percent per annum between 1980 and 1990, and 2.5 percent per annum between 1990 and 1998 (World Bank 2000). Assuming that the GDP growth in ROW will maintain this trend, the ROW GDP will be about US$100.3 trillion.[16]

China's annual new capital formation growth was 20.7 percent between 1985 and 1998 (SSB 1999), while domestic investment growth was 13.4 percent per annum between 1990 and 1998 (World Bank 2000). If this trend is maintained, China's capital stock will be as high as US$148 trillion by 2050, which is unrealistic. To be in line with the assumptions given above, and in Chao and Peck (2000), it is simply assumed that the interest rate and marginal extraction cost of energy are, respectively, 5 percent and $4.5 per gigajoule. The capital stock and energy consumption are derived from the assumption of their shares in GDP. The figure about capital stock implies no capital flows across borders at pre-control equilibrium. Plugging these values into the production functions gives the values of coefficient A_i, which are 4.08 for China and 29.93 for ROW. The difference in the values of this coefficient between China and ROW is mainly because the sizes of the two economies are different and the energy and capital share of total GDP is only 20–26 percent. Still, the marginal product of capital and energy are in the same order for both regions.

China's population was 1238.6 million by the end of 1998, and the average annual growth rate was 1.3 percent between 1980 and 1998. The rest of the world population was 4658 million in 1998. The World Bank (2000) estimates that the annual growth rates between 1998 and 2015 will be 0.7 and 1.1 percent, respectively, for China and ROW. Following these assumptions, the population in 2050 would be, respectively, 1780.2 million and 8227.3 million for China and ROW.

5.3.4 Numerical Results

Without environmental control, global energy consumption would be

1271.111 exajoules in 2050, and global warming would be 3.72°C. Correspondingly, the per capita utility of China and ROW would be 2.482 and 3.252, respectively, and global welfare would be 31.194 if both have the same utility weight (λ_i) of one (Table 5.4).[17] This is the baseline that will be used to compare different policy arrangements.

Table 5.4   Non-cooperative competitive equilibrium vs. global optimum

Indicator	Prior to environ. control	With environmental control	
		value	% change*
Capital used in China	48.000	47.632	-0.77
Capital used in ROW	300.000	300.368	0.12
Energy used in China	160.000	81.514	-49.05
Energy used in ROW	1111.111	571.137	-48.60
Output in China	12.000	11.506	-4.12
Output in ROW	100.000	96.745	-3.26
Per capita consumption in China	6.337	11.219	77.04
Per capita consumption in ROW	11.543	10.370	-10.16
Global warming	3.720	2.295	-38.31
Per capita utility in China	2.482	3.298	32.88
Per capita utility in ROW	3.253	3.133	-3.69
Total global utility	31.194	31.655	1.48
China	4.418	5.871	32.89
ROW	26.776	25.784	-3.70

Note: * Percentage change to the baseline outcome – competitive equilibrium prior to environmental control.

Source: Author's calculation.

Introducing environmental control will increase global welfare to 31.655 in a global social optimisation pattern (Table 5.4). However, this global optimisation is not attainable, because the underlying assumption is that US$ 8.812 trillion, amounting to 76.6 percent of China's GDP, has to be transferred to China from ROW. Correspondingly, China's per capita utility increases to 3.298, while ROW's decreases to 3.133.

Table 5.5 shows the results of imposing energy taxes, assuming that both China and ROW have the same bargaining power λ. As discussed in the previous section, a policy with uniform tax rate creates lower global welfare than one with differentiated tax rates, although both policies can achieve global utility higher than the baseline. Specifically, China's utility is lower while ROW's utility is higher in a uniform tax regime than would be the case in a differentiated tax regime.

Figure 5.3 shows the bargaining set with a differentiated tax regime. The bargaining set is larger than would usually be assumed. The tax rate imposed

Table 5.5   Outcome of energy taxes with equal bargaining power

Indicator	Differentiated rate[a]		Uniform rate[a]	
	Value	% change[b]	Value	% change[b]
Capital used in China	48.125	0.26	47.628	-0.78
Capital used in ROW	299.875	-0.04	300.372	0.12
Energy used in China	93.045	-41.85	80.880	-49.45
Energy used in ROW	552.165	-50.31	566.750	-48.99
Output in China	11.622	-3.15	11.501	-4.16
Output in ROW	96.558	-3.44	96.708	-3.29
Per capita consumption in China	6.291	-0.73	6.267	-1.11
Per capita consumption in ROW	11.431	-0.97	11.439	-0.90
Global warming	2.274	-38.87	2.281	-38.68
Per capita utility in China	2.490	0.32	2.485	0.12
Per capita utility in ROW	3.281	0.86	3.282	0.89
Total global utility	31.436	0.78	31.434	0.77
China	4.432		4.424	
ROW	27.004		27.011	
Marginal cost of global warming	0.210		0.136	
Energy tax in China	2.994		4.032	
Energy tax in ROW	4.244		4.032	

Notes:
a. Global optimisation with equal bargaining power and individual budget constraint.
b. Percentage change to the baseline outcome – competitive equilibrium prior to environmental control reported in Table 5.4.

Source: Author's calculation.

on ROW could be as high as \$14.328 per gigajoule for ROW to have the same utility as the baseline, if China could at the same time impose a tiny \$0.319 per gigajoule (about 7.09 percent of the extraction cost of energy). However, the bargaining set is not symmetric. The highest tax rate China would accept is only \$4.84 per gigajoule, on condition that ROW imposes a tax at the rate of \$4.108 per gigajoule.

Figure 5.4 compares the uniform tax regime with a differentiated tax regime. The optima with varying bargaining power (λ_i) are depicted. The variation of optima with uniform tax is much smaller than that of optima with differentiated tax. All the combinations of (U_1, U_2) under a uniform tax regime, as bargaining power varying from $\lambda_1 = 1$, $\lambda_2 = 0$ to $\lambda_1 = 0$, $\lambda_2 = 1$, are depicted in the diagram; while only a subset of (U_1, U_2) is depicted under a differentiated tax regime, with bargaining power varying from $\lambda_1 = 0.375$, $\lambda_2 = 0.625$ to $\lambda_1 = 0.970$, $\lambda_2 = 0.030$. It is clear from the diagram that the whole utility frontier with uniform tax rate falls into the utility frontier with differentiated tax rates, confirming the conjecture that a uniform tax regime cannot achieve higher global welfare than a differentiated tax regime.

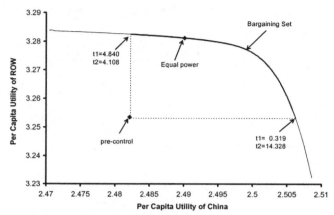

Source: Author's construction.

Figure 5.3   Bargaining set with differential taxes

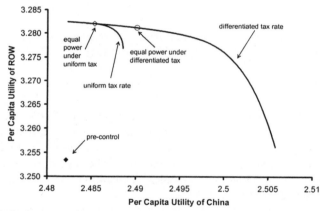

Source: Author's construction.

Figure 5.4   Uniform versus differential taxes

Another observation from Figure 5.4 is that, as the bargaining power of ROW increases, these two regimes tend to converge. This can be partly explained by the different size of China and ROW. When ROW dominates in the negotiation of a global energy tax policy, a uniform tax rate is likely to be adopted.

The results of a tradable permit system with equal bargaining power are listed in Table 5.6. Two scenarios are reported. One is the global optimisation of choosing a total permit number and an initial allocation without prior restrictions, in addition to the other control variables like capital and energy use and consumption. As discussed in the previous section, a tradable permit system can achieve the welfare optimum only if ROW can be allocated a negative amount of permits (-1648.805 exajoules). If a non-negative restriction is imposed on the initial allocation, it turns out that no permits are allocated to ROW. Needless to say, these two scenarios are not realistic and are not worth further exploration. Instead, an attempt is made to find the optimal number of permits to use energy with different allocation rules. The result is depicted in Figure 5.5. It can be seen that both allocation rules – allocating permits proportional to the population or pre-control energy use – are in the bargaining set. However, it can also be seen that China benefits less than the ROW from these two allocation rules.

Figure 5.6 shows the result of fixing the total amount of permits at the level of global optimisation with environmental control (652.651 exajoules). It is clear from the diagram that this kind of arrangement is always beneficial to ROW, but not necessarily to China.

Both Figures 5.5 and 5.6 show that, for China, an allocation of permits proportional to population is not as favourable as people usually assume. This can be explained by the fact that, compared to ROW, China has a higher

Table 5.6   Tradable permit with equal bargaining power

Indicator	Without non-negative restriction*	With non-negative restriction*
Capital used in China	47.632	47.682
Capital used in ROW	300.368	300.318
Energy used in China	81.514	89.237
Energy used in ROW	571.137	624.502
Permit allocated for China	2301.457	713.739
Permit allocated for ROW	-1648.805	0.000
Permit price	3.970	3.280
Output in China	11.506	11.571
Output in ROW	96.745	97.176
Per capita consumption in China	11.219	7.435
Per capita consumption in ROW	10.370	11.215
Global warming	2.295	2.458
Per capita utility in China	3.298	2.699
Per capita utility in ROW	3.133	3.247
Total global utility	31.655	31.529
China	5.871	4.804
ROW	25.784	26.725

Note: * Optimising permit number and initial allocation with individual budget constraint.

Source: Author's calculation.

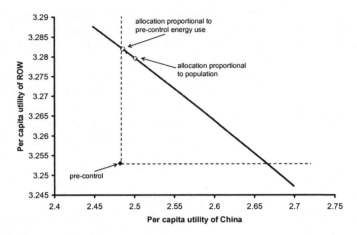

Source: Author's construction.

Figure 5.5   Tradable permit with endogenous number of permits, varying initial allocation

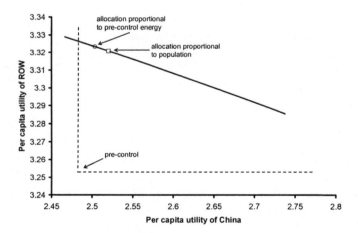

Source: Author's construction.

Figure 5.6   Tradable permit with fixed number of permits and varying initial allocation

preference for consumption and higher energy intensity in production. A restriction on the use of energy will hit China's production more than ROW's even if it is offered a seemingly favourable allocation of permits. Because

China has to use more energy to produce the same output and has to satisfy its own income constraint, China's benefit from this allocation is limited on the production side. On the other hand, due to its preference, China's benefit from improvement in global warming is also limited. Of course, this arrangement is more favourable than an allocation of permits proportional to the pre-control situation. Such an arrangement makes ROW much better off while leaving China at the margin if the total permit is endogenous (Figure 5.5). Given this fact, negotiation of an international agreement on permit allocation is doomed to be a painful process if the developing countries are covered.

5.3.5 Sensitivity Analysis

To test the robustness of the results, two sets of analyses are presented. First, the assumptions about parameters are changed in two ways: (1) the assumption about the preference is reversed, that is, the utility loss from a 3°C rise in average global temperature is 4 percent for China and 2 percent for ROW, and the utility losses increase in a cubic order as the average global temperature increases; (2) it is assumed that China has the same technology as ROW. The results are reported in Tables 5.7 and 5.8.

It is clear from the test that the qualitative result does not change even if the parameters change dramatically – a differentiated tax system is always better than a uniform tax system in terms of global welfare. China suffers from a uniform tax policy even if China cares more about global warming than ROW, or has the same technology as ROW.

Table 5.7   Sensitivity analysis of preference assumption

Indicator	Differentiated rates		Uniform rate	
	Old[a]	New[b]	Old[a]	New[b]
Total energy use (exa.j.)	645.210	790.630	647.630	792.275
Global warming (°C)	2.274	2.656	2.281	2.660
Energy tax, China (US$/g.j.)	2.994	2.016	4.032	2.547
Energy tax, ROW (US$/g.j.)	4.244	2.648	4.032	2.547
Per capita utility, China	2.490	2.470	2.485	2.468
Per capita utility, ROW	3.281	3.331	3.282	3.332
Total global utility	31.436	31.815	31.434	31.814

Notes:
a. Old preference assumption states that the utility loss from 3°C warming is 2 percent for China and 4 percent for ROW.
b. New preference assumption states that the utility loss from 3°C warming is 4 percent for China and 2 percent for ROW.

Source: Author's calculation.

Table 5.8   Sensitivity analysis of technology assumption

Indicator	Differentiated rates		Uniform rate	
	Old[a]	New[b]	Old[a]	New[b]
Total energy use (exa.j.)	645.210	630.231	647.630	632.183
Global warming (°C)	2.274	2.233	2.281	2.236
Energy tax, China (US$/g.j.)	2.994	3.011	4.032	4.063
Energy tax, ROW (US$/g.j.)	4.244	4.240	4.032	4.063
Per capita utility, China	2.490	2.505	2.485	2.501
Per capita utility, ROW	3.281	3.282	3.282	3.283
Total global utility	31.436	31.471	31.434	31.469

Notes:
a. Old assumptions about technology: capital share is 0.2 for China and 0.15 for ROW; energy share is 0.06 for China and 0.05 for ROW.
b. New assumptions about technology: China and ROW have same capital (0.15) and energy shares (0.05).

Source: Author's calculation.

Second, testing the impact of economic size on the result has also been attempted. The world is divided into three economies: China, rich countries (Rich), and the rest of the world (ROW). It is assumed that China and ROW have the same preference and production technology, but different population and GDP levels which are projected based on current and historical data. Rich countries have higher energy efficiency and care more about global warming.

Low- and middle-income countries had an annual growth rate of 3.5 percent between 1990 and 1998, and their GDP (excluding China) in 1998 was US$5.23 trillion. Following this trend, their GDP in 2050 will be US$31.32 trillion. Population was 3772 million in 1998. The growth rate is projected as 1.2 percent between 1998 and 2050. If this trend extends to 2050, population will be 7014.25 million.

High-income countries had an annual growth rate of 2.3 percent between 1990 and 1998 and 3.1 percent during the period between 1980 and 1990. Therefore it is assumed that rich countries will grow at the rate of 2.5 percent. Their total GDP in 1998 was US$22.54 trillion, so the level in 2050 would be US$81.41 trillion. Their population in 1998 was 886 million and the growth rate is estimated as 0.3 percent between 1998 and 2015. If this trend extends to 2050, the population in rich countries will be 1035.1 million. The detailed assumption of parameters is listed in Table 5.9.

Some stylised results are reported in Table 5.10. Again the qualitative results do not change after the regrouping of the world economy. The differentiated tax system is better than the uniform tax system. China and

Table 5.9 Numerical assumptions for the sensitivity analysis of economic size

	China	Rich	ROW
θ_i	0.9720	0.9459	0.9720
$\overline{T}_i$	6.03494	6.04728	6.03494
Production shifter, A_i	4.08	25.039	8.038
Capital value share, α_i	0.20	0.15	0.20
Energy value share, β_i	0.06	0.05	0.06
GDP (US$ trillion)	12.00	80.00	30.00
Population (billion)	1.78	1.04	7.01
Capital stock, $\overline{K}_i$, (US$ trillion)	48.00	240.00	120.00
Energy consumption, E_i, (exajoules)	160.00	888.889	400.00
Marginal cost of energy, c, (US$/g.j.)	4.50	4.50	4.50
Interest rate	0.05	0.05	0.50

Table 5.10 Simulation result for three country groups

Indicators	Pre-control	Diff. rate	Uniform rate
Capital use, China	48.000	48.861	47.652
Capital use, Rich countries	240.000	236.369	241.218
Capital use, ROW	120.000	122.770	119.130
Energy use, China	160.000	111.603	61.836
Energy use, Rich countries	888.888	334.984	347.798
Energy use, ROW	400.000	298.388	154.590
Output, China	12.000	11.785	11.318
Output, Rich countries	80.000	76.016	76.391
Output, ROW	30.000	29.612	28.295
Per capita consumption, China	6.337	6.315	6.211
Per capita consumption, Rich	73.077	71.811	71.893
Per capita consumption, ROW	4.023	4.014	3.943
Global warming	4.056	2.540	2.046
Per capita utility, China	2.477	2.492	2.477
Per capita utility, Rich	7.755	7.810	7.842
Per capita utility, ROW	1.986	2.000	1.986
Total global utility	26.394	26.575	26.486
China	4.408	4.436	4.409
Rich	8.065	8.122	8.155
ROW	13.921	14.017	13.922

Source: Author's calculation.

ROW suffer from the introduction of uniform tax, while rich countries benefit. The welfare optimum cannot be achieved without income redistribution.

5.4   CONCLUSION

The theoretical and numerical models show that an emission tax and a tradable permit policy are quite different. This is mainly because a tradable permit policy allows income transfer across borders while a tax does not. However, neither policy can achieve the first-best – welfare maximising – outcome. In order to achieve the first-best, an emission tax policy should be accompanied by a net transfer of income from rich to poor countries, while a tradable emission permit policy requires that rich countries be allocated a very small, or even negative number of permits. It is clear that neither arrangement is realistic.

In terms of achieving the second-best outcome, it is found that a differentiated tax system is better than a uniform tax system across countries. The difference in tax rate is justified by the fact that China and the rest of the world (or poor and rich countries) have different preferences regarding the environment and consumption and have different production technologies. Because China (or developing countries) prefers consumption more than developed countries and its energy intensity is higher, a lower emission tax (or energy tax) would provide a more favourable environment to produce what it consumes. And because rich countries care more about the environment, their willingness to pay for a clean environment is higher, therefore they could afford a higher tax rate. Thus, overall welfare could be enhanced by this arrangement.

Another benefit from a differentiated tax system is that it could gradually improve mutual trust and international cooperation because a small unilateral tax could improve an individual nation's welfare in addition to the global welfare. If the tax system could be carefully designed in the sense of combining global welfare with each nation's interest, the prisoner's dilemma could be solved.

Theoretically, a tradable permit system could produce higher global welfare if the initial allocation is carefully chosen. However, this is a centralised system, involving higher administrative demands. Moreover, the allocation of permits is a very sensitive issue, making it very difficult to reach an international agreement.

The above results should be interpreted cautiously. The numerical model presented here is very simple and is best interpreted as providing illustrative cases. For example, the Cobb–Douglas production function may not be the best functional form, as it allows substantial substitution between capital and energy input. After an environmental control is imposed, energy consumption falls by about half the previous level. Because global warming is related to the stock of GHG, a natural extension to the model is to introduce dynamics. Another extension could be to divide energy into several categories to allow energy switching and substitution.

NOTES

* This chapter draws heavily on Jiang (2002), 'China in International Action on Climate Change'. Permission to use this paper by Asia Pacific Press at the Australian National University is acknowledged.

1. When the Framework Convention was signed, the Annex I countries included the 24 original OECD members (Australia, Austria, Belgium, Canada, Denmark, Finland, France, Germany, Greece, Iceland, Ireland, Italy, Japan, Luxembourg, Netherlands, New Zealand, Norway, Portugal, Spain, Sweden, Switzerland, Turkey, United Kingdom of Great Britain and Northern Ireland, and the United States of America), the European Economic Community, and 11 countries with economies in transition (Belarus, Bulgaria, Czechoslovakia, Estonia, Hungary, Latvia, Lithuania, Poland, Portugal, Romania, Russian Federation, Ukraine). The Czech Republic and Slovakia later replaced Czechoslovakia.

2. Croatia, Liechtenstein, Monaco and Slovenia joined at COP-3, and Belarus and Turkey dropped from the list of Annex B countries. Therefore, there are 39 parties in the Annex B list.

3. CETA stands for Carbon Emissions Trajectory Assessment. An introduction to CETA can be found in Peck and Teisberg (1992) while an introduction to CETA-M can be found in Peck and Teisberg (1997).

4. To avoid confusion, the terms welfare optimum or the first-best outcome will be used in the remaining discussion.

5. This assumption implies full employment in the general equilibrium setting, that is, labour is fixed.

6. For simplicity, the energy is assumed to be of the same quality and carbon content. As the production cost of energy is assumed constant, the origin of energy is inessential – one nation could either produce or import the energy needed. These assumptions will be relaxed in Chapters 6–8 in a numerical dynamic general equilibrium model, G-Cubed-T.

7. The climate change, Q, is actually a function of all past and current energy uses. However, as the model presented here is static, only current energy use is controllable, while historical energy uses enter into the process as pre-determined parameters.

8. Equations (5.4), (5.6) and (5.8)–(5.12) form a system of $3N+4$ equations with $3N+4$ variables. If $P_iC_i^* = F^i(K_i^*, E_i^*, Q^*) - cE_i^* + r^*(\overline{K}_i - K_i^*)$ were included, the system would have $N-1$ more equations. The system would be insolvable unless N equations in the $4N+3$ equation system are linearly dependent.

9. Because the environmental quality is uniquely determined by (5.6), Q is used in these conditions to avoid excessive notation.

10. Because this is a global optimisation problem, the difference between the actual use and initial allocation of permits for individual countries and resulting payments cancel each other out. Therefore, the initial allocation of permits does

not enter the constraints and the first order conditions.

11. This simple stylised static model is presented because it is easy to handle and enables full demonstration of the above theoretical analyses. A much more complicated, dynamic general equilibrium model, G-Cubed-T, will be presented later, and some features of the theoretical analysis will be simulated and tested again using it.

12. A collection of these estimates can be found in Chapter 6 of this book.

13. It is fairly safe to make such an assumption as there is only one aggregated sector in the economy. The impact on production of global warming will be introduced later in the G-Cubed-T model where the economy has a more disaggregated structure.

14. In 1998, the state-owned and medium and large non-state-owned enterprises had a capital value of RMB 6483.205 billion yuan, and value-added of RMB 1942.193 billion yuan, implying a capital/GDP ratio of about 3.3. The interest rate fell from 10.08 percent on 23 August 1996 to 6.39 percent on 7 December 1998 for a capital investment loan of less than one year; and from 12.42 percent to 7.56 percent for a loan of more than five years during the same period (SSB 1999). According to Nehru and Dhareshwar (1993), China's capital/GDP ratio was 2.37 in 1990.

15. In 1998, China's total energy consumption was about 3984.8 exajoules, while GDP was US$959.03 billion (SSB 1999). The resulting energy/GDP ratio is as high as 41.55 megajoule/US$. It is still 36.63 megajoule/US$ even though the energy consumption is net of household use. However, the World Bank (2000) estimates that China's energy efficiency is in fact PPP$3.3 per kg oil equivalent. This figure gives a moderate energy/GDP ratio of 13.33 megajoule/US$, which implies the energy share is about 0.06.

16. Chao and Peck (2000) assume that OECD countries have an annual growth rate of 2.0 percent, while ROW has an annual rate of 3.5 percent; and the GDP in 2050 is US$40 trillion and US$25 trillion, respectively, for the OECD and ROW.

17. As utility levels are just for illustrative purpose, the unit is not included. However, it should be borne in mind that the figure for global welfare is about a billion times that of the per capita level.

6. A Dynamic General Equilibrium Model of the Chinese Economy

6.1 INTRODUCTION

Pioneered by Johansen (1960), computable general equilibrium (CGE) models have been rapidly applied in various areas of economics and policy studies because they have profound theoretical grounds and can provide systematic and comprehensive inquires of studied topics. There is a huge amount of literature about CGE modelling and application, making it impossible to conduct a complete survey, even in one particular area.[1] This section will briefly discuss the application of CGE modelling in CO_2 emission control policies.

Since Nordhaus (1977) first brought the problem of CO_2 to the attention of mainstream economists, and Edmonds and Reilly (1983) first built a large scale multi-country energy model, the literature applying CGE models to CO_2 emission control analysis has been rapidly growing. The reason is obvious: CO_2 emission control policies have economy-wide effects (Zhang 1998a, p. 92). However, early CGE models had some drawbacks. Some of them lacked industry detail while more attention was given to energy, for example, Edmonds and Reilly (1983), Whalley and Wigle (1990), Global 2100 (Manne and Richels 1990, 1992) and CRTM model (Rutherford 1992). Some are one-country models, or ignore the international trade and flows of capital and assets, for example, Cline (1992), Global 2100, CRTM, DICE model (Nordhaus 1994b), Jorgenson and Wilcoxen (1991a, 1991b), Goulder (1991), Goulder et al. (1996), GREEN model (Burniaux et al. 1992b) and Whalley and Wigle (1990). Some are recursive models, in which agents lack foresight, for example CRTM, GREEN, and Whalley and Wigle (1990). Most have restricted functional form with parameters chosen by judgement (or guesstimation) rather than by econometric estimation. The G-Cubed[2] model was developed to address these problems.

G-Cubed is a multi-country, multi-sector, intertemporal general equilibrium model which includes detailed energy producing sectors as well as financial sectors, international trade and capital flows. Most parameters in G-Cubed are econometrically estimated. It has been used to study a variety of policies in the areas of environmental regulation, tax reform, monetary and fiscal policy, international trade and currency crisis.[3]

There is also a growing literature on the application of general equilibrium models to the analysis of environmental policies in China. Xie (1996) and Xie and Saltzman (2000) present a static neo-classical environmental CGE model of the Chinese economy in which world prices are set exogenously. Seven production sectors in the model use intermediate inputs and two primary factors, capital and labour, whose supplies are also exogenously determined. Three general types of pollution, wastewater, smog dust and solid wastes, are included. The model is calibrated using an environmentally extended social accounting matrix (ESAM) based on the 1990 input–output table of China. Using the model, Xie (1996) simulates several environmental policy options, such as pollution emission taxes, subsidies for pollution abatement activities, household waste disposal tax, government purchase of pollution cleaning services, and the five-year environmental protection programme launched by the Chinese government in 1994.

Zhang (1998a, 1998c) presents a recursive CGE model to analyse China's energy and environmental policies. This model is also a single country model which takes the rest of the world as given. It disaggregates energy into coal, oil, natural gas and electricity, in addition to six other production sectors. The production technology is represented by nested CES–Cobb–Douglas–Leontief functions. It includes the rate of autonomous energy efficiency improvement in production functions to capture the effect of economic growth on energy use independent of changes in energy prices. Hicksian equivalent variation can be calculated to measure welfare changes.

Garbaccio et al. (1999a) develop a dynamic single country CGE model of the Chinese economy to examine the use of carbon taxes to reduce CO$_2$ emissions. They consider the dual feature of plan and market institutions in their model – a fixed amount of total output is sold at the planned price, while the remainder is sold on the market.[4] The model is built using the Chinese input–output table for 1992 and assuming Cobb–Douglas production functions. Twenty-nine sectors are included in the model, of which four are energy sectors. Using the model, they simulate a 5, 10 and 15 percent reduction in carbon emissions and find that a carbon tax can produce a 'double-dividend' – a decrease in CO$_2$ and a long run increase in GDP and consumption.

In order to examine China's CO$_2$ policy choices and the interaction between China and other countries on climate change issues, an aggregated G-Cubed model, G-Cubed-T, is constructed. It differs from the original model in three respects. Firstly, the original eight regions have been aggregated into three, China, the United States and the rest of the world, so as to focus on the China issue.[5] Secondly, the dynamics of climate change is included in the model. The impacts of climate change on the economy can be examined via revised production functions. Thirdly, some of the parameters for the Chinese economy are re-estimated using a new data set.

Compared to existing CGE models of the Chinese economy and environment, G-Cubed-T provides two additional features. Firstly, it is a multi-country model in which interaction between different countries can be explicitly examined. This is especially important for the issue of global warming. As discussed in Chapter 5, controlling greenhouse gas emission is an international game – each country chooses its best policy given the expectation of actions taken in other countries. A multi-country model provides a tool to run game theoretic simulations. Secondly, the model has an intertemporal optimisation structure where agents have foresight, and it is solved in annual interval of time, so that both short- and long-run effects of certain policy options can be examined.

This chapter will give a brief introduction about the structure of the G-Cubed-T model and its parameter estimation and calibration.

6.2   THE STRUCTURE OF G-CUBED-T MODEL

The original G-Cubed model presented in McKibbin and Wilcoxen (1999) has eight regions. In the current G-Cubed-T model designed for the purpose of analysing the interaction between China and the rest of the world on global warming issues, the regions are aggregated into three: China, the United States of America (USA) and the rest of the world (ROW). USA is separately included in the model because of the obvious fact that it is an important, and in most cases, dominant player in the world. Also relevant is the controversial stand of the USA in various issues of climate control, for example the Bush Administration's decision not to proceed to ratify the Kyoto Protocol.

Each region has three types of agents: firms in the 12 production sectors, a representative household and a government. The 12 production sectors include five energy sectors (electric utilities; gas utilities; petroleum refining; coal mining; and crude oil and gas extraction) and seven non-energy sectors (mining; agriculture, fishing and hunting; forestry/wood products; durable manufacturing; non-durable manufacturing; transportation; and services). Two additional sectors are also embodied in the model: investment and consumption good production.

6.2.1   Firms

It is assumed that each of the 12 production sectors is represented by a price-taking firm which chooses inputs and investment to maximise the firm's value.

Each firm's production technology is represented by a nest of constant elasticity of substitution (CES) functions (see Figure 6.1).

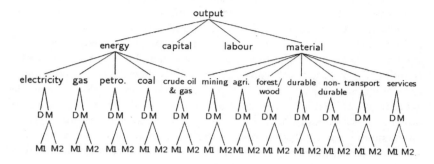

Notes: D – domestic output; M – imported good; M1, M2 – imports from country 1 and 2 respectively.

Figure 6.1   Production nesting in G-Cubed-T

At the top of the production nesting, the firm's output (Y_i, $i \in \{1,\cdots,12\}$) is a function of capital X_{iK}, labour X_{iL}, composite energy X_{iE} and composite material X_{iO}:

$$Y_i = A_i^Y \left[\sum_{j=K,L,E,O} \left(\delta_{ij}^Y \right)^{\frac{1}{\sigma_i^Y}} \left(X_{ij} \right)^{\frac{\sigma_i^Y - 1}{\sigma_i^Y}} \right]^{\frac{\sigma_i^Y}{\sigma_i^Y - 1}}, \tag{6.1}$$

where A_i^Y is a shifter representing industry i's technology level, which is affected by climate change and will be detailed later; δ the share (or weight) of different inputs in production; and σ the elasticity of substitution.

At the second level of the nesting, the inputs of composite energy, X_{iE}, and material, X_{iO}, are, respectively, CES aggregation of individual goods and services. X_{iE} is the aggregate of five energy goods (electricity through crude oil), and X_{iO} is the aggregate of seven non-energy goods and services (mining through services). The functional form used for these aggregations is identical to equation (6.1) except that the parameters are different, namely, superscript Y is replaced by E in the energy aggregation function and by O in the material aggregation function, and the domain for j is changed accordingly.

At the third level of the nesting, each good or service is an aggregate of domestic output and foreign good. The CES functional form represents the fact that domestic and foreign goods are imperfect substitutes.

At the bottom of the nesting, the composite imports of one good are, again, a CES aggregation of imports from different origins.

Following the conventional treatment, it is assumed the production process produces a by-product, the carbon dioxide emission, proportional to the use of particular types of energy, which will be discussed later.

Because of the nature of CES nesting production, the firm's production plan in each sector is determined in a multi-step manner. First, the firm's demand for labour, composite energy and materials and investment is determined according to an intertemporal optimisation problem. Second, once the demand for the composite factor is determined, the firm decides the demand for individual inputs according to a cost minimization problem.

At the top tier, each industry's composite capital stock (K_i) increases by the new capital formation (J_i), but decreases by the rate of depreciation (δ_i):[6]

$$\dot{K}_i = J_i - \delta_i K_i .\tag{6.2}$$

Because of the adjustment cost of installing capital (Lucas 1967a, 1967b; Tobin 1969, Treadway 1969, Uzawa 1969), more investment is required than the capital formation:

$$I_i = \left(1 + \frac{\phi_i}{2}\frac{J_i}{K_i}\right)J_i ,\tag{6.3}$$

where ϕ_i is a non-negative parameter. ϕ_i implies that no installation cost occurs.

The firm's instantaneous profit can be defined as:

$$\pi_i = (1 - \tau_2)(P_i^Y Y_i - W_i L_i - P_i^E X_{iE} - P_i^O X_{iO}) ,$$

where τ_2 is corporate income tax; P_i^Y is the producer price of firm's output; W_i, P_i^E and P_i^O are, respectively, the wage rate and the prices for composite energy and materials. The market value of the firm can then be defined as the profit net of investment:

$$V_i = \pi_i - (1 - \tau_4)P^I I_i ,$$

where τ_4 is the investment tax credit, and P^I is the price of investment good.

Thus the problem of each firm can be characterised as choosing a path of investment and inputs of labour, composite energy and material to maximise its intertemporal market value:[7]

$$\int_t^\infty V_i e^{-[R(s)-n](s-t)} ds \, , \tag{6.4}$$

subject to (6.1), (6.2) and (6.3). Solving this problem gives the firm's demand for inputs of labour, energy and other materials:

$$X_{ij} = \delta_{ij}^Y \left(A_i^Y\right)^{\sigma_i^Y - 1} Y_i \left(\frac{P_i^Y}{P_i^j}\right)^{\sigma_i^Y}, \quad \forall\, j \in \{L, E, O\}\, , \tag{6.5}$$

and the motion of the shadow value of an additional unit of investment in industry i, λ_i, which is the multiplier of (6.2) when constructing the Hamiltonian:

$$\lambda_i = \left(1 + \phi \frac{J_i}{K_i}\right)(1 - \tau_4)P^I \, , \tag{6.6}$$

$$\dot{\lambda}_i = (r + \delta_i)\lambda_i - (1 - \tau_2)P_i^Y \frac{\partial Y_i}{\partial K_i} - (1 - \tau_4)P^I \frac{\phi_i}{2}\left(\frac{J_i}{K_i}\right)^2 , \tag{6.7}$$

λ_i is related to Tobin's q in the following way:[8]

$$q_i = \frac{\lambda_i}{(1 - \tau_4)P^I} \, .$$

Using this relationship, (6.6) can be written as:

$$\frac{J_i}{K_i} = \frac{1}{\phi_i}(q_i - 1) \, .$$

Plugging this into (6.3) gives the firm's demand for investment good:

$$I_i = \frac{1}{2\phi_i}(q_i^2 - 1)K_i \, . \tag{6.8}$$

To be in line with the empirical evidence that actual investment is partly driven by cash flows (Hayashi 1982b), it is assumed that some firms are forward looking, that is, they follow the course defined by (6.8), and others are backward looking, that is, they decide investment based on the history of cash flows. Because the q measures the value of a firm, it is equivalent to modelling the investment of the second type of firms as a function of previous q in a similar way to (6.8). Therefore the demand for investment can be written as:

$$I_{it} = \alpha_1 \frac{1}{2\phi_i}(q_{it}^2 - 1)K_{it} + (1 - \alpha_1)\frac{1}{2\phi_i}(q_{it}^{*2} - 1)K_{it}, \qquad (6.9)$$

where α_1 is the share of forward looking firms in all firms; and q_{it}^* is the backward looking q, which follows the following rule:

$$q_{it}^* = q_{i,t-1}^* + \alpha_q(q_{i,t-1} - q_{i,t-1}^*).$$

This approach is superior to the previous treatment (McKibbin and Wilcoxen 1999, eqn.13) in the sense that it guarantees that these two types of firms act identically in the steady state, although the second type adjusts more slowly towards the steady state.

The investment good in turn is produced by a thirteenth sector whose functional form is identical to the 12 production sectors in production nesting. At the top, labour, capital, composite energy and materials are used to produce the good by CES technology; then the composite inputs are again CES aggregates of individual inputs.

Once the demand for composite input is determined by a rule like (6.5), the demand for individual inputs can be determined in a similar way. The firm chooses an appropriate amount of individual inputs to maximise the cost of producing the composite input, and the solution for this problem is:

$$X_k = \delta_k X \left(\frac{P_X}{P_k}\right)^{\sigma_k}, \qquad (6.10)$$

where X is the amount of a composite input; X_k the demand for individual input k; δ_k and σ_k, respectively, the share of and the elasticity of substitution between individual input k to produce the composite; and P_X and P_k, respectively, the prices of composite X and individual input X_k. It is clear that the above demand function is similar to (6.5). At the second level of nesting, X is E or O while X_k is one of the 12 goods; at the third level, X is one of the 12 goods, while X_k is domestic products or imports.

6.2.2 Household

There is a representative household in each region. The household chooses labour supply, saving and consumption to maximise its intertemporal utility:

$$U_t = \int_t^\infty (\ln C_s + \ln G_s) e^{-\theta(s-t)} ds , \tag{6.11}$$

where C_s is the household's composite consumption at time s, G_s is government consumption at s, and θ is the rate of time preference; subject to the budget constraint that the present value of its consumption is equal to human wealth (H) plus initial financial asset (F):

$$\int_t^\infty P_s^C C_s e^{-[R(s)-n](s-t)} ds = H_t + F_t . \tag{6.12}$$

Human wealth is defined as the expected present value of future after-tax labour income plus government transfers:

$$H_t = \int_t^\infty [(1-\tau_1)W(L_G + L_C + L_I + \Sigma_{i=1}^{12} L_i) + TR] e^{-[R(s)-n](s-t)} ds,$$

where τ_1 is the labour income tax rate, W the wage rate, TR is government transfers, and L_C, L_I, L_G, and L_i are, respectively, labour used in consumption good production, investment good production, government employment and in sector i. The financial asset is the sum of real money balances, MON/P, government bonds, B, net holding of foreign asset, A, and the value of capital in different sectors:

$$F = \frac{MON}{P} + B + A + q_I K_I + q_C K_C + \Sigma_{i=1}^{12} q_i K_i .$$

The solution of this dynamic optimisation problem gives the household's aggregate consumption in the usual form:

$$P^C C = \theta(F + H) .$$

Following Hayashi (1982a), it is assumed that some consumers are liquidity-constrained and consume a fixed proportion γ of their after-tax income (INC):

$$P^C C = \alpha_2 \theta(F + H) + (1 - \alpha_2) \gamma INC , \tag{6.13}$$

where α_2 is the share of first type households in all households. Households' current income is the sum of net government transfer, after-tax labour income, interests of bond and foreign assets and after-tax profit of investment and consumption goods production:

$$INC = TR + (1 - \tau_1)W(L_G + L_C + L_I + \Sigma_{i=1}^{12}L_i)$$
$$+ R(B + A) + (1 - \tau_2)\pi_I + \pi_C. \quad (6.14)$$

The aggregate consumption good is assumed to be produced by a fourteenth sector with a technology almost identical to (6.1), that is, a CES aggregation of household capital service (C_K), labour, energy and material. Demands for capital service, labour, composite energy and materials to produce the consumption good and individual goods to produce the composite good are similar to those given by (6.5) and (6.6).

Household capital services consist of the service flows of consumer durables and residential housing. The supply of household capital services is determined by consumers who invest in household capital K_C in order to generate a desired flow of capital services C_K, which is determined by the following production function:

$$C_K = \alpha K_C.$$

And, similar to (6.2) and (6.3), the formation of new household capital is also subject to an adjustment cost. Thus the household's investment decision is to choose household investment, I_C, to maximise:

$$\int_t^{\infty} (P^{C_K}\alpha K_C - P^I I_C)e^{-[R(s)-n](s-t)}ds,$$

where P^{C_K} is the imputed rental price of household capital. The solution to this problem is similar to (6.8).

Because leisure does not enter into household's utility, labour supply in the long run is exogenously given, being determined by the population growth rate, and the wage adjusts to ensure full employment. However, in the short run the wage adjusts slowly and short-run under or over full employment equilibria may arise. G-Cubed-T assumes that labour is perfectly mobile among sectors within a region but immobile across regions. Therefore wages are equal within a region but can differ across regions. This assumption may not be a good representation of the current situation in China. For example, China still implements the residence registration system, which prevents people living in one area from moving freely into another area, especially from rural areas to urban areas. However, as the primary focus here is not on the labour market and income issues, this simplified assumption does not much affect the discussion of other issues.

6.2.3 Government

It is assumed government spending is exogenous and is allocated among inputs in fixed proportions. Government income comes from corporate tax, labour income tax, sales tax, issues of new government bonds, and carbon taxes, while outlays include purchase of goods and services, interest payment on government bond, investment tax credits and transfers to households. The budget deficit is financed by issuing new bonds:

$$\dot{B}_t = r_t B_t + G_t + TR_t - T_t,$$

where B is the stock of debt, G is total government spending on goods and services, TR is transfer to households, and T is total tax revenue net of investment tax credits. However, the No-Ponzi-Game condition should be applied to government debt to prevent the per capita government debt from forever growing faster than the interest rate:

$$\lim_{s \to \infty} B_s e^{-[R(s)-n]s} = 0.$$

Therefore current government debt is always the present value of future budget surpluses:

$$B_t = \int_t^\infty (T - G - TR)e^{-[R(s)-n](s-t)}ds.$$

6.2.4 International Trade

Once the demand for import of one good, M_i, is determined, the demand for import of this good from different origins, M_{ij}, is determined by:

$$M_{ij} = \delta_{ij} M_i \left[\frac{P_i^M}{t_i^c + t_i^b + (1 + t_i^M)(E_{ju}/E_{jc})P_{ij}^X} \right]^{\sigma_i},$$

where δ_{ij} is the share of imports from country j in total imports of good i; σ_i is the elasticity of substitution between importing good i from different origins; P_i^M is the price of composite imports of good i; P_{ij}^X is country j's export price of good i; and t_i^c, t_i^b and t_i^M are, respectively, carbon import tax, energy (BTU) import tax and import tariff rates for good i.[9] E_{ju} and E_{jc} are, respectively, the exchange rates of the currencies of country j and China with respect to the US dollar.

6.2.5 Financial Markets and the Balance of Payments

The current account deficit is financed by the surplus on the capital account. The model distinguishes between the financial asset and physical capital. The asset market is assumed to be perfectly integrated globally. That is, expected returns on loans denominated in the currencies of various regions are equalised according to the following interest arbitrage relation:

$$i_k + \mu_k = i_j + \mu_j + \dot{E}_{jk}/E_{jk} ,$$

where i_k and i_j are interest rates in countries k and j, μ_k and μ_j are exogenous risk premiums demanded by investors, and E_{jk} is the exchange rate between the currencies of the two countries.

However, the physical asset is immobile and costly to adjust. As a shock occurs in a sector, the amount of physical capital stock in that sector remains unchanged initially, but the value of the stock will change accordingly.

6.2.6 Money Demand

The demand for real money balances is assumed to be a function of the value of aggregate output and the short-term nominal interest rate:

$$MON/P = Y\, i^{\varepsilon} ,$$

where Y is the aggregate output and P is a price index for Y, i is the nominal interest rate, and ε is the interest elasticity of money demand, which is set to be -0.6 following McKibbin and Sachs (1991).

6.2.7 Energy Use and Carbon Emissions

G-Cubed-T does not endogenise technological innovation and energy efficiency, which are simply treated as exogenous shocks under different assumptions and scenarios. Therefore, the demand for composite energy given by (6.5) can be slightly revised as:

$$X_{iE} = \delta_{iE}^{Y}(A_E B_i)^{\sigma_i^Y - 1} Y_i \left(P_i^Y / P_i^E \right)^{\sigma_i^Y} , \tag{6.15}$$

where A_E is the energy efficiency shock which is assumed to be identical across sectors in one simulation, and B_i is the production shock of sector i. The energy demands in investment and consumption good productions are the same as (6.15).

The carbon emission in each region is calculated as a fixed proportion (s_{ir}) of the energy use of each sector – energy production, Q_i, plus import, M_i, minus export, X_i – of the region:

$$EM_r = \sum_{i=2}^{4} s_{ir}(Q_{ir} + M_{ir} - X_{ir}), \quad r \in \{C, U, N\}.$$

6.2.8 Climate Change and Impacts

The common procedure for modelling the impact of climate change is as follows. First, the atmospheric CO_2 concentration is calculated according to the CO_2 emissions and the decay rate of CO_2 stock. Then the radiative force is determined according to the carbon concentration and other factors. Once the radiative force is determined, the temperature change in different boxes (atmosphere, sea surface and deep sea) can be modelled by a set of dynamic functions. And finally the damage is expressed as functions of temperature changes (for example, see Nordhaus 1994b; Nordhaus and Yang 1996; and Pizer 1999).

However, given the facts that a detailed general circulation model (GCM) can not be employed here and that most literature discusses the impact of doubling carbon concentration (see next section), the model can be simplified by linking carbon concentration to the economy directly.

Emissions of CO_2 accumulate in the atmosphere according to:

$$CO_t = \beta \, EM_t - \delta_m(CO_t - 590), \tag{6.16}$$

where CO_t is the atmospheric concentration of CO_2 in billions of tons of carbon equivalent, β is the retention rate of emissions, δ_m is the decay rate, and $EM (= \Sigma_r EM_r)$ is the total world emission of carbon dioxide.[10] The constant 590 in the above equation is the pre-industrial level of atmospheric concentration of CO_2 (in Gtc).

The next step is to link the increase in carbon concentration to damage to the economy, which is perhaps the most elusive aspect in the discussion of global warming. There is some agreement in academia that global warming affects the production of agriculture, forestry, fishery and agroindustry, energy demand and hydroelectricity production, human population health and settlement, and recreational activities, and that it causes sea-level rise which in turn increases the cost of protecting transportation infrastructure and industrial plants located in coastal regions and provides a market opportunity for the construction industry (Watson et al. 1996; IPCC 2001). However, there are diversified opinions about the degree of these impacts, and especially the monetary assessment of them.[11]

In relation to the treatment of these impacts in the current model, they can be divided into two types: direct and indirect impacts. The former includes impacts on agriculture, forestry, fishery, agroindustry and hydroelectricity production, while the latter includes all other impacts.[12]

The direct impacts can be measured as changes in output of specific sectors. Define the change in the atmospheric carbon concentration as $CC_t = CO_t/590$. The global warming is linked to the economy by affecting the shifter A_i^Y in equation (6.1):

$$A_{it}^Y = \Omega(CC_t)\overline{A}_{it}^Y .$$

In addition to the diverse estimation of impacts, one more difficulty emerges regarding the definition of $\Omega(CC_t)$: most current literature reports estimation of damages in only one equilibrium climate situation, for example doubling CO_2 concentration ($2 \times CO_2$) or $2.5°C$ increase of temperature. For simplicity, the relationship between global warming and output loss is assumed to be as follows,[13]

$$\Omega(CC_t) = CC_t^{\xi_1} . \tag{6.17}$$

The value of parameter ξ_1 will be discussed in the next section. The results of considering the direct impact on production will be compared with the results of not accommodating this impact in the Appendix to Chapter 7.[14] It will be seen that this seemingly small change in treatment makes a huge difference.

The indirect impacts affect the whole economy, not just specific sectors. Therefore, it is proper to model them as a proportion of GDP. Most studies assume that the ratio of damage to output is a nonlinear function of temperature change, for example, the DICE and FUND models assume that it is a quadratic function of the temperature change (Nordhaus 1994b, eq. 2.11; Tol 1999, eqn. 4a and 4b), while the CETA model assumes a cubic function (Peck and Teisberg 1995, eqn. 4), Cline (1992, p.100) assumes the power to warming is about 1.2. Following these studies, the indirect damage, defined as the ratio of GDP,[15] is determined as follows:

$$D_t/GDP_t = CC_t^{\xi_2} \tag{6.18}$$

where D_t is the loss due to indirect impacts, and ξ_2 is a parameter which will be discussed in the next section.

Finally, because the indirect impacts include costs of preventing adverse effects of global warming as well as some ethical, non-market costs, they are equivalent to a reduction in consumption goods available to the household. Given the high uncertainty of the indirect impacts, it is assumed that they do not directly affect the household's behaviour in the business-as-usual scenarios, and will be used as a reference to figure out possible gains under different policies.

6.2.9 Emission Taxes and Permits

G-Cubed-T can examine environmental policies in the form of carbon tax or tradable emission permits. The treatment of carbon tax is straightforward as the tax is a component of product prices (see next subsection for details) and the demand for energy changes in response to changes in taxes. However, emission trading involves more complicated treatment. The emission permit is set as an emission target for each region and permit price – in the form of emission taxes in the model – adjusts to achieve the target. If the permits trade within one region, the permit price in that region will be identical. If the permits trade across regions, the price will be identical in the involved regions due to arbitrage.

The revenues from carbon emissions taxes or permits go into the pool of government income which will be allocated according to the government's requirements as discussed in subsection 6.2.3.

6.2.10 Price Linkage

Each good in the model has an associated price. The linkages among prices are illustrated by Figure 6.2.

The description can be started from the production side. As previously discussed, the nominal wage rate is identical across sectors within one region because of the mobility assumption. However, to be in line with other factor prices in coding, the nominal wage rate in each sector is given a different name, which is set to be equal to an endogenously determined value through a set of assignment equations. The (next period's) nominal wage is calculated as:

$$W_t = \pi_{t+1}^{\alpha} \pi_t^{1-\alpha} L_t^{\beta} w_t \, ,$$

where W_t and w_t are, respectively, next period and current nominal wage rates at time t. π_{t+1} is the expected inflation at time $t+1$ while π_t is the inflation rate at time t, α is the weight on expected inflation, L_t is the total employment, β reflects the effect of labour market conditions on wage setting.

The price of capital used in sector i is determined by:

$$P_i^K = P_i^P \left(s_i Y_i / K_i \right)^{\frac{1}{\sigma_i^Y}} \left(\mu_i^Y \right)^{\frac{\sigma_i^Y - 1}{\sigma_i^Y}} , \qquad (6.19)$$

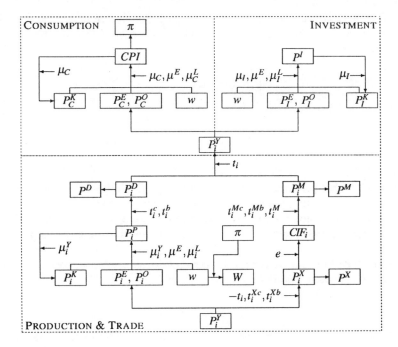

Figure 6.2   Price links in G-Cubed-T

where P_i^P is the producer price of good i which will be discussed below; μ_i^Y is the supply shock (including the impact of climate change) of good i; σ_i^Y, as in eq. (6.1), is the elasticity of substitution between capital, labour, energy and other material to produce good i.

Because the composite energy and material are CES aggregations of individual energy goods and materials, the prices of energy and material used in sector i, P_i^E and P_i^O, are calculated as:

$$
P_i^k = \begin{cases} \Pi_j \left(P_j^Y \right)^{\delta_{ij}^k} & \text{if } \sigma_i^k = 1 \\[2mm] \left[\Sigma_j \delta_{ij}^k \left(P_i^Y \right)^{1-\sigma_i^k} \right]^{\frac{1}{1-\sigma_i^k}} & \text{otherwise} \end{cases} \tag{6.20}
$$

$$
\forall \ k \in \{E, O\} \ \text{and} \ \begin{cases} j \in \{1,2,\cdots,5\} & \text{if } k = E \\ j \in \{6,7,\cdots,12\} & \text{if } k = O \end{cases}
$$

where δ's and σ's are shares and elasticities of substitution; P_j^Y is the price of final product j, which will be discussed below.

Next, because output is again a CES aggregation of labour, capital, energy and materials, the producer price of good i is determined in a similar way to (6.20):

$$
P_i^P = \begin{cases}
\dfrac{1}{\mu_i^Y} \prod_{j=E,L,O,K} \left(P_i^j / \mu_i^j\right)^{\delta_{ij}^Y} & \text{if } \sigma_i^Y = 1 \\[4mm]
\dfrac{1}{\mu_i^Y} \left[\displaystyle\sum_{j=E,L,O,K} \delta_{ij}^Y \left(P_i^j / \mu_i^j\right)^{1-\sigma_i^Y} \right]^{\frac{1}{1-\sigma_i^Y}} & \text{otherwise}
\end{cases}
\tag{6.21}
$$

where P_i^P is the producer price of individual good i; P_i^j, $j \in \{E, L, K, O\}$, is the price of input j, which is determined above, clearly $P_i^L = w$; μ_i^E (identical across sectors) and μ_i^L are shocks to energy efficiency and labour supply, respectively, and $\mu_i^O = \mu_i^K = 1$;[16] and others are the same as those in eq. (6.1).

Adding carbon and energy (BTU) taxes, t_i^c and t_i^b, to producer price gives the price of domestic product:

$$
P_i^D = P_i^P + t_i^c + t_i^b .
$$

The price of the final product is a combination of the prices of domestic product and imported product:

$$
P_i^Y = \begin{cases}
(1+t_i)\left(P_i^D\right)^{\delta_i}\left(P_i^M\right)^{1-\delta_i} & \text{if } \sigma_i = 1 \\[3mm]
(1+t_i)\left[\delta_i\left(P_i^D\right)^{1-\sigma_i} + (1-\delta_i)\left(P_i^M\right)^{1-\sigma_i}\right]^{\frac{1}{1-\sigma_i}} & \text{otherwise}
\end{cases}
$$

where P_i^M is the price of imported good i, which is in turn determined by:

$$
P_i^M = (1+t_i^M)CIF_i + t_i^{Mc} + t_i^{Mb},
$$

where t_i^M is the tariff rate; t_i^{Mc} and t_i^{Mb} are tax rates of carbon and energy, respectively; CIF_i, the price of imported good i when it enters the region, is a combination of export prices from the other two regions:

$$
CIF_{ri} = \begin{cases}
\displaystyle\prod_{j \neq r} \left((e_{ju}/e_{ru})P_{ji}^X\right)^{\delta_{ji}^M} & \text{if } \sigma_{ri}^M = 1 \\[4mm]
\left[\displaystyle\sum_{j \neq r} \delta_{ji}^M \left((e_{ju}/e_{ru})P_{ji}^X\right)^{1-\sigma_{ri}^M}\right]^{1/(1-\sigma_{ri}^M)} & \text{otherwise}
\end{cases}
\qquad \forall\, j, r \in \{c, u, n\}
$$

where CIF_{ri} is region r's price of imported good i;[17] c, u, n denote China, the United States and the rest of the world, respectively; e's are exchange rates; δ 's are shares of imports from different regions; σ is the elasticity of substitution between imports from different origins; and P_{ji}^X is region j's export price of good i, which is j's price of final good i adjusted by sectoral tax, t_{ji}, carbon and energy export taxes, t_{ji}^{Xc} and t_{ji}^{Xb}:

$$P_{ji}^X = P_{ji}^X \big/ (1 + t_{ji}) + t_{ji}^{Xc} + t_{ji}^{Xb} \, .$$

From the individual prices, P_i^D, P_i^M and P_i^X, the indexes of domestic product, imports and exports, P^D, P^M and P^X, can be calculated as:

$$P^j = \prod_{i=1}^{12} \left(P_i^j \right)^{\rho_i^j}, \quad \forall \, j \in \{D, M, X\} \, .$$

The prices of inputs in consumption good production are calculated in a similar way to the 12 production sectors, although only two tiers of prices are calculated. The prices of energy and materials in consumption are determined from prices of individual final output P_i^Y using eq. (6.20). The determination of the price of capital in consumption is identical to eq. (6.19) in form, except that Y_i is replaced by C and K_i by K_C, the producer price P_i^P is replaced by the consumer price index CPI, and the parameters are replaced accordingly. The real wage rate in consumption is the same as the rate in production sectors because labour is mobile. The calculation of the consumer price index CPI is identical in form to that of the producer price given by eq. (6.21).

The prices in investment production are determined in exactly the same way as in consumption good production. Two tiers of prices are calculated: prices of energy, material, capital and labour are calculated first using formulas similar to (6.19) and (6.20). Then the price of the investment good is calculated using (6.21).

6.3   PARAMETERS ESTIMATION AND CALIBRATION

Parameters in G-Cubed-T can be divided into three categories: elasticities, shares or weights, and other parameters. Most parameters for the US economy are econometrically estimated using data from the detailed benchmark US input–output transactions tables produced by the Bureau of Economic Analysis for the years 1958, 1963, 1967, 1972, 1977 and 1982. The detailed procedure of estimation can be found in McKibbin and

Wilcoxen (1994).[18] Because of limitation of data availability, the elasticities for China are adopted from US values in consultation with other studies; while the shares are calculated from the latest input–output data (SSB Department of National Accounts 1999).

The rationale of this approach is illustrated by Figure 6.3. On the supply side, an economy can be characterised by three sets of parameters: the curvature of the frontier – elasticity, the height of the frontier – output level, and the specific position in the frontier – input shares in the output. The last two, which are correlated, determine the position of an economy at a specific point of time, for example, point C in A′B′ and the U points on AB. The shares of individual inputs can easily be observed for both country C and country U. The curvature of AB can be estimated by observation of the U points. However, the curvature of the curve passing through point C cannot be estimated because there are not enough data (it is possible to have an infinite number of curves passing through point C). Therefore, it is natural to assume that the curve A′B′ has the same curvature as AB. Empirical studies find that the hypothesis that A′B′ and AB have the same elasticity can not be rejected (Kim and Lau 1995).

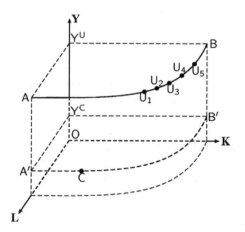

Figure 6.3   Curvature and position of production frontiers

6.3.1 Elasticities

The elasticities used in the G-Cubed-T model are listed in Table 6.1. σ_i^Y is the elasticity of substitution between capital, labour, aggregate energy and aggregate material in the production of good i; σ_i^E is the elasticity of substitution between individual energy to produce aggregate energy used in

Table 6.1   Elasticities used in G-Cubed-T

Sector i	σ_i^Y	σ_i^E	σ_i^O	σ_i^{DM}	σ_i^M
1. Electric utilities	0.7634	0.2000	1.0000	1.0000	1.0000
2. Gas utilities	0.8096	0.9325	0.2000	1.0000	1.0000
3. Petroleum refining	0.5426	0.2000	0.2000	1.0000	1.0000
4. Coal mining	1.7030	0.1594	0.5294	1.0000	1.0000
5. Crude oil and gas extraction	0.4934	0.1372	0.2000	1.0000	1.0000
6. Mining	1.0014	1.1474	2.7654	1.0000	1.0000
7. Agriculture, fishing & hunting	1.2830	0.6277	1.7323	1.0000	1.0000
8. Forestry/wood products	0.9349	0.9385	0.1757	1.0000	1.0000
9. Durable manufacturing	0.4104	0.8045	0.2000	1.0000	1.0000
10. Non-durable manufacturing	1.0044	1.0000	0.0573	1.0000	1.0000
11. Transportation	0.5368	0.2000	0.2000	1.0000	1.0000
12. Services	0.2556	0.3211	3.0056	1.0000	1.0000
Y. Firm investment	1.0000	1.0000	1.0000		
Z. Household consumption	0.8000	1.0000	1.0000		

Source: McKibbin and Wilcoxen (1992, 1999).

sector i's production; σ_i^O is the elasticity of substitution between individual material to produce aggregate material used in sector i's production. σ_i^{DM} is the elasticity of substitution between domestically produced and imported good i, while σ_i^M is the elasticity of substitution between different origins of imported good i.

Some related elasticities used in other studies (Xie 1996 and Zhang 1998a) are listed in Table 6.2. However, because of differences in model structure, such as production tiers, sector classification, consumption and so on, these parameters may not be directly comparable.

6.3.2 Shares and Weights

The latest input–output table of the Chinese economy (SSB Department of National Accounts 1999) has been used to calculate the shares or weights of different goods used in each sector. Based on the 1997 economic data, this input–output table includes 124 sectors, of which there are five agricultural sectors, 12 energy sectors, 70 other industrial sectors, one construction sector, 10 transportation sectors and 26 services sectors. The classification of sectors in the 1997 input–output table into G-Cubed-T sectors is detailed in Table 6.3 and the resulting shares and weights are reported in Table 6.4.

6.3.3 Impact of Climate Change

As discussed in the previous section, two sets of parameters are related to the impact of climate change: ξ_1 in eq. (6.17) and ξ_2 in eq. (6.18), which,

Table 6.2   Elasticities used in other China models

Sectors	Production[a]		Armington[b]		CET[c]		Income[d]
	Xie 1996	Zhang 1998a	Xie 1996	Zhang 1998a	Xie 1996	Zhang 1998a	Zhang 1998a
Mining	1.0	n.a.	0.75	n.a.	1.1	n.a.	n.a.
Energy	1.0	n.a.	n.a.	n.a.	0.5	n.a.	n.a.
Electricity	n.a.	0.3	n.a.	n.a.	n.a.	n.a.	0.9
Coal	n.a.	0.3	n.a.	0.7	n.a.	1.5	0.7
Oil	n.a.	0.3	n.a.	0.7	n.a.	1.5	0.8
Natural Gas	n.a.	0.3	n.a.	n.a.	n.a.	n.a.	0.8
Agriculture	1.0	0.3	2.0	0.6	2.0	0.9	0.7
Heavy Industry	1.0	0.3	0.5	0.5	0.9	1.05	0.6
Light Industry	1.0	0.3	0.75	0.7	1.1	0.3	1.0
Transp. & telecom	n.a.	0.3	n.a.	n.a.	n.a.	0.9	1.1
Construction	1.0	0.3	n.a.	n.a.	n.a.	n.a.	0.9
Services	1.0	0.3	n.a.	0.6	0.5	0.3	1.1

Notes:

n.a. not available.

a.   Xie's (1996) model uses Cobb–Douglas production, therefore the elasticity of substitution between inputs are one; while the elasticity of substitution is between value added aggregate and energy aggregate in Zhang (1998a).

b.   The price elasticity of substitution between imported and domestically-produced goods.

c.   The price elasticity of transformation between foreign and domestic sales of good (in the CET export supply function).

d.   The income elasticity of consumption of consumer good by household.

Table 6.3   Sector mapping in G-Cubed-T and China input–output table

G-Cubed-T Sector	In 124-sector 1997 China I/O Table
1. Electric utilities	86, 87
2. Gas utilities	88
3. Petroleum refining	36
4. Coal mining	6, 37
5. Crude oil and gas extraction	7, 8
6. Mining	9–12
7. Agricultural, fishing and hunting	1, 3–5
8. Forestry/wood products	2, 13, 30
9. Durable manufacturing	31, 48–81, 83, 84
10. Non-durable manufacturing	14–29, 32–35, 38–47, 85
11. Transportation	91–96, 102–105
12. Services	82, 89, 90, 97–101, 106–124

Source: Author's construction.

respectively, describe the impacts on individual sectors and on the overall economy. For the first type of impacts, two sectors, agriculture and forestry, are investigated.

Table 6.4 Shares of individual inputs for China in G-Cubed-T sectors

Inputs							Sectors							
	1	2	3	4	5	6	7	8	9	10	11	12	Y	Z
In top-tier output														
Capital(K)	0.2658	0.0805	0.0911	0.1371	0.5679	0.1270	0.0546	0.1097	0.1072	0.1248	0.2644	0.1832	0.0377	0.1757
Labour(L)	0.1201	0.2006	0.0444	0.3303	0.1512	0.2214	0.5314	0.3934	0.1279	0.1178	0.2734	0.2806	0.1150	0.0027
Energy(E)	0.3089	0.4587	0.6909	0.1402	0.0668	0.1100	0.0176	0.0272	0.0576	0.0397	0.1349	0.0330	0.0210	0.0161
Material(M)	0.3052	0.2601	0.1735	0.3925	0.2142	0.5415	0.3964	0.4698	0.7072	0.7177	0.3274	0.5032	0.8264	0.8056
In composite energy input														
Energy1	0.1220	0.1194	0.0237	0.3700	0.4912	0.6333	0.4284	0.4424	0.4641	0.4867	0.1032	0.4550	0.1936	0.6748
Energy2	0.0004	0.1049	0.0000	0.0036	0.0002	0.0001	0.0000	0.0013	0.0063	0.0046	0.0010	0.0201	0.0024	0.1257
Energy3	0.1841	0.1887	0.0777	0.0954	0.3245	0.2948	0.4966	0.3082	0.1994	0.1839	0.8431	0.4053	0.7781	0.0807
Energy4	0.6209	0.5220	0.0104	0.4970	0.0881	0.0435	0.0518	0.2468	0.3097	0.2065	0.0470	0.1172	0.0259	0.1034
Energy5	0.0726	0.0650	0.8882	0.0339	0.0961	0.0283	0.0232	0.0013	0.0205	0.1182	0.0057	0.0024	0.0000	0.0153
In composite material input														
Material1	0.0076	0.0003	0.0001	0.0031	0.0022	0.2264	0.0006	0.0001	0.0536	0.0084	0.0076	0.0015	0.0131	0.0006
Material2	0.0001	0.0000	0.0000	0.0152	0.0000	0.0028	0.4143	0.0397	0.0063	0.2368	0.0001	0.0405	0.0199	0.3301
Material3	0.0035	0.0035	0.0030	0.1159	0.0095	0.0072	0.0080	0.4480	0.0125	0.0124	0.0066	0.0054	0.0242	0.0028
Material4	0.4769	0.2820	0.3217	0.4589	0.5435	0.2801	0.0586	0.1116	0.6322	0.0571	0.3815	0.2618	0.8134	0.0000
Material5	0.0426	0.1108	0.1668	0.1074	0.2035	0.1678	0.3787	0.1817	0.1448	0.5604	0.1146	0.2442	0.0179	0.3831
Material6	0.1078	0.1575	0.1265	0.0628	0.0304	0.1122	0.0270	0.0430	0.0307	0.0193	0.1586	0.0561	0.0145	0.0198
Material7	0.3614	0.4459	0.3819	0.2368	0.2108	0.2035	0.1129	0.1759	0.1199	0.1055	0.3310	0.3906	0.0970	0.2636

Source: Author's calculation based on 1997 Input–output Table of China (SSB Department of National Accounts 1999).

173

Table 6.5   *Selected estimations of climate change impact on agriculture*

Study	Climate change	Scenario	Crop	Yield impact (%) China	USA	ROW
Cline (1992)[a]	2×CO_2	440 ppm carbon fertilisation	Various	-10	-20	-6.9
Kane et al. (1992)[b]	2×CO_2	Moderate	Wheat	10	-10	1.27[c]
			Corn	10	-15	4.33[c]
			Soybean	10	-15	0.52[c]
			Rice	10	0	0.10[c]
			Other	10	10	0.93[c]
		Severe	Wheat	-15	-20	-10.26[c]
			Corn	-15	-40	-5.10[c]
			Soybean	-15	-40	-2.81[c]
			Rice	-15	-15	8.83[c]
			Other	-15	-20	6.98[c]
Tao (1992)[d]	2×CO_2 +1.5°C	With direct CO_2 effect	Wheat	-8		
			Rice	-6		
			Cotton, fruits, oil corps, potatoes and corn	-4~+1		
Rosenzweig and Hillel (1993)				0~+10	0~+10	-30~30
Zhang, H. (1993)[d,e]	+1.5°C	Double-crop, with direct CO_2 effect	Rice	-11~-7		
Jin et al. (1994)[d,e]	2×CO_2	GCMs[f], without direct CO_2 effect	Rainfed rice	-78~-6		
			Irrigated rice	-37~15		
Mendelsohn et al. (1994)	+2.5°C +8% precip.	Cropland weight Crop revenue weight	Farmland rent[g]		-4.2 1.2	
Rosenzweig and Parry (1994)	2×CO_2	GCMs[f] without direct CO_2 effect, no adaption		-30~-10	-50 ~-10	-19.6 ~-10.9[h]
		GCMs[f] with direct CO_2 effect, no adaption		-10~10	-30~10	-7.6 ~-1.2[h]
		GCMs[f] with direct CO_2 effect, minor adaption		0~10	-20~10	-5.2~0[h]
		GCMs[f] with direct CO_2 effect, major adaption		0~10	-10~10	-2.4 ~1.1[h]
Darwin et al. (1995)[i]	2×CO_2	GCMs[i], no adaption			-37.8 ~-21.5	-29.3 ~-18.6
		GCMs[j], land use fixed			-22.3 ~-8.7	-6.4 ~-2.4
		GCMs[j], land use fixed			-5.6 ~-2.0[h]	-0.6 ~-0.2

Study	Climate change	Scenario	Crop	Yield impact (%) China	USA	ROW
Darwin et al. (1995)[i]	$2 \times CO_2$	GCMs[j], no restrictions			-5.2	~-2.0[h]
Lin (1996)[e]	$2 \times CO_2$	GCMs[k], without direct CO_2 effect	Wheat Maize	-21~55 -19~5		
Wang and Lin (1996)[e]	$2 \times CO_2$	GCMs[k], without direct CO_2 effect	Corn	-0.1 ~-9.3		
Schimmelpfennig et al. (1996)[l]	$2 \times CO_2$	GCMs[f], without direct CO_2 effect, no adaptation	Maize Soybeans Winter wheat	-31 -28 -28		
		GCMs[f], without direct CO_2 effect, with adaptation	Maize Soybeans Winter wheat	3 15 -4		
Reilly et al. (1996)	$2 \times CO_2$	GCMs[f]	Maize		-55~62	-58.6 ~2.4[m]
Reilly and Schimmelpfennig (1999)			Wheat		-100 ~180	-62.7 ~74.7[m]
			Soybean		-96~58	-10~40[m]
			Rice	-78~15		-33.6 ~29[m]

Notes and sources:

a. Table 3.2, p. 99 of Cline (1992).

b. Kane et al.'s (1992) assumption based on Santer (1985), Parry et al. (1988), Peart et al. (1990), Ritchie et al. (1990), and Rosenzweig (1990).

c. The cited study author's own estimation of the world average based on the impact values of other regions in Kane et al. (1992) and the 1990 regional production data (as weights) in United Nations Food and Agriculture Organization (FAO) Statistical Database.

d. Quoted from Table 13–6, p. 440 of Reilly et al. (1996).

e. Quoted from Table 1, p. 737 of Luo and Lin (1999).

f. Generic Circulation Models, including Goddard Institute for Space Studies (GISS), Geophysical Fluid Dynamics Laboratory (GFDL) and United Kingdom Meteorological Office (UKMO). The global mean changes of $2 \times CO_2$ are +4.2°C and +11% precipitation for GISS; +4.0°C and +8% precipitation for GFDL; and +5.2°C and +15% precipitation for UKMO (Reilly 1995).

g. Change in farmland rents as percentage of 1982 farm marketing; truncating impact if they drive land values below zero.

h. Changes in cereal production represent changes in equilibrium quantities.

i. Quoted from Table 2, p. 729 of Reilly (1995).

j. Including GISS, FGDL, UKMO and Oregon State University (OSU). The global mean change of $2 \times CO_2$ is 3.3°C for OSU (Reilly 1998).

k. Including GFDL, Max-Planck Institut für Meteorologie (MPI) and High-Resolution UKMO Model (UKMOH).

l. Quoted from Table 1, p. 246 of Reilly (1998).

m. The cited study author's own estimation of weighted average based on the regional impact ranges in Reilly et al. (1996) and Reilly and Schimmelpfennig (1999) and the 1995 production level (as weight) in FAO Statistical Database. The calculation is based on available regional estimations. The value for maize is the average of Latin America, Europe, Africa, and South Asia; the value for wheat is of Latin America, Former Soviet Union, North America (other than United States), South Asia and other Asia and Pacific Rim, the value for rice is of South Asia and other Asia and Pacific Rim, while the value for soybean is the impact on Latin America only.

Table 6.5 is an incomplete collection of estimates of the impact on agriculture of climate change. Although the results are diverse, a careful reading of these studies finds that the damage to US agriculture is more severe than to the China's agriculture, and the damage to the rest of the world is the least severe because favourable impacts in some regions offset adverse impacts in others. More specifically, the central estimate of yield change caused by a doubling of CO_2 concentration is -11.6 percent for China, -15.8 percent for USA and -5.305 percent for the rest of the world. Most General Circulation Models (GCMs) predict that a doubling of CO_2 concentration leads to about 4°C warming, so the above figures suggest ξ_1's in agriculture are -2.90, -3.95 and -1.326, respectively, for China, USA and ROW (see Table 6.8).

Table 6.6 lists the estimates of impacts on forest area and wood production of climate and land use changes cited in IPCC's Second Assessment Report (Watson et al. 1996). The values in these estimates are so diverse that a convincing figure for climate change impacts cannot be concluded. In the same report, Kirschbaum et al. (1996, p. 97) state, 'although net primary

Table 6.6   Selected estimations of impacts on forestry of climate and land use change

Study	Scenario and model	Indicator	Percentage change			
			Tropical	Temperate	Boreal	Global
Kirschbaum et al. (1996)	BIOME[a,b], MAPSS[c,b] and IMAGE-TVM[d]	Area	-14.4[e] -9.3[f]	4.5	-17.1	
Solomon et al. (1996)	BIOME 1.0[a], GCMs[g]	Area[h]	10.3~16.6	25.5~51.9	-49.7 ~-19.2	0.9 ~9.4
	IMAGE 2.0[i]	Area[j]	-47.8	-1.9	10.9	-25.2
	IMAGE 2.0[i]	Volume[k]	-47.9	-1.7	10.8	-22.0

Notes and sources:
a.   BIOME (Prentice et al. 1992).
b. $2 \times CO_2$ equilibrium climate change scenario generated by GFDL.
c.   Mapped Atmosphere-Plant-Soil System (Neilson 1993).
d.   Terrestrial Vegetation Model (TVM) (Leemans and van den Born 1994) from Integrated Model to Assess the Greenhouse Effect (IMAGE 2.0) (Alcamo 1994) generates the climate change internally, based on comparable assumptions about greenhouse gas concentrations and land-use changes.
e.   Value for tropical rain forest.
f.   Value for tropical dry forest.
g.   GFDL, GISS, OSU and UKMO.
h.   Percentage changes are the projected changes in forest areas with different GCMs relative to the modelled areas.
i.   Under a single, self-generated future climate and land-use scenario, using the IMAGE 2.0 model (from data of Zuidema et al. 1994).
j.   Projected changes in forest areas in 2050 relative to the 1990 level.
k.   Projected changes in volume in 2050 relative to the 1980 level.

Table 6.7   Selected estimations of global warming damages

Study	Global warming	Damage (% of GDP)		
		China	USA	World
Nordhaus (1991)[a]	+3°C		1.00^b 0.98^c	
Cline (1992)	$2 \times CO_2$ (+2.5°C)		1.10^d 0.73^c	
	Very long term warming (+10°C)		6.04^d 4.21^c	
Titus (1992)	4°C		2.50^e 1.70^c	
Fankhauser (1995)	$2 \times CO_2$ (+2.5°C)	4.70^f 2.50^c	1.30^f 1.13^c	$1.35^{f,g}$ $1.17^{c,g}$
Tol (1995)	$2 \times CO_2$ (+2.5°C)	$8.60^{h,i}$ $5.23^{c,i}$	$1.50^{h,j}$ $1.30^{c,j}$	$1.70^{h,k}$ $1.85^{c,k}$
Mendelsohn et al. (1996)	+2.5°C			-0.08
Fankhauser et al. (1997)	Based on Fankhauser (1995)			$1.09{\sim}2.12^l$ 1.38^m $0.33{\sim}1.17^n$
	Based on Tol (1995)			$2.03{\sim}5.22^l$ 3.03^m $0.44{\sim}1.64^n$

Notes and sources:

a.   Transformed to 1990 base as cited in Pearce et al. (1996).

b.   Original estimate in Nordhaus (1991) includes impacts on farms, energy and real estate damage from sea level rise. Pearce et al. (1996) assumes an additional 0.75 percent of GDP for other damage categories.

c.   Excluding impact on agriculture, fishery, and/or forestry, if applicable.

d.   Including agriculture, forest loss, species loss, sea-level rise, electricity requirements, nonelectric heating, human life, migration, hurricanes, leisure activities, water supply, urban infrastructure, air pollution.

e.   Including impact on agriculture, forest, sea level rise, electricity, human life, water supply, air pollution, and mobile air condition.

f.   Including damages of agriculture, forestry, fishery, energy, water, coastal protection, dryland loss, wetland loss, ecosystem loss, health/mortality, air pollution (tropical O_3, and SO_2), migration and hurricanes.

g.   Value for Rest of the World.

h.   Including coastal defence, dryland loss, wetland loss, species loss, agriculture, amenity, life/mortality, migration and natural hazards.

i.   Value for Region 1 (USA and Canada).

j.   Value for Region 2 (South and South East Asia).

k.   Excluding Regions 1 (USA and Canada) and 7 (South and South East Asia).

l.   Damage corrected for inequality according to utilitarian welfare function with e varying from 0.5 to 1.5, where e is the parameter in the iso-elastic utility function that depends solely on income Y : $u = aY^{1-e} /(1 - e)$.

m.   Damage corrected for inequality according to Bernoulli–Nash welfare function whose weights are independent of e, and corresponding to the case $e = 1$ of the utilitarian welfare function.

n.   Damage corrected for inequality according to maximin welfare function with e varying from 0.5 to 1.5.

productivity may increase, the standing biomass of forests may not increase because of more frequent outbreaks and extended ranges of pests and pathogens and increasing frequency and intensity of fires (medium confidence)'. Therefore it is assumed that the overall impact of climate change on forestry is zero.

As illustrated by Table 6.7, empirical studies also show a wide range of global warming damage to the whole economy, but the degree of diversity is smaller than that in the case of agriculture and forestry. Because only two of these studies (Fankhauser 1995 and Tol 1995, which are also cited by the SAR) estimate damages to the three regions of interest here, they are used to calculate the central estimates. It should also be pointed out that the impact on agriculture and forestry should be extracted from their estimates because those effects are separately addressed. From their results, the values of ξ_2 are calculated and reported in Table 6.8.

Table 6.8   Damage parameters used in G-Cubed-T

	Parameter	China	USA	ROW
ξ_1	G-Cubed-T sector 7	-0.17788 (11.5984[a])	-0.24811 (15.7987[a])	-0.07864 (5.3060[a])
	G-Cubed-T sector 8	0.0	0.0	0.0
ξ_2		0.00616 (3.865[b])	0.00192 (1.200[b])	0.0024 (1.500[b])

Notes:
a.   Corresponding percentage change in output with $2 \times CO_2$.
b.   Corresponding percentage change in output with 2.5°C warming.

NOTES

1. Beaver (1993) compares the structure of 14 models included in the Energy Modeling Forum (EMF) 12. Xie (1996, Ch.2) discusses the definition and classification of CGE models, and gives a review of environmental CGE models. He also mentions some surveys, for example, de Melo's (1988) survey on trade policy, Bergman's (1988) survey on energy policy and Devarajan's (1988) survey on natural resources. McKibbin and Wilcoxen (1992) discuss the evolution of general equilibrium analysis of controlling CO_2 emissions, and Zhang (1998a, p. 94) lists some examples of such an application at national and global levels. Pezzey and Lambie (2001) systematically evaluate G-Cubed and the other three major models of greenhouse policies used in Australia.
2. G-Cubed stands for 'Global General equilibrium Growth model'.
3. See, for example, McKibbin and Wilcoxen (1992, 1999) for a general

introduction to G-Cubed model, and McKibbin (1997, 1998), McKibbin, Ross, Shackleton and Wilcoxen (1999) and McKibbin, Shackleton and Wilcoxen (1999) for applications on global warming issues.

4. There is a moderate literature on CGE modelling of the Chinese economy with two-tier plan and market structure, which can be traced to Byrd (1987, 1989) for the Chinese economy and Sicular (1988) for a theoretical analysis of the Chinese agricultural sector. Following them, many authors have devoted their efforts to modelling this peculiar feature during the transition period of the Chinese economy. An incomplete list includes Martin (1993), Xu (1990, 1993, 1996), Garbaccio (1994, 1995), and Xiaoguang Zhang (1998). However, after more than 20 years of economic reform, this system is no longer a common practice. The price of almost every commodity has been freed. In the energy sector, for example, the government freed all coal prices by 1994, subsidy rates fell from 37 percent in 1990 to 29 percent in 1995, and the petroleum subsidy rates fell from 55 percent to 2 percent during the same period (Zhang 1998b). Therefore, the G-Cubed-T model described in this chapter does not consider the two-tier price.

5. This is achieved at the cost of overlooking some emission trading potentials as a large amount of trading would happen among countries in the ROW.

6. To save space the time subscription is suppressed in all equations.

7. $R(s)$ is the long-term interest rate between period t and s, see the $R(s)$ equation on page 44 for details.

8. See Tobin (1969), Abel (1979) and Hayashi (1982b) for details.

9. Carbon and BTU taxes are identical for all imported goods. However as the contents of carbon and/or energy in goods are different, the excise tax rate are different.

10. According to Nordhaus (1994b, Chapter 3), $\beta = 0.64$ and $\delta_m = 1/120 = 0.00833$ per year.

11. For example, see the debate about the impact of global warming on agriculture (Mendelsohn et al. 1994; Cline 1996; Mendelsohn and Nordhaus 1996) and the critiques (Mendelsohn 1998; Demeritt and Rothman 1999; Ekins 1999) and defence and extensions (Fankhauser et al. 1997; Cline 1998; Reilly 1998; Tol 1998; Fankhauser and Tol 1999) of the social cost chapter (Pearce et al. 1996) in IPCC's second assessment report (Bruce et al. 1996).

12. It is clear that this classification is different from that of market and non-market impacts. Some indirect impacts, for example, the impact on building and infrastructure in coastal regions, have market values.

13. Cline (1992, pp.100) proposes a mildly non-linear relation between warming T_t and damage: $D_t = kT_t^{1.2}$. In DICE, the shifter is related to both global warming and the reduction in GHG emissions level: $\Omega = (1 - 0.686\mu_t^{2.887})/(1 + 0.00144T_t^2)$, where μ_t is the fractional reduction in emissions.

14. The comparison is postponed because the prerequisite of making such a comparison is level projections which will be the topic of the next chapter.

15. This approach has been criticised as unjust because the evaluation depends on income, and, in absolute terms, the damage imposed on a poor person or country is less important than the same damage imposed on a rich person or country. Therefore it is proposed to use uniform values (as at the level of developed

countries) for all countries (Erkins 1995; Meyer and Cooper 1995). However, Fankhauser et al. (1997) point out that this approach is also problematic because it causes inconsistencies of risks from different sources for developing countries – damage from climate change is valued more highly than domestic risks. They argue that differentiated value in absolute terms is not unfair per se because income disparities are possible and people have different preferences for environmental goods. The disparities provide important and necessary signals for decision makers.

16. All price variables and shocks in the model take the form of logarithm. Therefore the value of one denotes zero shocks in logarithm.

17. The subscript r is suppressed from previous expressions for simplicity, and enters into one expression only when several regions are involved.

18. Most studies follow the approach developed in Mansur and Whalley (1984). However, McKibbin and Wilcoxen (1994, 1999) point out that estimating production parameters should account for the fact that capital is fixed in the short run. Their result shows a significant difference if this fact is considered.

7. Projection of China's Carbon Dioxide Emissions

In this chapter, the G-Cubed-T model developed in Chapter 6 is used to project China's future energy consumption and CO_2 emissions. These projections are business-as-usual (BAU) or non-intervention projections without including any climate change policies or measures to reduce emissions, although different scenarios of underlying assumptions about economic, population and technological growth may emerge. They serve as the baseline projections for the discussion of different environmental policies which is the topic of the next chapter.

The projections presented in this chapter consider CO_2 emissions from energy use only. They seek to refine the existing analysis in two respects. First, the model described in the previous chapter has important advantages. It is a dynamic multi-region general equilibrium model with both macro- and microeconomic details as well as the interaction between the economic activity and climate change. Second, the scenarios developed in this chapter utilise the new findings about the underlying driving forces and future development paths in China.

This chapter is organised as follows. The next section briefly introduces the development and projections of energy consumption and CO_2 emissions in China. Section 7.2 discusses the driving forces of different scenarios, and section 7.3 quantifies the scenario assumptions and presents the results of these scenarios. The last section gives some concluding remarks.

7.1 INTRODUCTION

7.1.1 Energy Consumption and CO_2 Emissions in China

Since the late 1970s, China has experienced rapid growth at an annual real rate of about 10 percent. Along with this rapid economic growth, total energy consumption, and thus GHG emissions, have increased sharply. Between 1980 and 1998, total energy consumption more than doubled, with an annual rate of increase of 4.63 percent (see Table 7.1), while carbon dioxide

Table 7.1   China's energy consumption

Year	Total (million tce)	Per capita (kg tce)	Coal	Petroleum	Natural gas	Hydro-power
1957	96.44	14.92	92.3	4.6	0.1	3.0
1962	165.40	24.58	89.2	6.6	0.9	3.2
1965	189.01	26.06	86.5	10.3	0.9	2.7
1970	292.91	35.29	80.9	14.7	0.9	3.5
1975	454.25	49.15	71.9	21.1	2.5	4.6
1978	571.44	59.36	70.7	22.7	3.2	3.4
1980	602.75	61.07	72.2	20.7	3.1	4.0
1985	766.82	72.44	75.8	17.1	2.2	4.9
1986	808.50	75.20	75.8	17.2	2.3	4.7
1987	866.32	79.26	76.2	17.0	2.1	4.7
1988	929.97	83.76	76.2	17.0	2.1	4.7
1989	969.34	86.01	76.0	17.1	2.0	4.9
1990	987.03	86.33	76.2	16.6	2.1	5.1
1991	1 037.83	89.60	76.1	17.1	2.0	4.8
1992	1 091.70	93.17	75.7	17.5	1.9	4.9
1993	1 159.93	97.87	74.7	18.2	1.9	5.2
1994	1 227.37	102.41	75.0	17.4	1.9	5.7
1995	1 311.76	108.30	74.6	17.5	1.8	6.1
1996	1 389.48	113.53	74.7	18.0	1.8	5.5
1997	1 381.73	111.77	71.5	20.4	1.7	6.2
1998	1 322.14	105.93	69.6	21.5	2.2	6.7
1999*	1 220.00	96.90	67.1	23.4	2.8	6.7

Note: * Data for 1999 are estimates.

Source: SSB (1990–98, 1999).

emissions increased at an annual rate of 5.28 percent between 1980 and 1996 (see Table 5.2). Zhang (1998b) decomposes the change in China's CO_2 emissions between 1980 and 1997 into five components. He finds that, although economic growth and population expansion would have caused CO_2 emissions to increase by 799.13 and 128.39 percent, respectively, the total increase in emissions was only 488.65 percent. This is because China's energy efficiency has improved during the same period. In 1997, China's energy efficiency, measured in PPP GDP per unit of energy use, was $3.3 per kilogram of oil equivalent, while it was only $0.7 in 1980 (World Bank 2000). Zhang (1998b) finds that the change in energy intensity reduced total emissions by 432.32 percent. Switching between alternative energy sources also played a moderate role, reducing total emissions by 6.51 percent. This can be seen very clearly from the pattern of energy consumption in Table 7.1. From the 1950s to the 1970s, China underwent a major change in the composition of energy consumption. Due to the discovery and exploration of several big oil fields, the share of oil increased steadily from 5 percent to 20 percent and, consequently, the share of coal decreased from more than 90 percent to around 70 percent. However, the pattern has not changed significantly since the late 1970s.

Although population growth contributes to the increase in CO_2 emissions, China's rigorous and controversial population policy does play an important role in the change of emissions.´ Since the 1970s, due to continuous birth control activities over a long period, China has reduced what otherwise would have been its population by 300 million people (Wu et al. 1998, p. 548). If the population policy had not been implemented, China's total CO_2 emission would had been 4203.4 million metric tons in 1996, 25 percent higher than the actual level.

One of the important factors that have improved China's energy efficiency is price reform. In order to expand industry, China underpriced energy for a long time. The price of coal was set so low that even the best coal mines could not make a profit (Laffont and Senik-Leygonie 1997; Smil 1998). This low price system hurt the economy in two ways: inefficient production and over consumption of energy. In 1984 the Ministry of Finance introduced a two-tier price system and by 1994 the government finally freed all coal prices. Subsidies for energy consumption have been reduced significantly. Coal subsidy rates fell from 61 percent in 1984 to 37 percent in 1990 and to 29 percent in 1995; and petroleum subsidy rates fell from 55 percent in 1990 to 2 percent in 1995 (Zhang 1998). However, China's energy prices are still lower than those of the resource-rich United States (World Bank 1997, Table 4.4, p. 53).

Although China has significantly improved energy efficiency, it still has a long way to go. First, the current level of energy efficiency is still quite low compared to industrialised countries (see Table 5.2).[1] Second, a coal dominant energy structure, which may be responsible for the low energy efficiency and high CO_2 emissions, is likely to last for a very long time due to the fact that China has relatively abundant coal reserves. China's global rank of coal deposits is third behind Russia and the United States. In any case, its coal resources could last for several hundreds of years at the mid-1990s rate of extraction. In terms of verified coal reserves, China again ranks third in the world, with roughly 115 billion tons (Gt) or one-ninth of the world's total. In contrast, at the end of 1996, China's proved oil reserves amounted to just over 2 percent of the global total; and proved natural gas reserves are much smaller, amounting to a mere 0.8 percent of the global total (Smil 1998).

Another issue is that China is likely to experience an energy shortage in the near future. Using Engle–Granger's error correction model and data between 1954 and 1994, Chan and Lee (1997) find that China's coal demand would exceed the official output target by 5 percent in the year 2000 under the most optimistic scenario.[2] According to *The Study on China's Energy Strategy* reported on *Industry and Commerce Times*, 30 November 1999, total energy demand will be 1.9 billion ton standard coal in 2010, and be as high as 3.5–4.4 billion ton standard coal in 2050. Among the demand in 2010, coal is 1.86 billion tons, petroleum 0.25–0.27 billion tons, and natural gases 60–100 billion cubic metres; while the supply of petroleum is only 0.16–0.21 billion tons, and natural gases 51.6–71.3 billion cubic metres. The petroleum supply will be 40–80 million tons in 2050, leaving a shortage of about 600–700 million tons.

7.1.2 Existing Projections of CO$_2$ Emissions in China

The literature about CO$_2$ emissions projection is huge. The writing team of IPCC's Special Report on Emissions Scenarios (SRES) conducted a comprehensive literature review with over 400 scenarios examined (Nakićenović and Swart 2000, Chapter 2).[3] Due to differences in methodology and model structure, data source and definition, understanding of driving forces and assumption of scenarios, the resulting projections of future CO$_2$ emissions have been quite disparate, with the global emissions being from negative to 60 GtC in 2100 (Nakićenović and Swart 2000, Figure 2-1).

Based on a review of these scenarios, SRES (Nakićenović and Swart 2000) identifies population growth, economic development, and structural and technological change as the main scenario driving forces. Four scenario families with a total of 40 scenarios are developed in the report. The A1 family 'describes a future world of very rapid economic growth, low population growth, and the rapid introduction of new and more efficient technologies. Major underlying themes are convergence among regions, capacity building, and increased cultural and social interactions, with a substantial reduction in regional differences in per capita income.' It consists of three scenario groups characterising alternative developments of energy technologies: A1FI (fossil fuel intensive), A1B (balanced) and A1T (pre-dominantly non-fossil fuel). The A2 family 'describes a very heterogeneous world. The underlying theme is self-reliance and preservation of local identities. Fertility patterns across regions converge very slowly, which results in high population growth. Economic development is primarily regionally oriented and per capita economic growth and technological change are more fragmented and slower'. The B1 family 'describes a convergent world with the same low population growth as in the A1 storyline, but with rapid changes in economic structures toward a service and information economy, with reductions in material intensity, and the introduction of clean and resource-efficient technologies'. The B2 family describes 'a world with moderate population growth, intermediate levels of economic development, and less rapid and more diverse technological change than in the B1 and A1 storylines. While the scenario is also oriented toward environmental protection and social equity, it focuses on local and regional levels' (Nakićenović and Swart 2000, Box TS–1). The scenarios are quantified by six modeling teams.[4] The projected global CO_2 emissions from fossil fuels vary from 7.8 to 14.7 GtC per year in 2020, from 8.5 to 26.8 GtC per year in 2050, and from 3.3 to 36.8 GtC per year in 2100 (Nakićenović and Swart 2000, Table SPM-3a).

There are 144 scenarios of China's CO_2 emissions in the IPCC Scenario Database (Morita and Lee 1998a, 1998b; Morita 1999),[5] of which 69 scenarios are identified as intervention scenarios, 45 are non-intervention scenarios, and 30 are not classified. As with global scenarios, the ranges of projections of China's CO_2 emission are very wide (Figure 7.1). For example, projected non-intervention emissions vary from 4.486 GtC/year to 0.185 GtC/year in 2050 and from 13 GtC/year to 0.15 GtC/year in 2100 (see Table 7.2). The upper bound of the non-intervention scenarios is the highest, while the upper bound of the intervention scenarios is the lowest among the three categories. However, the lower bound values of these categories are more or less similar. The histograms (Figure 7.2) show that the frequency distribution of emissions projections is skewed: about 63 percent of all scenarios project that CO_2 emissions in 2050 will be less than three times the 1990 level, while the highest projection extends to 6.6 times; and about 56 percent of scenarios project that emissions in 2100 will be less than four times that of the 1990 level, while the highest value reaches 20 times. In the case of non-intervention scenarios, the variance across scenarios is even larger (Table 7.2 and Figure 7.3). This is understandable because the emission levels are exogenously set targets in some of the intervention scenarios.

The scenarios come from 40 sources, where most studies are conducted by research teams in developed countries and do not focus specifically on China. Only four scenarios can be identified as the work of a Chinese team. Jiang et al. (1999) have argued that this collection of studies does not sufficiently reflect the circumstances of developing countries. They develop four storylines of future Chinese and world demographic, economic and technological situations. Using the AIM/emission linkage model, they project that China's CO_2 emissions from energy use will be 1.95–5.4 GtC in 2050, and will decline to 0.8–5.1 GtC in 2100, while total CO_2 emissions will be slightly higher than those figures, being 2.0–5.5 GtC in 2050 and 0.85–5.2 GtC in 2100. Their major finding is that 'it is possible for China to pursue high economic growth while maintaining GHG emissions at a lower level'. However, this result relies heavily on their assumptions, especially that of the decline in China's population in the second half of 21st century.

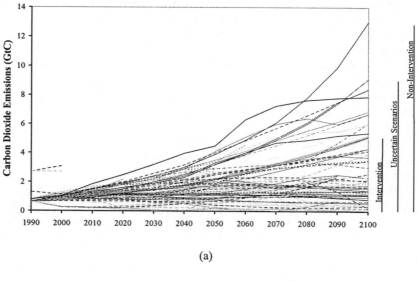

(a)

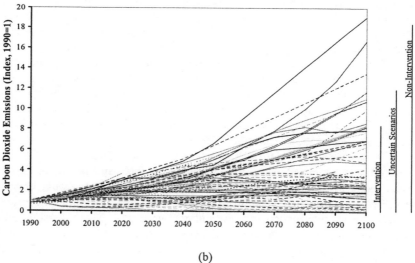

(b)

Source: Author's construction based on the data extracted from IPCC SRES Database version 1.0 maintained by the National Institute of Environmental Studies in Japan (http://www-cger. nies.go.jp/cger-e/db/ipcc.html).

Figure 7.1   Projections of China's CO₂ emissions in literature

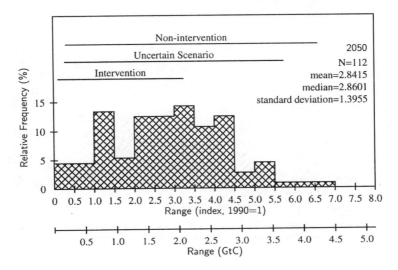

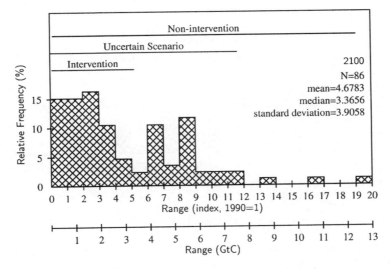

Note: The numbers of scenarios for index is less than the number of projections due to missing values in 1990.

Source: Author's construction based on the data extracted from IPCC SRES Database version 1.0 maintained by the National Institute of Environmental Studies in Japan (http://www-cger. nies.go.jp/cger-e/db/ipcc.html).

Figure 7.2   Frequency distribution of China's projected CO_2 emissions

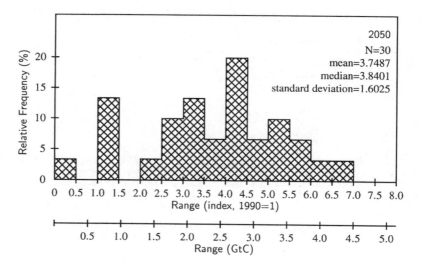

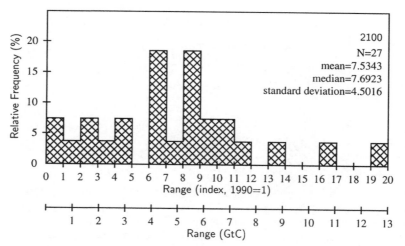

Note: The numbers of scenarios for index is less than the number of projections due to missing values in 1990.

Source: Author's construction based on the data extracted from IPCC SRES Database version 1.0 maintained by the National Institute of Environmental Studies in Japan (http://www-cger. nies. go.jp/cger-e/db/ipcc.html).

Figure 7.3   Frequency distribution of China's projected non-intervention CO₂ emissions

Table 7.2   Scenario statistics of China's CO_2 emissions projections

Scenarios Year	Maximum (GtC)	Minimum (GtC)	Mean (GtC)	Median (GtC)	Standard deviation	Number of projections
All scenarios						
2000	3.186	0.2265	0.9810	0.8863	0.5119	140
2010	1.853	0.156	1.0792	1.1107	0.3075	130
2050	4.486	0.1049	1.8868	1.8238	0.9837	114
2100	13.000	0.033	3.5241	2.6295	2.9287	88
Non-intervention scenarios						
2000	3.186	0.241	1.0233	0.8915	0.5963	42
2010	1.853	0.2191	1.1113	1.1184	0.3610	38
2050	4.486	0.1846	2.5025	2.533	1.1195	31
2100	13.000	0.1509	5.5751	5.1073	3.2863	28
Intervention scenarios						
2000	2.700	0.2343	0.9174	0.8921	0.3497	68
2010	1.379	0.1560	1.0513	1.0556	0.2597	65
2050	3.241	0.1049	1.5555	1.6430	0.6678	63
2100	5.236	0.1000	2.0050	1.5730	1.5717	39
Uncertain scenarios						
2000	3.078	0.2265	1.0661	0.8705	0.6717	30
2010	1.853	0.1912	1.1013	1.1107	0.3374	27
2050	4.486	0.1718	1.9759	2.0607	1.1536	20
2100	9.100	0.0330	3.6105	3.4312	2.7643	21

Source: Author's calculation based on the data extracted from IPCC SRES Database version 1.0 maintained by the National Institute of Environmental Studies in Japan (http://www-cger.nies. go.jp/cger-e/db/ipcc.html).

7.2   SCENARIO DRIVING FORCES

A popular way to organise the discussion of the scenario driving forces, as followed by SRES (Nakićenović and Swart 2000), is through the Kaya Identity. The identity states that CO_2 emissions are a multiple of population growth, per capita income (GDP), energy efficiency and emissions per unit of energy use (Kaya 1990; Yamaji et al. 1991). It is implicitly assumed that policies are underlying factors affecting population growth, economic development and technological change.

7.2.1 Population

Population is an important driving force of emissions scenarios. This is especially true for dynamic models like G-Cubed-T because the variables at the steady state grow at a rate being equal to the sum of population and productivity growth rates which are set exogenously. Therefore a reliable population projection is crucial to the result of emission projections.

The widely used world population projections are those by the World Bank (up to 2015), the United Nations (up to 2150), the International Institute for Applied System Analysis (IIASA, up to 2100), and the US Bureau of the Census (up to 2050). These projections, which are summarised in Figure 7.4, give large differences in future world population due to different assumptions.

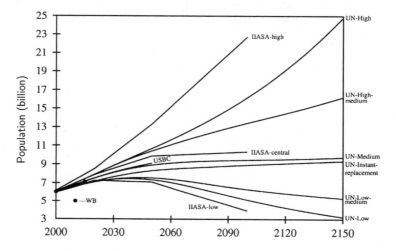

Note: IIASA–high refers to the scenario with high fertility and low mortality, IIASA–central refers to the scenario with central fertility and mortality, and IIASA–low refers to the scenario with low fertility and high mortality.

Source: Author's construction based on the United Nations (2000), the World Bank (2000), US Bureau of the Census (2000c) and Lutz (1996).

Figure 7.4   World population projections

The United Nations (2000) revised its previous results (United Nations 1998) downward. For example, the figure for the world population in 2100 was reduced by about 10 percent. Seven scenarios are considered in the UN projections. Despite the *constant-fertility* scenario where the world population will surge to 14.4 billion in 2050, 52.5 billion in 2100 and 255.8 billion in 2150, the other six scenarios project the world population will vary from 5.15 to 16.18 billion in 2100 and from 3.24 to 24.83 billion in 2150. The IIASA projection (Lutz 1996) considers nine scenarios with different fertility and mortality rates, and the range of projections is even wider than the six UN projections, varying from 3.94 to 22.74 billion in 2100. However, the central projection of IIASS and the medium projection of UN are close to each other.

Both the World Bank (2000, 2001) and the US Bureau of the Census (2000c) provide projections which are close to the medium or central projections of UN and IIASA.

China's population has doubled in the past 50 years. The recent national census reveals that about 1.27 billion people live in mainland China (SSB 2001), which is close to previous projections (for example, 1.28 billion by Tian 1998; 1.28–1.30 billion by the United Nations 2000, 1.26 billion by the US Bureau of the Census 1999). However, due to the strict 'one-child' policy, the population growth rate in China has been steadily declining since 1987 (Figure 7.5).

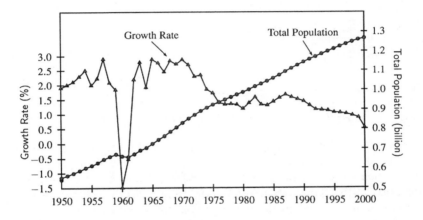

Sources: SSB (1990–98,1999); 2000 data from SSB (2001).

Figure 7.5 Population and population growth rate in China, 1950–2000

The UN projections show that China's population will be 1.25–1.686 billion in 2050, 0.71–2.09 billion in 2100 and 0.395–2.926 billion in 2150. Unlike the trend for world population under the constant fertility scenario, China's population under this scenario will slowly grow up to 1.509 billion in 2050, before declining to 1.121 billion in 2150, lower than the current level (United Nations 2000). The other projections are much shorter in period than the UN projections. Projections by the World Bank (2000, 2001) and the US Bureau of the Census (2000a) are very close to the UN-Medium projection, while the projections by a Chinese scholar (Tian 1998) approach the high value of UN projections (see Figure 7.6).

These projections also show that an ageing population is a common feature of demographic dynamics in both China and the world. China will experience the most rapid ageing among the developing countries because fertility has

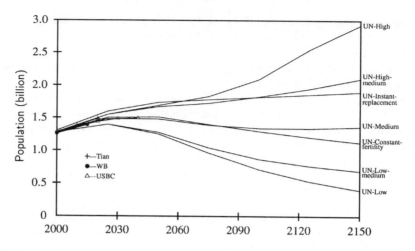

Sources: Author's construction based on the United Nations (2000), the World Bank (2000), Tian (1998), and the US Bureau of the Census (2000a).

Figure 7.6   Projections of China's population, 2000–2150

already declined dramatically (Lutz 1996). The current population above age 65 in China is 88.11 million, accounting for 6.96 percent of the total population, which is about 1.39 percentage point above the 1990 value revealed by the Fourth National Census (SSB 2001). The percentage of people above age 60 in the total Chinese population is projected by the United Nations (2000) to rise from only 9 percent in 2000 to 19–31 percent in 2050, 25–48 percent in 2100, and 28–54 percent in 2150 (Table 7.3). An ageing population may affect the economy and emissions in several aspects. First, the supply of labour per head of population might decline. Second, the higher elderly dependency ratio may imply a lower saving rate and higher government spending on social security and health care programmes.

Another demographic trend is urbanisation. Currently 36.09 percent of Chinese people live in the urban area (defined as cities and townships, SSB 2001). The figure will be 55–69 percent in 2020 (Tian 1998). Urbanisation will lead to the expansion of infrastructure and transportation services. In addition, urban people in developing countries tend to use more fossil fuels than rural people (Nakićenović and Swart 2000).

7.2.2 Economic Development

As discussed in Bagnoli et al. (1996) and McKibbin and Huang (1997), a country's sources of economic growth include increases in the supply and

Table 7.3   Percentage of ageing population[a]

Regions/Sources/Scenarios	2000	2025	2050	2100	2150
World					
United Nations (2000)					
Low	11.00	18.00	32.00	49.00	56.00
Medium	11.00	17.00	26.00	36.00	40.00
High	11.00	16.00	22.00	27.00	31.00
Lutz (1996)					
Low fertility, high mortality		13.70	23.40	33.40	
High fertility, low mortality		12.80	17.00	17.20	
China					
United Nations (2000)					
Low	9.00	15.00	31.00	48.00	54.00
Medium	9.00	14.00	24.00	34.00	39.00
High	9.00	13.00	19.00	25.00	28.00
US Bureau of the Census (2000a)	10.20	19.69			
Tian (1998)	12.80	14.83[b]			

Notes:
a.   Percentage of the population above age 60 except the values in Tian (1998) which refer to population above age 65.
b.   Value in the year of 2020.

Sources: As indicated in the table.

quality of labour, capital and other inputs; improvements in technology which affect the way inputs are used; and structural change affecting the way inputs are allocated. All of these sources will be explicitly considered in the model, exogenously or endogenously. The labour supply in the long run is determined by population which has been discussed in the previous subsection. The production functions used in G-Cubed-T allow for improvements in labour quality or labour augmenting technical change. The model determines material use and the evolution of the capital stock endogenously. Structural change, induced by changes in the price level, is also modelled endogenously. This subsection discusses the achievement and future prospects of economic growth in China and the world to shed light on the assumptions about economic growth sources specified elsewhere.

China has experienced rapid growth in the past two decades. China's GDP growth rate was 10.1 percent per annum between 1980 and 1990, and 10.7 percent per annum between 1990 and 1999. Growing 6 percent a year over the past 40 years, China has increased its GDP per capita more than sevenfold (World Bank 2001, p. 185).

Figure 7.7 clearly shows that the growth rates of GDP and per capita GDP in China have fluctuated over time. These variations have been closely

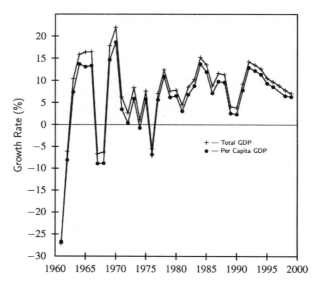

Sources: SSB (1990–98, 1999), World Bank (2000, 2001).

Figure 7.7   China's GDP growth rate, 1960–2000

associated with the political situation in China. This suggests that appropriate assumptions about future development growth are highly dependent on expectation about the political situation in China.

Maddison (1998) projects that per capita GDP growth in China will be 4.5 percent during the period 1995 to 2015. The per capita GDP growth potential for the USA and the world would be 1.3 and 1.73 percent, respectively. The Chinese government wants the per capita GDP level in 2050 to be the same as the middle income countries. If that target is the current level of $2000, fulfilling the task requires annual growth rates to 2050 of 1.9 percent for per capita GDP or 2.9 percent for GDP (assuming population growth is 1 percent per annum). If it means catching up and if middle income countries follow the same path as before – 1.5 percent per annum, the annual growth rates to 2050 should be 3.4 and 4.4 percent, respectively, for per capita and total GDP.

7.2.3 Technology and Energy Efficiency

The literature about technological change and energy efficiency in China is diverse, especially as it relates to quantitative estimation. Jefferson et al. (1996) find that collectively owned enterprises have a higher total factor productivity (TFP) growth rate than state-owned enterprises (SOEs): during the period between 1980 and 1992, the former had 7.15 percent TFP growth, or 3.43 percent, if applying the price index for state-sector industrial output, while the latter had 2.50 percent TFP growth during the same period. Li (1997) observes that TFP growth of China's SOEs between 1980 and 1989 was 4.68 percent, and nearly half of this growth is attributed to incentives and competition and more than a third to reallocation. Both Li et al. (1993) and Ezaki and Sun (1999) explore the TFP growth of the whole Chinese economy. Li et al. (1993) find that TFP growth between 1981 and 1990 was about 2.73 percent. Ezaki and Sun (1999) find that TFP growth between 1980 and 1995 was 3.8 percent. However, Kong et al. (1999) analyse Chinese SOEs in four sectors between 1990 and 1994, and find no evidence of technological change in the building materials, chemicals and textiles industries, a neutral technological progress in the machinery industry, and significant reduction of technical efficiency in chemicals, machinery and textiles. Consequently, chemicals and textiles experienced a negative TFP growth, while building materials and machinery displayed negligible FTP change. The detailed results of these studies are reported in Table 7.4. From examining the table, it might be concluded that the TFP growth in China was around 3 percent in the 1980s and early 1990s.

Table 7.4   Selected estimations of China's TFP growth

Study	E-S	Kong et al.				Li	Jefferson et al.			Li et al.
Year	Nation	BM	Chem	Mach	Textile	SOE	SOE	Col	Col-R	Nation
1981	-0.1					-2.18	2.24	3.29	2.80	-0.6
1982	3.4					6.18	2.24	3.29	2.80	4.4
1983	5.3					6.26	2.24	3.29	2.80	3.4
1984	8.1					10.75	2.24	3.29	2.80	7.8
1985	4.9					2.15	3.68	8.73	4.52	4.9
1986	0.7					4.08	3.68	8.73	4.52	0.7
1987	3.4					8.36	3.68	8.73	4.52	4.5
1988	3.2					7.35	3.68	8.73	4.52	4.4
1989	-2.0					-0.12	1.58	9.44	2.98	-1.7
1990	-1.1						1.58	9.44	2.98	-0.1
1991	4.3	-0.019	-0.059	0.001	-0.053		1.58	9.44	2.98	
1992	9.2	-0.004	0.020	0.124	-0.016		1.58	9.44	2.98	
1993	7.6	-0.019	-0.023	-0.005	-0.034					
1994	5.6	0.018	-0.073	-0.060	-0.049					
1995	3.7									
Average	3.8	-0.006	-0.033	0.015	-0.038	4.68	2.50	7.15	3.43	2.7

Notes:
E-S – Ezaki and Sun (1999) study; Nation – national economy; BM – building materials; Chem – chemicals; Mach – machinery; SOE – state owned enterprise; Col – collectively owned enterprise; Col-R – revised calculation for Col; Average – average for the studied period.

Sources: Ezaki and Sun (1999), Kong et al. (1999), Li (1997), Jefferson et al. (1996), Li et al. (1993).

Table 7.5   AEEI assumption for China in selected studies

Study	Period	Sector	Annual AEEI (%)
Manne (1992)[a]			1.00
Bagnoli et al. (1996)	1990–2020		0.00
Rose et al. (1996)	1990–2000		2.50
	2000–2010		1.50
	2010–2025		1.00
McKibbin and Huang (1997)	1990–2019		1.00
Zhang (1998a)	1987–2000	Fossil fuels	1.0~4.5
		Electricity	0.0~0.3
	2000–2010	Fossil fuels	1.0~2.7
		Electricity	0.0~0.2
Jiang et al. (1999)	1990–2100		0.8~1.8
EMF14[b]	1990		0.87
	1990–2000		0.85
	2000–2050		0.92
	2050–2100		0.64

Notes:
a.   Cited from Zhang (1998).
b.   Energy Modeling Forum (EMF) 14 Common Assumptions Scenario, from IPCC SRES Database (Morita 1999).

Sources: As shown.

Closely related to the technological change, autonomous energy efficiency improvement (AEEI) is also important for the projection of CO_2 emissions. AEEI 'accounts for all but energy price-induced energy conservation' (Zhang 1998a, p. 123). Higher AEEI means lower emissions to achieve a given level of economic growth. Assumptions about AEEI in China used by some studies are given in Table 7.5. Most are around 1 percent per annum, however, Zhang (1998a) claims the figure was too low compared to the significant achievement of 3.6 percent per annum AEEI over the period between 1980 and 1990.

From the above discussion, changes in the energy demand in production can be considered in two categories: price induced and non-price induced effects. The former may be characterised by the elasticity and the latter by AEEI. These two effects have been estimated, assuming a CES functional form of production, and the estimation process is given in the Appendix and the results in Table 7.6.

Table 7.6 shows that energy conservation in most sectors is predominantly attributed to the price-induced changes. Only three sectors have an AEEI significantly different from zero. However, this result is not as surprising as it first seems. As pointed out in the introduction, the period from which the

Table 7.6   Estimated elasticity of substitution between energy and other inputs and implied AEEI

Sectors	Elasticity[a]	Implied AEEI (%)[a]	R^2	Durbin–Watson Statistics[a]	Number of Observations
Metallurgy[b]	0.4880	9.866	0.2542	2.0849	15
	(0.237)	(0.208)		(0.4440)	
Electricity	3.4741	1.487	0.3563	2.3669	16
	(0.015)	(0.341)		(0.7607)	
Coal and coke	3.4295	-1.625	0.2639	1.7941	15
	(0.050)	(0.046)		(0.3858)	
Petroleum	5.7364	-0.724	0.7130	2.7391	15
	(0.000)	(0.248)		(0.9238)	
Chemical industry[b,c]	0.6931	17.833	0.2386	2.6116	13
	(0.010)	(0.028)		(0.8092)	
Machinery	1.9486	-4.101	0.5089	2.0630	15
	(0.003)	(0.383)		(0.4672)	
Food industry[c]	0.9821	1.007	0.5576	2.7352	12
	(0.005)	(0.992)		(0.8914)	
Textile[c]	0.5700	3.983	0.8676	1.4951	14
	(0.000)	(0.050)		(0.1308)	
Tailoring[c,d]	2.6341	6.083	0.6061	1.8987	6
	(0.068)	(0.247)		(0.6314)	
Paper[c]	0.3982	4.195	0.4295	1.6806	14
	(0.011)	(0.164)		(0.2312)	

Notes:
a. Numbers in parentheses are *p*-values. Low *p*-values of elasticity and implied AEEI denote that they are significantly different from zero, while high *p*-value of Durbin–Watson statistics denotes that the hypothesis of no autocorrelation in the residuals cannot be rejected.
b. Including dummy variable for samples after 1990.
c. Outlier deleted.
d. Only seven samples available before deleting outliers.

Source: Author's estimation.

data are obtained witnessed significant price reform. Moreover, the specification that implicitly assumes instant adjustment of capital may overstate the elasticity (see discussion in McKibbin and Wilcoxen 1999).

7.3   SCENARIOS AND RESULTS

7.3.1   Scenarios

As discussed above, there are three major types of exogenous inputs for G-

Cubed-T to produce baseline projections: population growth, productivity growth and the autonomous energy efficiency index (AEEI). It turns out that the number of possible combinations of these factors is huge.[6] However, it is unnecessary to explore all of these possibilities. For example, the number of scenarios can be significantly reduced by assuming that the USA and the rest of the world follow a similar path of population, economic growth and technological change to enable a detailed study of China. From the above discussion, the following scenarios can be developed (Table 7.7).[7]

Table 7.7   Scenario assumptions

	Scenarios							
	R1	R2	R3	H1	H2	M1	M2	M3
Population Growth	H	H	M	L	M	H	M	L
Productivity Growth	H	H	H	H	H	M	M	M
AEEI (%)	3	1	0	1	1	0	0	0

Notes: H – High, M – Moderate or Medium, L – Low.

Rapid Growth – R. So-called both because China's productivity will have a high growth rate and population growth will be high or moderate. It is assumed China's population growth will follow the path of UN high or medium scenario projections to 2150 (see Figure 7.6) and then stabilise. The productivity growth rate, starting from 5.6 percent which is slightly lower than the upper bound of estimated TFP growth rates reported in Table 7.4, will gradually approach the US level (1.6 percent, Figure 7.8). Accompanying this rapid growth, AEEI may be high or low. Thus, this scenario family is in turn divided into three scenarios:

  R1 – High population and productivity growth and high AEEI. In this scenario, the AEEI is set to be 3 percent per annum, which is close to the upper bound of assumptions in the literature (Zhang 1998).
  R2 – High population and productivity growth and low AEEI. This scenario sets AEEI to be 1 percent per annum which is a common assumption in most studies.
  R3 – Moderate population growth, high productivity growth and zero AEEI.

Healthy Growth – H. So-called because it assumes China will have low or moderate population growth (the UN low scenario, see Figure 7.7), high productivity growth, and low AEEI. This scenario family is divided into two scenarios:

H1 – Low population growth, high productivity growth and low AEEI.
H2 – Moderate population growth, high productivity growth and low AEEI.

Moderate Growth – M. In contrast to the rapid progress scenarios, this scenario family assumes a moderate productivity growth rate starting from 3.97 percent (Figure 7.8). To be consistent with the moderate productivity growth, AEEI is assumed to be zero. However, the population could grow rapidly or slowly. Therefore, this family is also divided into three scenarios: High population growth (M1), moderate population growth (M2) and low population growth (M3).

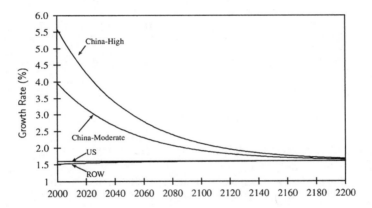

Figure 7.8   Productivity growth assumptions

The assumption for US population is drawn from the middle series of USBC projections (US Bureau of the Census 2000b), while that for ROW population is drawn from the medium scenario of UN projections (United Nations 2000). It is assumed that the US has a constant productivity growth rate (1.6 percent) and ROW productivity growth rate is slightly lower than the US rate at the beginning and then gradually catches up (Figure 7.8). Their AEEI is assumed to be 1 percent.

7.3.2 Results

The results of simulating these scenarios are reported in Tables 7.8–7.12 and Figures 7.9–7.11. The demand for coal in China will be 61.28–64.4 EJ in 2010 and 265.5–432.1 EJ in 2050. The demand for crude oil and natural gas will be 35.2–38.1 EJ in 2010, and 191.2–250.8 EJ in 2050. China's CO_2 emissions under these scenarios will be 1.47–1.53 GtC in 2010, 2.38–2.62

Table 7.8   Projected carbon emissions (Mtc)

Year	R1	R2	R3	H1	H2	M1	M2	M3
China								
2000	874.2	878.0	879.2	876.2	877.2	875.1	874.3	873.3
2010	1511.7	1529.6	1532.4	1506.3	1523.5	1506.6	1491.7	1466.0
2020	2604.4	2616.9	2621.7	2576.2	2615.5	2492.8	2456.9	2386.7
2050	10879.6	10756.4	10133.2	9340.3	10194.8	8102.2	7465.6	6634.2
United States								
2000	1605.7	1599.4	1596.8	1600.6	1599.9	1597.6	1598.0	1598.4
2010	2134.8	2039.2	2006.4	2070.3	2054.3	2027.8	2037.4	2048.0
2020	2747.8	2518.0	2447.5	2609.4	2562.4	2508.5	2536.5	2567.4
2050	5706.3	4606.3	4312.0	5127.7	4862.0	4638.2	4793.9	4963.0
Rest of the World								
2000	4148.5	4129.5	4119.6	4128.6	4129.1	4119.0	4118.7	4118.4
2010	5948.4	5634.0	5457.9	5594.5	5615.1	5430.2	5417.8	5403.7
2020	8392.1	7619.4	7173.9	7496.7	7560.3	7088.8	7050.6	7008.1
2050	19922.0	16228.3	14026.5	15512.0	15873.4	13604.7	13396.1	13176.5

Source: G-Cubed-T simulation.

Table 7.9   Projected GDP (2000 US$ billion)

Year	R1	R2	R3	H1	H2	M1	M2	M3
China								
2000	1047.1	1046.3	1044.3	1042.7	1044.7	1038.6	1037.2	1035.5
2010	1968.7	1912.9	1859.2	1847.6	1887.1	1801.1	1772.3	1730.4
2020	3511.1	3340.0	3186.5	3160.6	3272.1	2953.1	2873.9	2755.5
2050	14578.9	13545.1	11815.0	10860.5	12332.0	9185.3	8212.8	7067.3
United States								
2000	9205.1	9190.3	9182.0	9188.4	9189.4	9180.9	9180.4	9179.7
2010	12249.1	11935.5	11806.7	11992.2	11963.5	11845.0	11861.7	11879.3
2020	15861.0	15006.6	14691.8	15233.9	15119.0	14834.0	14900.9	14972.0
2050	34005.7	29446.3	27833.6	30774.7	30113.3	28561.2	28935.6	29325.9
Rest of the World								
2000	20629.3	20593.1	20576.0	20595.2	20594.1	20577.6	20578.3	20579.0
2010	28952.3	27943.0	27369.9	27800.6	27874.6	27271.1	27226.7	27177.0
2020	40495.6	37630.7	35939.3	37096.0	37371.7	35573.1	35408.9	35228.2
2050	92358.2	77017.3	67535.1	73408.1	75205.6	65561.7	64544.7	63507.4

Source: G-Cubed-T simulation.

GtC in 2020, and 6.63–10.88 GtC in 2050. The real GDP will be US$1.73–1.97 trillion in 2010, US$2.76–3.51 trillion in 2020, and US$7.07–14.58 trillion in 2050, implying annual growth of 3.96–5.45 percent. However, the carbon intensity, defined as the carbon emission per unit of real GDP, will change only marginally.

Table 7.10 Projected per capita carbon emission (ton)

Year	R1	R2	R3	H1	H2	M1	M2	M3
China								
2000	0.691	0.694	0.695	0.692	0.693	0.691	0.691	0.690
2010	1.103	1.116	1.137	1.145	1.131	1.099	1.107	1.114
2020	1.754	1.763	1.828	1.884	1.823	1.679	1.713	1.745
2050	6.453	6.380	6.856	7.472	6.898	4.806	5.051	5.307
United States								
2000	5.833	5.809	5.800	5.814	5.811	5.803	5.804	5.806
2010	7.119	6.800	6.691	6.904	6.851	6.762	6.794	6.830
2020	8.457	7.749	7.532	8.031	7.886	7.720	7.806	7.901
2050	14.135	11.410	10.682	12.702	12.044	11.489	11.875	12.294
Rest of the World								
2000	0.921	0.917	0.915	0.917	0.917	0.915	0.915	0.915
2010	1.180	1.117	1.082	1.110	1.114	1.077	1.075	1.072
2020	1.511	1.372	1.292	1.350	1.361	1.277	1.270	1.262
2050	3.042	2.478	2.141	2.368	2.423	2.077	2.045	2.012

Source: G-Cubed-T simulation.

Table 7.11 Projected per capita GDP (2000 US$)

Year	R1	R2	R3	H1	H2	M1	M2	M3
China								
2000	827.2	826.6	825.0	823.7	825.3	820.5	819.4	818.0
2010	1436.1	1395.4	1379.7	1404.4	1400.4	1313.8	1315.3	1315.3
2020	2365.0	2249.7	2221.4	2311.5	2281.1	1989.1	2003.5	2015.2
2050	8647.1	8033.9	7993.9	8688.4	8343.7	5448.0	5556.7	5653.8
United States								
2000	33435.9	33382.1	33351.9	33375.3	33378.8	33348.1	33346.0	33343.6
2010	40849.2	39803.3	39373.8	39992.4	39896.7	39501.6	39557.2	39616.0
2020	48814.0	46184.6	45215.6	46884.1	46530.3	45653.3	45859.3	46077.9
2050	84237.8	72943.4	68948.5	76234.0	74595.7	70751.0	71678.4	72645.1
Rest of the World								
2000	4582.2	4574.2	4570.4	4574.7	4574.4	4570.8	4570.9	4571.1
2010	5742.2	5542.0	5428.4	5513.8	5528.5	5408.8	5400.0	5390.1
2020	7292.6	6776.6	6472.0	6680.3	6730.0	6406.1	6376.5	6344.0
2050	14100.5	11758.4	10310.7	11207.3	11481.8	10009.4	9854.1	9695.8

Source: G-Cubed-T simulation.

China's share in total world CO_2 emissions will steadily increase in all scenarios. The share will be 15.75–17.03 percent in 2010, 18.95–21.41 percent in 2020, and 26.78–35.59 percent in 2050. The R2 and R3 scenarios suggest China could surpass the United States to become the world's number one CO_2 emitter as early as in 2019. Even if China has a moderate growth, it

Table 7.12   Projected carbon emission intensity (kgC/US$)

Year	R1	R2	R3	H1	H2	M1	M2	M3
China								
2000	0.8349	0.8392	0.8419	0.8403	0.8397	0.8426	0.8429	0.8433
2010	0.7678	0.7996	0.8243	0.8153	0.8073	0.8365	0.8417	0.8472
2020	0.7418	0.7835	0.8228	0.8151	0.7993	0.8441	0.8549	0.8662
2050	0.7463	0.7941	0.8577	0.8600	0.8267	0.8821	0.9090	0.9387
United States								
2000	0.1744	0.1740	0.1739	0.1742	0.1741	0.1740	0.1741	0.1741
2010	0.1743	0.1708	0.1699	0.1726	0.1717	0.1712	0.1718	0.1724
2020	0.1732	0.1678	0.1666	0.1713	0.1695	0.1691	0.1702	0.1715
2050	0.1678	0.1564	0.1549	0.1666	0.1615	0.1624	0.1657	0.1692
Rest of the World								
2000	0.2011	0.2005	0.2002	0.2005	0.2005	0.2002	0.2001	0.2001
2010	0.2055	0.2016	0.1994	0.2012	0.2014	0.1991	0.1990	0.1988
2020	0.2072	0.2025	0.1996	0.2021	0.2023	0.1993	0.1991	0.1989
2050	0.2157	0.2107	0.2077	0.2113	0.2111	0.2075	0.2075	0.2075

Source: G-Cubed-T simulation.

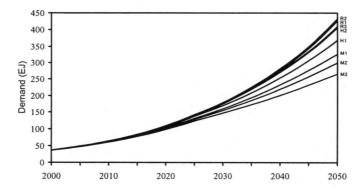

Sources: G-Cubed-T simulation

Figure 7.9   Projections of China's demand for coal

may catch up with the United States in 2023 as suggested by the M3 scenario. These results support the point that China will be an important player in the climate change policy debate and will be pressed more vigorously to participate in international actions.

On the other hand, China's per capita CO₂ emission and per capita GDP level will still be quite low compared to the industrialised countries represented by the United States. The per capita emission in China is only

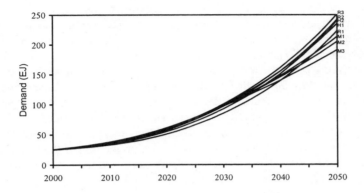

Source: G-Cubed-T simulation.

Figure 7.10 Projections of China's demand for crude oil and natural gas extraction

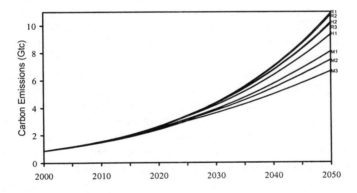

Source: G-Cubed-T simulation.

Figure 7.11 Projections of China's carbon emissions

one quarter to one third of that in the US in 2020, and increases to about 40–60 percent in 2050. The gap of per capita GDP between both countries is even wider: China's per capita GDP level is only 5 percent of the USA level in 2020 and 7.7–11.6 percent in 2050.[8] These results suggest that economic development will remain a top priority for China for a very long period and it will be very hard to convince China to adopt any rigorous efforts of reducing CO_2 emissions which may hinder its economic growth.

The first impression from comparing the results of these scenarios is that they are very close, especially during the period of the next 20 years. For example, the dispersion ratio of China's CO_2 emissions, defined as the ratio of difference between the maximum and minimum values over the minimum value of projected CO_2 emissions, is only 9.85 percent in 2020. This result is understandable because the underlying assumptions, especially about population, are close during this period (Figure 7.6). However, the underlying assumptions generate greater differences among scenarios over a longer period of time, so that the projections differ significantly in the long run. The ratio of maximum to minimum projected emissions increases to 64 percent in 2050. Similarly, the standard deviation of these projections is 0.09 in 2020, and increases to 1.60 in 2050. Although the dispersion is in the same range as those of previous projections in terms of standard deviation (see Figure 7.2), it is still too high to provide a concrete reference. Therefore, the interpretation of long-run projections should be very cautious and they are at best used for illustrative purposes.

The underlying assumptions about future productivity, population and energy efficiency growth lead to the dispersion of CO_2 emission projections, but their contributions are different. The largest contributor is productivity growth. For example, the scenario R3 differs from M2 only in productivity growth. The difference in CO_2 emissions between these two scenarios is 2667.69 Mtc in 2050, accounting for about 62.8 percent of the total dispersion of projected emissions among all scenarios. Different assumptions about population growth also make a significant difference to projections. For example, R2 and H1 differ only in the population growth, which changes from high to low growth, as do M1 and M2. The difference of projections in the first group accounts for about 33.4 percent of total dispersion, while the second accounts for about 34.6 percent. However, differences in the assumption about energy efficiency improvement make a much smaller difference in projected emissions. For example, R1 differs from R2 only in AEEI which changes significantly from 3 to 1 percent per annum, but their projected emissions in 2050 are very close, with the difference accounting for less than 3 percent of the total dispersion. The reason for this seemingly controversial result is that the demand for energy and economic growth are endogenous in each scenario. Under the scenario with higher AEEI, it pays for the economy to consume more energy (and thus produce more emissions) to achieve higher economic growth as evidenced by the higher GDP level (US$14 578.94 trillion versus US$13 545.08 trillion, Table 7.9). However, higher AEEI enables the economy to use less energy (thus fewer CO_2 emissions) to achieve a given GDP level, that is, the carbon emission intensity of higher AEEI scenarios is lower than that of lower AEEI scenarios (0.7463 versus 0.7941 kgC/US$, Table 7.12).

Comparing with other projections, it is found that the projected emissions in 2010 and 2020 fall in the range reported by other studies. However, the emissions in the later period exceed the upper bound of other studies (comparing Tables 7.2 and 7.8). Because the underlying assumptions of most studies are not given in the database, it is hard to trace the source of this difference. However, it can be conjectured that the differences come from the different views about the future paths of productivity, population and technological growth (Zhang 1998c). For example, many studies assume some kind of backstop technologies in the future while G-Cubed-T does not make such an assumption. Without significant improvement in technology, the energy consumption and thus the CO_2 emissions may grow along with the economic growth. However, given the fact that the picture of future technology is not clear, making assumptions about backstop technology is somehow arbitrary.

Before concluding this chapter, it is useful to discuss the impact of linking climate change to the economy in the current model. The detailed discussion is given in Appendix 7.B to this chapter.

It is found that, with the same assumptions about future population, productivity and energy efficiency growth, considering the direct adverse impact of global warming on the production of the agricultural sector will significantly reduce the projected level of agricultural output and total output in the long run (Figures 7.A–7.B). For example, the annual growth rate of China's agricultural output decreases from 3.3 percent to 1.4 percent, leading an 85 percent decline in agricultural output by 2100. On the other hand, because of decline in the agricultural sector, resources are relocated to other sectors, leading to higher total output levels for a shorter period of time. Because other sectors have higher CO_2 emission rates than the agricultural sector, the projected world CO_2 emissions are slightly higher up to 2095, which is mainly driven by higher emissions in the US.

The patterns of emission changes are different across regions. This is because the final emissions are affected by two opposing effects and the degree of these effects is different for individual countries. One is the above-mentioned 'expanding effect' that tends to increase CO_2 emissions because other sectors with higher emission rates will boost them. The other one is the 'feedback effect': higher emissions will have higher adverse impact on the agricultural sector. If the agricultural sector accounts for a very small share of an economy, as in the US, the adverse impact would be overlooked, the expanding effect would play a dominant role, and the emissions would increase. In contrast, the agricultural output has a higher share in China's total output, so more attention would be paid to the feedback effect. As a result, China's 'with feedback' projections of CO_2 emissions fall below the 'without feedback' projections after 2076 and are 44 percent lower than the 'without feedback' projections in 2100.

7.4   CONCLUDING REMARKS

Eight scenarios are developed based on the analysis of the existing literature and Chinese data. These scenarios give very different projections about China's future energy consumption and CO$_2$ emissions. Although the projections presented in this chapter mainly serve as the baseline for policy discussions in the following chapter, some insights can still be drawn.

First, given the information available today, as long as the economy continues to grow, it is not likely that China will have lower emissions than the current level.

Second, China's share in total world CO$_2$ emissions will steadily increase and China could surpass the United States to become the number one emitter in the world in the first half of the 21st century. However, the per capita emission, and especially the per capita GDP level in China, will still be quite low compared to the industrialised countries. This implies that it is not likely that China will compromise too much economic development to achieve emission stabilisation or reduction targets.

Third, the projection results are mainly determined by the underlying scenario assumptions. Assuming different population and productivity growth leads to significant difference in long-run emissions. Therefore long-term projection can at best be illustrative because knowledge about the future is limited and thus the assumptions are somehow arbitrary.

Some improvements can be made to refine the scenario assumptions. First, more effects of demographic dynamics such as ageing and urbanisation could be embedded into the scenario assumptions. For example, ageing may lead to a reduction in savings, and urbanisation may lead to an increase in household demand for energy. These effects can be captured by introducing a negative shock to saving and a positive shock to household energy demand. Second, elimination of trade protection could be an alternative scenario, given the fact that China has been admitted to the World Trade Organization.

APPENDIX

7.A   Estimation of Elasticity and AEEI

This Appendix describes the identification of price- and non-price-induced changes in energy conservation in the Chinese economy through the estimation of elasticities of substitution between energy, labour, capital and materials and autonomous energy efficiency index (AEEI).

It is useful to discuss the Chinese data before detailing the estimation procedure. Despite the accuracy problem, the sector classification in China's statistics varies over time. The statistics in the early 1980s have a simpler and broader classification which prevents perfect mapping from Chinese sectors to G-Cubed sectors.

Table 7.A contrasts the new sector classification (post-1993) in Chinese energy statistics against the pre-1985 classification. There were also minor changes in the classification between 1985 and 1993. It is clear that the pre-1985 classification can not be transformed to G-Cubed sectors without bias. However, it is possible to map the post-1985 classification to the previous one. In order to use all available data, it was decided to aggregate the sectors into the pre-1985 sectors.

Data available are output value, producer price indexes, and energy use in each sector between 1980 and 1996. Energy is aggregated according to the coal equivalence, and the energy price index in each sector is calculated by

$$p_i^E = \prod_j \left(p^{E_j}\right)^{s_{ij}},$$

where p_i^E is the price index of aggregate energy used in sector i, p^{E_j} is the price index of individual energy j, s_{ij} is the share of individual energy j in total energy used in sector i.

From eqn. (6.5) and (6.15), the energy demand can be obtained:

$$E_{it} = \delta_{iE}^Y \left(A_{it}^Y\right)^{\sigma_i^Y-1} \left(P_{it}^Y Y_{it}\right)\left(P_{it}^Y\right)^{\sigma_i^Y-1}\left(P_{it}^E\right)^{-\sigma_i^Y}, \tag{7.A.1}$$

$$E_{it-1} = \delta_{iE}^Y \left(A_{it-1}^Y\right)^{\sigma_i^Y-1} \left(P_{it-1}^Y Y_{it-1}\right)\left(P_{it-1}^Y\right)^{\sigma_i^Y-1}\left(P_{it-1}^E\right)^{-\sigma_i^Y}, \tag{7.A.2}$$

where E_i is the amount of energy used in producing good i, Y_i is the output of good i, P_i^Y and P_i^E are, respectively, prices of output and aggregate energy used in sector i, δ_{iE}^Y is the share of energy in the production of good i, σ_i^Y is the elasticity of substitution between energy and other inputs, and A_i^Y is the shifter. Dividing (7.A.1) by (7.A.2), taking logarithm of both sides and collecting terms lead to:

$$\ln e_{it} - \ln y_{it} + \ln p_{it}^y = \sigma_i^Y (\ln p_{it}^y - \ln p_{it}^e) + (\sigma_i^Y - 1)\ln(A_{it}^Y / A_{it-1}^Y). \tag{7.A.3}$$

where e_{it} is the index (the growth rate plus one) of demand for energy in sector i at time t, y_{it} is the index (the growth rate plus one) of sector i's output value (not physical amount), p_{it}^y and p_{it}^e are, respectively, the price indexes of product i and energy. From (7.A.3), the change of energy use per unit of output is attributed to two factors: price-induced and non-price-induced changes.

Table 7.A   Evolution of sector classification in Chinese statistics

Pre-1985 classification	New classification (post-1993)	1997 I/O sectors
Agriculture	Agriculture, forestry, animal husbandry, fishery and water conservancy	1–5
Metallurgical industry	Ferrous metal mining and processing;	9
	Nonferrous metal mining and processing;	10
	Ferrous metal smelting and pressing;	55–58
	Nonferrous metal smelting and pressing	59, 60
Power industry	Electricity, steam and hot water production and supply	86, 87
Coal & coking industry	Coal mining and processing;	6
	Gas production and supply	88
Petroleum industry	Crude oil and natural gas extraction;	7, 8
	Petroleum processing and coking	36, 37
Chemical industry	Raw chemical materials and chemical products;	38–43
	Medical and pharmaceutical products;	44
	Chemical fibres;	45
	Rubber products;	46
	Plastic products	47
Machinery	Ordinary machinery;	62–64
	Equipment for special purposes;	65–66
	Transportation equipment;	67–72
	Electric equipment and machinery;	73–75
	Electronic and telecommunication equipment;	76–79
	Instruments, meters, cultural and office machinery;	80, 81
	Other manufacturing industry;	84
	Metal products	61
Building materials	Non-metal minerals mining and dressing	11, 12(part)
	Non-metal mineral products	48–54
Forestry industry	Timber and bamboo logging and transportation;	13
	Timber processing, bamboo, cane, palm fibre and straw products	30
Food processing	Food processing;	14–17
	Food production;	18
	Beverage;	19, 20
	Tobacco processing	21
Textile	Textile	22–27
Tailoring	Garments and other fibre products	28
Leather	Leather, furs, down and related products	29
Paper industry	Papermaking and paper products	32
Cultural, educational handicraft articles	Printing and record medium reproduction	33
	Cultural, educational and sports articles	34, 35 83
Other industry	Other minerals mining and dressing	12 (part)
	Tap water production and supply	89
	Furniture manufacturing	31 82
Construction	Construction	90
Transportation and services	Transportation, storage, postal and telecommunications services	91–99, 102–105
	Wholesale, retail trade and catering services	100, 101
Others	Others	106–124

To capture the autonomous change, it is assumed that the shifter A_{it}^Y has the form $\overline{A_i}^Y e^{\lambda_i t}$, where λ is the autonomous change ratio. Therefore eqn. (7.A.3) becomes

$$\ln e_{it} - \ln y_{it} + \ln p_{it}^y = \sigma_i^Y (\ln p_{it}^y - \ln p_{it}^e) + (\sigma_i^Y - 1)\lambda_i .$$

It can be used to estimate the elasticity of substitution between labour, energy, capital and other materials, and the AEEI or more precisely, the autonomous change in the shifter. The results are reported in Table 7.6.

7.B   Impact of Linking Climate Change to Production

This section compares the results of considering the direct impact of climate change on production (denoted 'with feedback') with the results of not considering the impact (denoted 'without feedback'). As discussed in Chapter 6, it is assumed that global warming adversely affects the production of sector 7 (agriculture, fishing and hunting). The scenario M3 is chosen to make such a comparison based on the following considerations. First, as discussed in this chapter, the results of all eight scenarios are very close during the period between 2000 and 2020, so that it will not make much difference to choose from one of these scenarios. Second, referring to the other long-run projections in the literature, the projected emission of M3 is one of the closest projections. Third, the underlying assumptions seem reasonable. Zero AEEI assumption is consistent with the findings of historical energy conservation as discussed in Appendix 7.A. Low population growth could be achieved if China sticks to the current strict 'one-child' policy. Although the moderate productivity growth assumption seems conservative to some people, it is consistent with the findings in the literature (Table 7.4).

As expected, the output level of sector 7 differs quite significantly between these two treatments, however, the degree of these effects is different across regions (Figure 7.A). China's agricultural output projection changes the most: the output predicted by the model with feedback will be 13.4, 39.4 and 84.6 percent lower than that by the model without feedback in 2020, 2050 and 2100, respectively. The changes in the US's output projections are the lowest: the output is about 57 percent of the level without feedback effect in 2100. The change in the rest of the world is close to that of the US: the output is about 53 percent of the 'without feedback' level in 2100.

The changes in the total output projections follow a similar pattern but to a smaller extent than the agricultural output projections (Figure 7.B). This is an understandable result if other sectors are not directly affected. Moreover, as the agricultural sector is adversely affected by global warming, resources move to other sectors where the marginal returns are higher, thus boosting

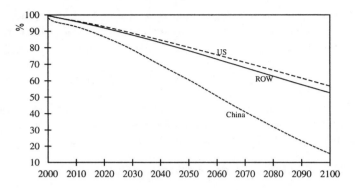

Source: G-Cubed-T simulation.

Figure 7.A   Agricultural output relative to 'without feedback' level

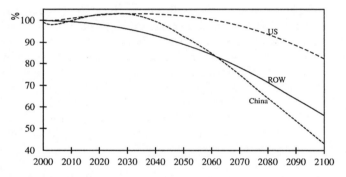

Source: G-Cubed-T simulation.

Figure 7.B   Total output relative to 'without feedback' level

other sectors. In fact, the resource relocation effects are so high for China and the US that the total output level will be slightly higher for a while than that without considering the feedback effect of climate change.

Because of the expansion of other sectors, a paradoxical result is derived: considering the adverse effect of global warming may even increase the projected carbon emissions during a certain period of time (Figure 7.C)! This could be explained by looking at the different patterns of China and the US emissions which in effect come from the fact that the share of agricultural output in total output differs for regions. China is affected the most because its agricultural share is the highest. At the beginning, the shares are 12.5 and 2.6 percent for China and the US, respectively. Because the agricultural

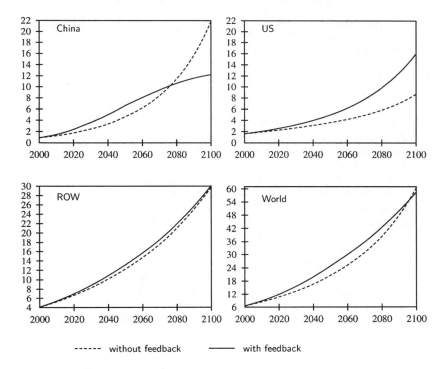

----- without feedback ——— with feedback

Source: G-Cubed-T simulation.

Figure 7.C Carbon emissions with and without feedback (GtC)

sector is relatively important in the Chinese economy, China eventually reduces its emissions to prevent the agricultural sector from further deterioration. On the other hand, agricultural output accounts for only a very small part of the US's total output, and boosting of other sectors leads to higher CO_2 emissions.

NOTES

1. This cross country comparison of broad energy efficiency might be inappropriate because the resource endowment differs significantly across countries. However, it still gives some rough idea about the gaps between China and other countries. A more appropriate approach would be the direct comparison of physical output level per unit of energy use for specific products. This comparison shows that China's factories typically use 20 percent more energy to produce chemicals, building materials and electricity, and 40 percent more energy to produce iron

and steel than their counterparts in industrialised countries. For a collection of such comparisons, see Zhang (1998a, Section 3.5).

2. The Chinese government has planned to supply 1.40 billion tons for the year 2000 in its Ten Year's Social and Economic Development Strategy and the Eighth Five-Year Plan. Assuming the economy growing at 8 percent per annum, coal prices rising 4 percent per annum and the share of heavy industry's output in national income declining 1 percent per annum between 1996 and 2000, Chan and Lee (1997) forecasted the coal demand would be 1.48 billion tons, 5.7 percent higher than the official supply target.

3. This is the second review undertaken by the IPCC. The first was conducted to evaluate the IPCC Scenarios 1992 (IS92) set of scenarios in comparison to other GHG emissions scenarios found in the literature (Alcamo et al. 1995).

4. These models are: Asian Pacific Integrated Model (AIM) from the National Institute of Environmental Studies in Japan (Morita et al. 1994); Atmospheric Stabilization Framework Model (ASF) from ICF Consulting in the USA (Lashof and Tirpak 1990; Pepper et al. 1992, 1998; Sankovski et al. 2000); Integrated Model to Assess the Greenhouse Effect (IMAGE) from the National Institute for Public Health and Environmental Hygiene (Alcamo et al. 1998; de Vries et al. 1994, 1999, 2000) in connection with the Dutch Bureau for Economic Policy Analysis WorldScan model (de Jong and Zalm 1991); Multiregional Approach for Resource and Industry Allocation (MARIA) from the Science University of Tokyo in Japan (Mori and Takahashi 1999; Mori 2000); Model for Energy Supply Strategy Alternatives and their General Environmental Impact (MESSAGE) from the International Institute of Applied Systems Analysis (IIASA) in Austria (Messner and Strubegger 1995: Riahi and Roehrl 2000); and Mini Climate Assessment Model (MiniCAM) from the Pacific Northwest National Laboratory (PNNL) in the USA (Edmonds et al. 1994, 1996a, 1996b).

5. This database was developed for the IPCC Special Report on Emission Scenarios. The main sources of data are from the International Energy Workshop Poll (Manne and Schrattenholzer 1995, 1996, 1997), Energy Modeling Forum (for example, Weyant 1993), and previous database for the IPCC Supplement Report (Alcamo et al. 1995) as well as direct individual contact.

    The number of available Chinese scenarios in the database is different from that reported in IPCC SRES (Nakićenović and Swart 2000, Table 2–1) as SRES used the Database version 0.1.

6. If considering two possible situations for each driving force in each country region, there will be $(2^3)^3 = 512$ scenarios. If considering three possibilities for each factor, the number of scenarios will be 19 683!

7. These scenarios typically represent possible ranges of individual factors. However, they are not assumed to be associated with higher probabilities.

8. The current figure is about 2.5 percent.

8.   Policy Options of Carbon Dioxide Emissions Control in China

This chapter compares the effects of different climate change policy targets and instruments on the Chinese economy using the G-Cubed-T model developed in Chapter 6. The simulation results of policy options are mainly represented as the deviation from the baseline projections.

Eight scenarios for baseline projections were presented in the previous chapter. However, to save space, only one scenario – the M3 scenario assuming low population growth, medium productivity growth and zero AEEI – will be used for the analysis. As shown in Chapter 7, the eight scenarios produce very close CO_2 emissions during the period to 2020, so, over this time horizon, it will not make much difference to choose one from those scenarios. With regard to long-term projections, M3 is closest to the projections in the literature, although as discussed in Chapter 7, caution should be exercised when interpreting them. Moreover, the underlying assumptions of M3 seem reasonable. The zero AEEI assumption is consistent with the findings of historical energy conservation as discussed in Appendix 7.A. Low population growth could be achieved if China sticks to the current strict 'one child' policy. Although the moderate productivity growth assumption seems conservative to some, it is consistent with the findings in the literature (Table 7.4).

This chapter is organised as follows. The next section discusses possible CO_2 emission targets that China could adopt. The discussion focuses on the impact of these targets on China's economic development and the interaction between regions. It is followed by the analysis of policy instruments – uniform international emission tax, differential tax and emission trading – for achieving the targets. It will be shown that, as predicted by the theoretical analysis, different instruments have different outcomes, and a differential emission tax produces a better outcome for China than a uniform tax.

8.1   POLICY TARGETS

Although developing countries have not been specifically required to set CO_2

emission targets in the international negotiation, discussion of such targets is not rare in the literature. As discussed in Chapter 5, setting such targets is a sensitive issue. Developing countries wish to negotiate a relaxing term so that their economic development will not be hindered. For example, Gupta and Bhandari (2000) argue that targets set on the basis of per capita emissions are the most equitable, effective and implementable.

As regards China, the discussion has focused on the measures of achieving some pre-determined targets rather than on how to determine such targets. For example, using a dynamic computable general equilibrium model of the Chinese economy with a sub-model of the health effects of burning fossil fuel, Garbaccio et al. (2001) estimate the required level of a carbon tax that reduces carbon emissions from the base case by 10 percent in each year. Rose et al. (1996) simulate several abatement strategies to achieve a 20 percent reduction in year 2000 baseline CO_2 emissions in China.[1] Zhang (2000a) implicitly suggests some possible targets by listing the following strategies at the climate change negotiations for China in ascending order of stringency. First, China could regard its active participation in CDM as meaningful participation. Second, China could commit demonstrable efforts towards slowing its greenhouse gas emissions growth at some point between the first commitment period and 2020. Third, China could make voluntary commitments to specific policies and measures to limit greenhouse gas emissions at some point between the first commitment period and 2020. Such policies and measures might include abolishing energy subsidies, improving the efficiency of energy use, promoting renewable energies, and increasing the R&D spending on developing environmentally sound coal technologies. Fourth, China could voluntarily commit to total energy consumption or total greenhouse gas emissions per unit of GDP at some point around or beyond 2020. Fifth, China could make a voluntary commitment to an emission cap on a particular sector at some point around or beyond 2020. Finally, the bottom line for China is to offer a combination of a targeted carbon intensity level with an emission cap on a particular sector at some point around or beyond 2020.

From the above discussion, there are several ways that the target could be set. First, the target could be set in the form of a cap, that is, each country is required to stabilise its emissions at a certain level. In turn, this cap will be determined or negotiated according to certain principles. As one extreme, it could be determined according to the current emission levels. However, this would be strongly opposed by the developing countries because such targets would impose a very heavy burden on them. For example, suppose the target is to stabilise the emissions at the year 2000 level. Under the most conservative scenario (M3) as discussed in Chapter 7, China would have to cut its emissions by 40.4 percent in 2010, and by 63.4 percent in 2020. On the other hand, the corresponding figures for the US would be 22.0 percent and 37.7 percent. This case will be analysed in the experiment C1.

At another extreme, the cap could be set in terms of per capita emissions. The base year CO_2 emissions from fuel combustion in the United States is 4 840 483 gigagrams (1320.13 MtC). The US agreed to a target of 93 percent of the base year emissions in the commitment period (2008 to 2012) (Table 8.1). Suppose this target is achieved at the end of the commitment period (2012). By that time, the US population will be 304.764 million (US Bureau of the Census 2000c). This means the per capita carbon emissions would be 14.771 megagrams (4.028 tc). If applying this standard and using the current Chinese population level in order not to encourage population growth, China would be allowed to emit 5115.56 Mtc per year. According to the baseline projections presented in the previous chapter, China would reach this cap around year 2033–34 (R1) to year 2040–41 (M3). This case will be analysed in the experiment C2.

Alternatively, the cap could be set according to the principle of cost sharing. That is, the target could be set such that it has the same impact on the economy (same reduction in output level) for each country. Two experiments will be conducted in this regard. The first one supposes that the US will stabilise its emissions at the year 2000 level (C3) and the second supposes that the US will stabilise its emissions at the Kyoto target after year 2012 (C4). China will be set a target such that its reduction in production will be in line with that of the US in the two situations.

The target may take the form of a percentage reduction in emissions, that is, each country commits to the same or similar percentage reduction relative to its baseline emission level. Although some studies discuss emission control in this way, it might not be practical as it is set on a hypothetical basis.[2] Three experiments will be conducted: 5 percent (P1), 10 percent (P2) and 20 percent (P3) reduction from baseline emission level. These experiments are summarised in Table 8.2. Results from these experiments are reported in Figures 8.1–8.3.

Among these experiments, stabilising emissions at 2000 level (C1) has the most severe impact on China's economy. The output level will decrease more than 8 percent from the baseline (M3) level around the year 2030. As expected, setting the cap according to per capita emissions at the US level is a more favourable option. The output level increases slightly[3] until 2043 when the emission is capped. After that, it declines rapidly, but to a lesser extent than C1 – the deviation from baseline level is less than 5.5 percent (Panel (a), Figure 8.1).

Although setting a target in per capita terms has strong grounds, as argued by Gupta and Bhandari (2000), the international community will not let China stay away from emission control for so long a period. In this case, cost

Table 8.1 CO_2 emission target under Kyoto Protocol and implied per capita emissions[a]

Country	Base year emissions (gigagram)	Target % of base year	Population (million) 2010	Population (million) 2015	Per capita emissions (t) 2010	Per capita emissions (t) 2015
Australia	265 289	108	20.4	21.5	14.021	13.326
Austria	46 685	92	8.2	8.0	5.249	5.369
Belgium	104 190	92	10.1	10.3	9.513	9.306
Bulgaria	95 495	92	7.9	7.3	11.115	12.035
Canada	415 690	94	34.3	33.5	11.399	11.664
Croatia	n.a.	95	4.6	4.3	n.a.	n.a.
Czech Republic	160 073	92	10.5	9.9	14.082	14.875
Denmark	51 516	92	5.5	5.4	8.691	8.777
Estonia	37 184	92	1.3	1.3	25.741	26.315
Finland	53 889	92	5.2	5.3	9.590	9.354
France	357 723	92	59.7	61.1	5.517	5.386
Germany	986 832	92	81.0	79.4	11.207	11.434
Greece	77 292	92	11.0	10.3	6.474	6.904
Hungary	80 089	94	10.0	9.4	7.556	8.009
Iceland	1 674	110	0.3	n.a.	6.416	n.a.
Ireland	29 577	92	3.8	4.3	7.142	6.328
Italy	398 320	92	55.3	54.8	6.627	6.687
Japan	1052 964	94	127.1	124.3	7.785	7.963
Latvia	24 209	92	2.2	2.2	10.350	10.124
Liechtenstein	n.a.	92	n.a.	n.a.	n.a.	n.a.
Lithuania	37 332	92	3.5	3.6	9.782	9.540
Luxembourg	12 133	92	0.5	n.a.	24.587	n.a.
Monaco	106	92	n.a.	n.a.	n.a.	n.a.
Netherlands	159 040	92	16.2	16.8	9.009	8.709
New Zealand	22 397	100	4.0	4.2	5.559	5.333
Norway	26 370	101	4.6	4.7	5.829	5.667
Poland	462 998	94	39.9	38.8	10.900	11.217
Portugal	39 020	92	9.6	9.9	3.723	3.626
Romania	185 575	92	22.3	21.3	7.660	8.015
Russian Federation	2 298 900	100	143.9	134.5	15.974	17.092
Slovakia	56 691	92	5.6	5.4	9.254	9.658
Slovenia	13 294	92	2.0	1.9	6.190	6.437
Spain	205 673	92	39.2	38.1	4.830	4.966
Sweden	51 328	92	9.1	8.7	5.181	5.428
Switzerland	39 673	92	7.4	7.1	4.965	5.141
Ukraine	672 075	100	47.6	44.0	14.122	15.274
United Kingdom	557 666	92	58.0	59.8	8.842	8.579
United States	4 840 483	93	299.9	312.3	15.012	14.416
Total	13 919 445	94.7[b]	1167.0	1159.4	11.296	11.370

Notes:
a. CO_2 emissions from fuel combustion.
b.   Base year emissions weighted average.
n.a.   Not available.

Sources: Kyoto Protocol; 2010 population from the US Bureau of the Census (1999); 2015 population of the United States from US Bureau of the Census (2000b), of other countries from World Bank (2000).

Table 8.2   Target options for China's CO_2 emission control

Form	Targets	Code
Cap	Stabilised at year 2000 level	C1
	Per capita emission at the US level (Kyoto target)	C2
	Same impact as the US whose emissions stabilised at year 2000 level	C3
	Same impact as the US whose emissions stabilised at the Kyoto target after year 2012	C4
Percentage	5% reduction in baseline level	P1
	10% reduction in baseline level	P2
	20% reduction in baseline level	P3

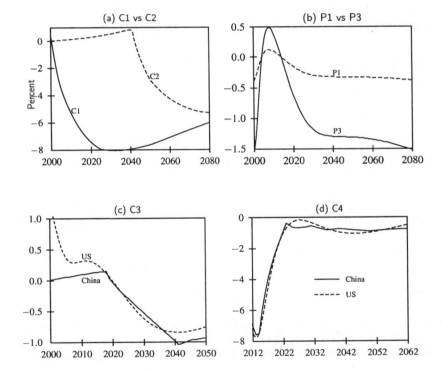

Source: G-Cubed-T simulation.

Figure 8.1   Changes in China's output level

sharing may be a better approach. Panels (c) and (d) of Figure 8.1 contrast
the output losses of China against those of the US under certain targets. Panel

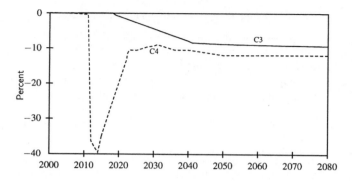

Source: G-Cubed-T simulation.

Figure 8.2   Reduction in China's emissions from baseline level

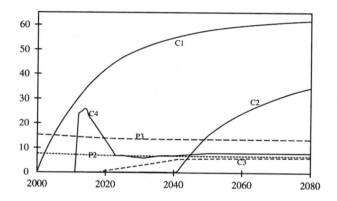

Source: G-Cubed-T simulation.

Figure 8.3   Required carbon tax rates for China (US$)

(c) shows that the US stabilises its emissions at the level of year 2000. As the growth rate of CO_2 emissions in the US is relatively small, the required emission control is not very strict in the early days, and because the resources are attracted from the rest of the world, the US actually boosts its output slightly. If China argues that its CO_2 emissions control target can be set such that its economic loss is no larger than that of the US, it will start to control its emissions around 2019, and then gradually increase the control strength such that the reduction from baseline emissions will be about 8.4 percent around 2040. That reduction will stay virtually the same – from 8.4 to 9.3 percent – over a longer period (Figure 8.2).[4]

Panel (d) of Figure 8.1 shows a similar idea. But this time it is assumed the US will meet its Kyoto obligation in 2012 but not do anything before that time. That is why there is an abrupt and severe decline in output level after 2012.[5] In this case, China would have to cut emissions by almost 40 percent in 2012, but would lessen the control to about 11 percent by around 2023 (Figure 8.2). If a smarter strategy were taken by the US to meet the Kyoto target, this abrupt and severe control could be avoided. The corresponding target for China would be to gradually strengthen its control on emissions.

The required carbon tax rates for China to meet these targets are reported in Figure 8.3. The order of tax rates is in line with the strength of CO_2 emission control targets and therefore the economic losses. Concentrating on the period before 2040, C1 has the strictest target and requires the highest carbon tax. On the other hand, C2 represents the most relaxing target – with no actions necessary before 2040, that is, the tax rate is virtually zero. In between these two extremes are, in order of strength, P3, P2 and C3. If C4 could be done in a smooth way, it could lie between P3 and P2 in terms of required tax rate.

As discussed in Chapter 5, China and other developing countries set economic development as their first priority and argue that the industrialised countries have contributed the most to the global CO_2 stock and thus have the responsibility and ability to rigorously control their emissions. From this stance, China can not adopt a target that would hinder its economic growth more severely than the developed countries. Therefore, it could be concluded from the above experiments that the bottom line for China would be a target close to C3 and/or C4 if early actions were taken to smooth the path. That is, China would commence the control on CO_2 emissions between the end of the first commitment period and 2020 and gradually increase the extent of emission cut to around 10 percent in 2040. Consequently, it would start to impose a carbon tax between 2012 and 2020 and gradually increase the rate to about US$5–7 per tce in 2040. This kind of target is broadly in line with the suggestion by Zhang (2000a).

Another conclusion drawn from the above analysis is the need for early action. The required cut in the US's emissions in 2012 of C3 (stabilising at year 2000 level) and C4 (meeting Kyoto obligation) are close; however, delaying the control activity until 2012 would bring about a much more severe loss to the economy (comparing panels (c) and (d) in Figure 8.1).

8.2 UNIFORM TAXES VS. DIFFERENTIAL TAXES

This section discusses the effect of a carbon tax system. First, a uniform international carbon tax is analysed and it is found that this has different impacts on China and other countries and that a differential tax system is needed, which is in line with the discussion in Chapter 5 and the previous section. Second, the discussion is brought into the domestic arena to ask whether a differential tax system is justified in domestic policy design. It is found that a uniform domestic tax is preferred because the domestic economy is integrated.

8.2.1 Impact of a Uniform International Carbon Tax

It is here assumed that a uniform carbon tax of US$10 per tce will be imposed from 2010.[6] The simulation results generated by G-Cubed-T are reported in Table 8.3 and Figures 8.4 and 8.5.

Table 8.3   Effects of a uniform carbon tax of US$10/tce[*]

Variable	China		USA		ROW	
	2010	2015	2010	2015	2010	2015
Carbon emissions	-15.05	-15.08	-0.96	-0.97	-0.94	-0.96
World emissions	-4.72	-4.76	-4.72	-4.76	-4.72	-4.76
Total output	-2.85	-2.06	-0.14	0.01	-0.43	-0.22
Total wealth	-12.05	-6.74	0.73	2.26	-1.61	-0.49
Total private consumption	-0.49	-0.42	-0.02	0.01	-0.10	-0.09
Total saving	-0.03	0.02	0.10	0.16	-0.05	0.05
Total investment	-0.05	0.14	0.10	0.17	-0.05	0.05
Current account	0.04	0.05	0.01	0.01	-0.01	-0.01
Producer price index	1.24	0.84	0.10	-0.02	0.26	0.12
Consumer price index	0.59	0.22	0.00	-0.12	0.21	0.07

Note: [*]The tax, in 1999 US dollars, is imposed from 2010 onwards. The effects are expressed as the percentage change from the baseline.

Source: G-Cubed-T simulation.

With this tax, China's carbon emissions drop by 15 percent, while emissions from the United States and the rest of the world are reduced by less than 1 percent. Consequently, world emissions decline by about 5 percent (Figure 8.4). This is often presented as evidence to justify permit trading. Because a small amount of carbon tax induces a large amount of reduction in emissions in China, or developing countries by and large, emission trading is said to be a cost-efficient way to control CO_2 emissions.

However, the US$10 carbon tax only measures the direct costs of controlling emissions. Total domestic output declines by 2.85 percent in China, but only by 0.14 percent and 0.43 percent, respectively, in the United States and the rest of the world.[7] Moreover, the total wealth of Chinese people drops by 12.05 percent in the first year of implementing the tax. In

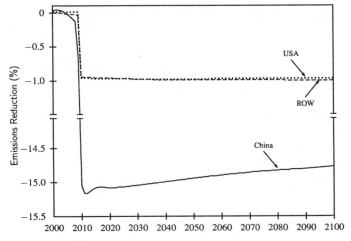

Source: G-Cubed-T simulation.

Figure 8.4   Emissions reduction caused by a uniform tax of US$10 per tce

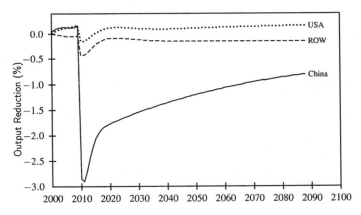

Source: G-Cubed-T simulation.

Figure 8.5   Output reduction caused by a uniform tax of US$10 per tce

contrast, total wealth decreases by only 1.61 percent in the ROW, and even increases by 0.73 percent in the US (Figure 8.6). This imbalance in the economic impact of a uniform carbon tax is mainly due to the fact that the world market is not fully integrated. This uniform tax causes different relative prices (of emission control) in different countries, which can be seen from the change in price indices. The producer price index increases by more

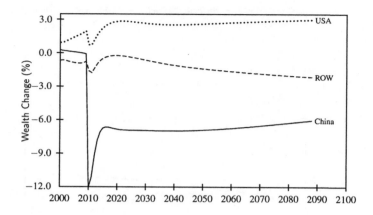

Source: G-Cubed-T simulation.

Figure 8.6   Wealth changes caused by a uniform tax of US$10 per tce

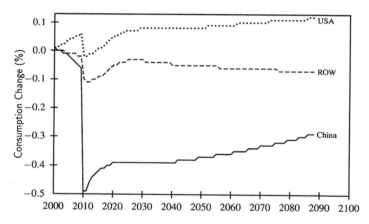

Source: G-Cubed-T simulation.

Figure 8.7   Consumption changes caused by a uniform tax of US$10 per tce

than 1 point in China, but only by 0.1 point in the US and 0.26 point in the ROW. Therefore, a uniform tax damages the Chinese economy more severely than others.

8.2.2 How About a Tax on a Particular Sector?

Zhang (2000a) suggests that, in response to the pressure from developed countries, China could make a demonstrative effort in one particular sector. It is an attractive suggestion because it could limit the adverse effect of carbon emission control on growth to a specific amount. And it seems a natural extension and application of the idea of a differentiated tax system to the domestic context. However, as the income transfer is not, or is not assumed to be, restricted within the boundary of one nation, and people's preference and firms' technology do not differ, this appeal is not in line with the principle of the differentiated tax proposal. In fact, because it adds further distortions to the economy it may further deteriorate the adverse effect on growth. The following experiment demonstrates this argument.

Suppose China proposes a 10 percent rise in its tax on coal from 2010. This measure would bring the CO_2 emissions down by about 6.5 percent from the baseline (Figure 8.8). An alternative way to achieve the same amount of reduction in emissions is to adopt a uniform carbon tax. G-Cubed-T shows that it would require a carbon tax of US$4.3 per tce (Figure 8.9).

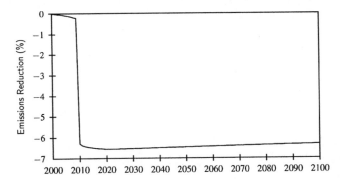

Source: G-Cubed-T simulation.

Figure 8.8   Emissions reduction of 10 percent increase in coal tax

Although both policies can achieve the same reduction of CO_2 emissions, their effects on output level are different. Despite the fact that its initial impact on output is slightly larger than a 10 percent tax increase in coal production (-1.16 percent versus -1.09 percent), a uniform carbon tax results in a lower reduction in output level over a long period between 2013 and 2098 (Figure 8.10).

Because coal constitutes a very high proportion of China's energy structure, a tax on coal production is closer to a uniform carbon tax than other energy taxes. In other words, the difference in output between a carbon tax and taxes in other energy sectors would be larger for a similar cut in emissions.

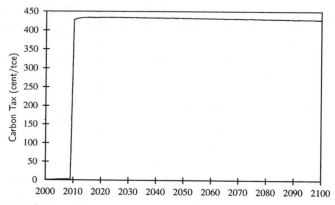

Source: G-Cubed-T simulation.

Figure 8.9 Carbon tax to achieve emissions reduction of 10 percent increase in coal tax

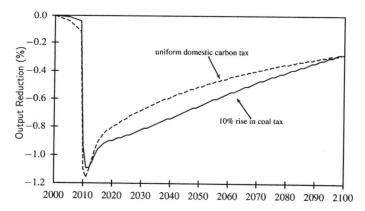

Source: G-Cubed-T simulation.

Figure 8.10 Output deviation from baseline

8.3 EMISSION PERMIT TRADING

The previous sections focus on the use of carbon taxes. This section discusses the issue of emission permit trading and compares it with emission taxes. As no uncertainty and no domestic distribution and transfers are considered in the model, the tax rate is virtually the permit price in the domestic market. Therefore, the discussion will concentrate on international trading. Moreover, as the current model is highly aggregated, with only three country regions included, a full discussion of emission trading is impractical and inaccurate. Rather, the analysis focuses on the examination of previous theoretical arguments, especially those made in Chapter 5. To that end, two sets of stylised experiments are conducted (Table 8.4).

Table 8.4   Emission trading experiments

Experiment	2000–09	2010–20	2021 onwards
1	no control	CO$_2$ emission allocation: USA: 1598.44mtc; ROW: 4118.37mtc; China: 1466.02mtc	an emission tax same as previous year's permit price or emission tax imposed
2	no control	CO$_2$ emission allocation: USA: 1227.72mtc; ROW: 4118.37mtc; China: 2386.78mtc	an emission tax same as previous year's permit price or emission tax imposed

Both experiments try to stabilise CO$_2$ emissions at a certain level over the period between 2010 and 2020,[8] but differ in the specific level of emission stabilisation. In the first experiment, the USA and the ROW are allocated permits equivalent to their emissions at the year 2000 level, while China is allocated permits equivalent to the year 2010 level. In the second experiment, the USA is assigned a harder target than in the first one, meeting the Kyoto requirement – stabilising its emissions 7 percent lower than the base year level. On the other hand, China is given a more favourable deal, being allocated permits equivalent to its projected emissions in 2020. The rest of the world has the same target or emission allocation as that in the first experiment. Three instruments – an emission trading system, a uniform international emission tax and a decentralised differential emission tax – are tested to obtain these targets in each experiment. The differential emission tax is different from that discussed in Chapter 5 in the sense that it does not intend to maximise the world welfare, but simply to induce each country to meet its emission control target. The results of these experiments are reported in Tables 8.5–8.6 and Figures 8.11–8.13.

The first observation from these results is that an emission tax and an emission trading system are not equivalent. From Table 8.5, it can be seen that permit prices are slightly higher than the tax rates under a uniform tax system although both systems try to obtain the same emission control target. The difference arises from income transfers associated with an emission trading system. China's income from permits sales boosts the economy, partly

Table 8.5   Emission permit prices and tax rates (US$)

Year	Experiment 1					Experiment 2				
	Permit Price	Uniform Tax	Differential Tax			Permit Price	Uniform Tax	Differential Tax		
			China	USA	ROW			China	USA	ROW
2010	31.29	31.03	0.00	40.74	50.81	21.47	21.03	0.00	72.46	51.08
2011	35.11	34.82	3.80	43.69	54.98	25.62	25.13	0.00	74.44	55.28
2012	38.97	38.66	7.57	46.55	59.23	29.74	29.23	0.00	76.56	59.53
2013	42.79	42.49	11.30	49.45	63.45	33.84	33.29	0.00	78.73	63.74
2014	46.59	46.25	15.08	52.27	67.62	37.83	37.28	0.00	80.81	67.86
2015	50.25	49.90	18.83	54.99	71.56	41.73	41.15	0.00	82.82	71.80
2016	53.82	53.47	22.57	57.65	75.42	45.53	44.93	0.00	84.78	75.60
2017	57.31	56.96	26.30	60.21	79.12	49.23	48.63	0.00	86.68	79.27
2018	60.71	60.36	30.03	62.68	82.70	52.84	52.26	0.00	88.51	82.81
2019	64.04	63.70	33.75	65.09	86.16	56.36	55.81	0.00	90.21	86.23
2020	67.24	66.92	37.45	67.40	89.36	59.78	59.23	0.33	91.95	89.42

Source: G-Cubed-T simulation.

Table 8.6   Emission permit trade volume (mtc) and revenue (US$ billion)[*]

Year	Experiment 1				Experiment 2			
	China		USA		China		USA	
	Volume	Revenue	Volume	Revenue	Volume	Revenue	Volume	Revenue
2010	586.46	18.35	-108.16	-3.38	1 307.08	28.06	-586.18	-12.59
2011	605.07	21.24	-100.70	-3.54	1 324.46	33.93	-578.00	-14.81
2012	621.13	24.21	-91.96	-3.58	1 339.79	39.85	-568.94	-16.92
2013	635.74	27.20	-82.41	-3.53	1 354.80	45.85	-558.62	-18.90
2014	650.62	30.31	-71.60	-3.34	1 368.47	51.77	-548.01	-20.73
2015	663.75	33.35	-60.82	-3.06	1 381.51	57.65	-536.75	-22.40
2016	676.06	36.39	-49.62	-2.67	1 393.68	63.45	-525.12	-23.91
2017	687.50	39.40	-37.83	-2.17	1 404.76	69.16	-513.14	-25.26
2018	697.59	42.35	-25.60	-1.55	1 414.80	74.76	-500.69	-26.46
2019	706.55	45.25	-12.65	-0.81	1 423.65	80.24	-487.77	-27.49
2020	712.90	47.94	0.36	0.02	1 431.01	85.55	-474.35	-28.36

Note: [*]Positive (negative) figures are for sale (purchase) of CO_2 emission permits.

Source: G-Cubed-T simulation.

offsetting the contracting effect of an emission tax (permit price). Therefore a higher permit price is needed to obtain the same control target.

As discussed in Chapter 5 and the previous section of this chapter, a differential emission tax system is better for China than a uniform tax system, which can be seen from Figure 8.11. The dashed lines depicting the relationship between these two taxes lie above zero, indicating that a differential tax system generates higher wealth, private consumption and gross national product (GNP) than a uniform tax system.

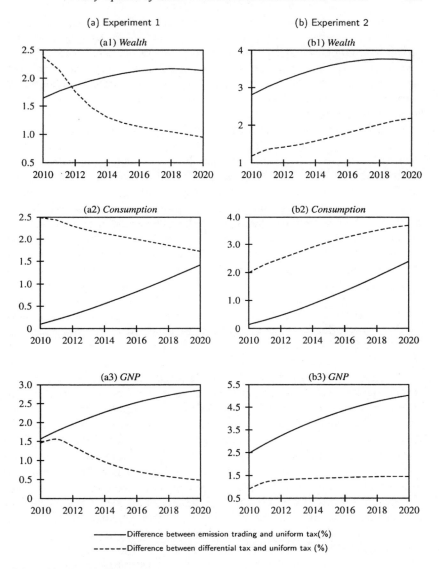

(a) Experiment 1   (b) Experiment 2

(a1) *Wealth*   (b1) *Wealth*

(a2) *Consumption*   (b2) *Consumption*

(a3) *GNP*   (b3) *GNP*

———Difference between emission trading and uniform tax(%)

-----Difference between differential tax and uniform tax (%)

Source: G-Cubed-T simulation.

Figure 8.11   Effects on China of different policy instruments (percentage points above/below [+/–] uniform tax)

A uniform emission tax is also worse than an emission trading system, which can be evidenced by Figure 8.11. The solid lines depicting the relationship between the emission trade and the uniform tax also lie above zero, indicating that the emission trading system produces higher wealth, private consumption and GNP than the uniform tax system. Although the permit price is slightly higher than the emission tax rate, revenues from selling permits boost the economy, leading to higher welfare as indicated by consumption and GNP. In sum, a uniform emission tax is the worst instrument for China among the three instruments discussed.

In contrast, an emission trading system is the best instrument for China. As shown in Figure 8.11, solid lines lie above dashed lines in panels (a1), (b1), (a3) and (b3), indicating that the emission trading generates higher wealth and GNP for China than the differential tax system. Although the wealth is higher under an emission trading system, the private consumption is smaller (solid lines in a2 and b2 of Figure 8.11 lie below dashed lines), because of the assumption of backward-looking household behaviour. Private consumption is determined by two factors: present value of future wealth and the current income (see equation 6.13 in Chapter 6). Net government transfer is a part of the current income (equation 6.14 in Chapter 6) and is exogenously fixed in current experiments. That is, the revenue of permit sales goes into the government's pockets and is not transferred to the household accordingly. In addition, other income components are depressed by the higher effective emission tax rate as indicated by the higher permit price. Consequently private consumption is less under the emission trading regime than under the differential tax regime. However, as private consumption does not capture the effect of the increase in government revenue and household wealth, it is not a good indicator for welfare in this case.[9] A better one would be the sum of private and public consumption as expressed by equation (6.11) in Chapter 6. GNP is such an indicator because it includes private and government consumptions and investment.

However, the difference in GNP between the emission trading and the differential tax is not very great, being less than 2.5 percentage points in experiment 1 and less than 3.5 percentage points in experiment 2. There are two reasons for this. First, the regions in the model are highly aggregated, so the potential from emission trading is lessened. Second, after 2020, China is given a more favourable treatment – the tax rate imposed after 2020 is smaller under the differential tax regime than under the emission trading or uniform tax regimes (see Tables 8.4 and 8.5).[10] Therefore, caution should be exercised when interpreting the results.

Consequently, the estimated emission trading volumes and revenues may be smaller than those predicted by a more disaggregated model. However, these 'conservative' estimates still show that a large amount of cash flows. In experiment 1, China's emission permit sales revenue accounts for 1.1 to 1.7 percent of GDP, and in experiment 2, the corresponding figures are 1.6 to 3.1

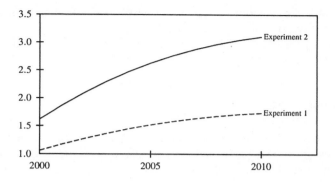

Source: G-Cubed-T simulation.

Figure 8.12   Share of permit sales revenue in China's GDP (%)

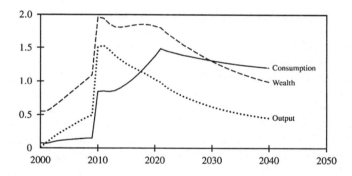

Source: G-Cubed-T simulation.

*Figure 8.13   Experiment 1 versus experiment 2 under emission trading
(percentage points of experiment 2 above experiment 1)*

percent of GDP (Figure 8.12). The US's trade deficit was US$371 billion in 2000 (Office of the US Trade Representative 2001). A Kyoto-like arrangement (experiment 2) would add about 4–8 percent more to the deficit. Considering the Sino–US trade relationship, the payment for purchasing permits would be equivalent to one sixth to one third of the current US deficit with China.[11] Clearly it is not a desirable outcome for the US.

Finally, needless to say, China is better off in experiment 2 than in experiment 1 because it is allocated a larger number of emission permits. As shown in Figure 8.13, China has higher private consumption, wealth and output in experiment 2 than in experiment 1.

In a word, the experiment results presented in this section confirm the findings of theoretical analysis in Chapter 5. An emission trading system is the best policy for China and a differential emission tax is a better choice for China than a uniform tax.

8.4   CONCLUSION

This chapter discusses the climate change policy arrangement for China, which consists of two parts: setting a proper policy target and choosing efficient instruments to meet the target. As regards the first components of policy design, several alternative options for a CO_2 emission control target in China have been examined. These options are designed according to certain principles, such as stabilising emissions at year 2000 level, reducing emissions by a certain percentage from baseline, and setting the emission cap according to principles of equal per capita emissions (the cap is calculated based on the population and a standard of per capita emissions which is set as the same as that of the US at one point in time), or sharing economic losses (the target will be set such that the percentage change in output level would be the same for both China and the US). As expected, the simulation shows that stabilising emissions at the year 2000 level has the most severe impact on the Chinese economy, with the output level reduced by more than 8 percent. Clearly China will not accept such a target. On the other hand, a target set according to the equal per capita emissions principle is the most favourable for China. China would not have to do anything until 2040. Equally clearly, this target is not acceptable to other countries. A better argument for China would be to adopt an emission control target which would bring about economic losses no larger than developed countries. According to this principle, the experiment finds that China could start its control on CO_2 emissions between the end of the first commitment period and 2020 and gradually increase the reduction in emissions to about 10 percent in 2040. Consequently, the required carbon tax to fulfil this task would be around US\$5–7 per tce in 2040.

As regards the second component, the analysis compares emissions tax and emission trading systems. Simulations confirm that a differential international carbon tax system is better than a uniform one if wealth transfer is restricted. However, as the economy is assumed to be integrated and transfers are not restricted within one country, a uniform domestic carbon tax achieves better results than a differential one. It is also shown that an emission trading system is the best instrument for China among the three instruments discussed. However, the large amount of cash flow may cause resistance from countries buying permits, for example, the US, because it will worsen their trade balances. Moreover, as the current model aggregates the world into only three regions and may overlook emission trading potentials, caution should be exercised when interpreting these results. An extension to the analysis in this chapter would be to disaggregate the ROW further to enable a full exploration of the emission trading.

NOTES

1. They are: change in sectoral mix, mandated conservation, interfuel substitution with current technology, interfuel substitution with technological advances, and combination of strategies.
2. The target could also be set in the form of emission intensity as implied by Zhang (2000a). However, as revealed by Table 7.12, China's projected carbon emission intensity, measured as the ratio of carbon emission to GDP, is about five times the US level, and about four times the ROW level. The intensities are more or less the same over time and across scenarios, which implies huge difficulties in achieving an emission intensity target. The intensities may be better measured in PPP terms. Moreover, this broad definition is not technically a good measure of emission intensity. As the emissions are controlled, the GDP level is also reduced, leading to a much smaller change in the ratio. Therefore, this type of target will not be analysed in this study.
3. This is because resources are attracted from other countries where emissions are controlled.
4. It should be noted that experiments C3 and C4 are approximate, that is, the evolution of China's output paths roughly follows that of the US.
5. Clearly it is not a practical approach because early action would have been taken to smooth the paths. In that case, the lines will be of similar shape as those of C3, but with a lower position.
6. This figure is drawn from the McKibbin–Wilcoxen Proposal (McKibbin and Wilcoxen 2000), which is close to the required tax rates in experiments C3 and C4 discussed above, and moderate compared to other studies, for example, US$8–20 in GREEN (Martins et al. 1993), US$18–35 in Zhang (2000a), and US$58–166 in GLOBAL 2100 (Manne 1992).
7. China is a bigger loser even in absolute terms. For example, in 2010, China will lose output by US$49.3 billion, while the US will lose only US$16.6 billion. In the long run, the US will experience an increase in output, while China and the ROW will remain at a net loss in output.
8. Because of the uncertain nature of long-term projection of CO_2 emissions, the stabilisation target is kept for only ten years. An emission tax being equal to the permit price or tax rate at 2020 will be imposed after 2020.
9. Technically it is possible to make private consumption a better indicator by introducing positive shocks to the government transfer along with the emission trading.
10. It might be a more 'reasonable' experiment design that the same tax rate is

imposed on the three regions after year 2020 to make the results 'comparable'. However, this design has its own problems. As the tax rates under a differential tax regime are different for the three regions, imposing an identical tax rate after year 2020 would cause an abrupt change in tax rates in at least two regions, no matter at what level the tax rate is set. Therefore the current design is legitimate – that is what the 'differential tax' means.

11. According to the US Bureau of the Census (2001) and the Office of the US Trade Representative (2000), the trade deficit of the US with China was US$68.7 billion and US$ 83.83 billion, respectively, in 1999 and 2000.

9.   Conclusion

Economic instruments (EIs) for environmental policy have gained popularity in the last two decades because of their flexibility and cost-effectiveness. There are two basic categories of EIs: price-based instruments exemplified by an emission tax, and quantity-based instruments exemplified by an emission permit trading system. Economic theory suggests that these two EI categories are equivalent under some assumptions, such as no distortion, no transaction cost, and no uncertainty. However, these perfect assumptions are hardly justified in the real world. Therefore choosing appropriate EIs is an important task in designing environmental policies. Although there is a vast amount of literature on this issue, some areas are yet to be further explored, for example, the use of pollution charges, instrument choices under uncertainty and for international cooperation. This study provides both theoretical and empirical analyses of these topics.

9.1   MAJOR FINDINGS

EIs may differ in the way they generate revenues for a government. A pollution tax can generate revenues, while a permit trading scheme cannot, unless the permits are auctioned by the government. If an environmental policy generates revenues, how to use the revenues is thus an integral part of that policy. The current literature suggests using these revenues to replace pre-existing distorting taxes to achieve the so-called 'double dividend': sound environment and less distortion. This book argues that another possible use of such revenues should be considered, that is, earmarking for environment-related activities. In fact, both replacing pre-existing taxes and earmarking are special cases of a general tax-income scheme which sets no prior restriction on the use of revenues. According to the optimisation principle, these two special arrangements are usually welfare-decreasing except under certain circumstances. Nevertheless, it is also found that a fully earmarked scheme might be a better choice than a pure tax scheme if the marginal utility of environment is high, relative to that of consumption, and the pollution tax revenue is small.

Considering the possibility of earmarking necessitates re-examination of the Pigouvian tax. Under the principle of Pigouvian tax, the tax rate is set equal to the marginal damage cost of the pollution in order to internalise the external cost. However, it is not necessarily the case if the pollution tax revenues can be used for environmental purposes. In a partial equilibrium setting, as a pollution tax affects the output level, the optimal tax rate may be higher (smaller) than the marginal external cost if the output level is inelastic (elastic) to the tax. In a general equilibrium setting, the optimal tax rate should be set equal to the marginal cost of producing environmental good and services, but not necessarily the marginal cost of pollution. This may imply that less information is required than thought to design an environmental policy, and partly justifies some common practices, that is, employing 'schedules of fees that generate revenues sufficient to cover the cost of public pollution-abatement programs'.

Another difference between price- and quantity-based economic instruments is their consequence with the presence of uncertainty. Weitzman's rule of choosing policy instruments was developed in a partial equilibrium setting. This book explores this issue in a general equilibrium framework. It is found that Weitzman's rule is not valid in the general equilibrium setting, except when restrictions on consumers' preference are imposed. Such restrictions include risk neutrality and utility separability. Introducing risk aversion and environmental spending changes the relative advantage of one policy instrument over the other. A quantity-based instrument is more likely to be favourable in these two situations, *ceteris paribus*.

It is more complicated to design a policy to address global environmental issues such as climate change. One of the complications is related to national sovereignty. Centralised instruments such as international emission permit trading and international emission tax require the establishment of international agencies administering such schemes, and result in huge wealth transfers across national boundaries. In addition, both developed and developing countries fear that combating CO$_2$ emissions would damage their economy. These concerns make it very difficult to reach an international agreement. This study finds that the first-best outcome, that is, welfare maximum, is usually not achievable in reality because the underlying wealth transfer is too big to be realistic. For example, under an international permit trading scheme all emission permits would be allocated to developing countries. In terms of achieving the second-best outcome, and acknowledging the restriction on income transfers, a differentiated emission tax scheme is found to be better than a uniform tax scheme because countries have different technology and different preference over environment and consumption. This result deviates from the conventional recommendation that a uniform price signal is required to minimise the abatement cost. This is because a different objective is set in this study, that is, maximising the welfare, or minimising the overall cost of reducing CO_2 emissions, including both direct abatement costs and indirect impact on production. Consistent with the previous discussion of the emission tax rate, it is found that a smaller emission tax rate should be imposed on developing countries than on developed countries, because their output level is more elastic to a CO_2 emission tax than that of developed countries, that is, CO_2 emission tax has a higher impact on developing countries.

China's pollution control policies have been criticised as inefficient and ineffective, but in contrast this study finds they are effective. This conclusion is backed by two pieces of evidence. First, China's pollution intensity has decreased significantly over time, and the decomposition process shows that nearly half of the reduction in the discharge of some pollutants could be attributed to pollution control policies. Second, an econometrically estimated demand and supply system of pollution rights shows that firms respond well to the pollution levy rates. However the pollution supply functions are not well-behaved, suggesting that the government sets environmental controls without reference to the preference of households. In that sense, the policies may not be efficient and could be improved. It is also found that policies tackling more local problems (for example water pollution) tend to be more efficient. This is not surprising because the government and local public pay more attention to these problems when designing the policies.

In addition to the overview of China's pollution control policy, the empirical analysis has concentrated on developing a dynamic general equilibrium model of the Chinese economy and applying it to run baseline projections of China's future CO_2 emissions and to examine the effects of different policy arrangements. The projection shows that, given the currently available information, it is not likely that China will have lower emissions than the current level as long as GDP continues to increase, which appears inevitable, unless the population declines significantly to offset the efficiency growth of the economy. It is also shown that, in most scenarios, China's share in total world CO_2 emissions will steadily increase and could surpass the United States to become the number one emitter in the world in the first half of the 21st century. However, the per capita emissions and GDP level will still be quite low compared to the industrialised countries. This implies that China will not compromise economic development too much to achieve CO_2 emission stabilisation or reduction targets.

Several alternative options for possible CO_2 emission control targets in China have been examined. These options are designed according to certain rules, such as stabilising emissions at year 2000 level, reducing emissions by a certain percentage from baseline, setting the cap according to the same per capita emissions as the US, or sharing economic losses. As expected, the simulation shows that stabilising emissions at year 2000 level has the most severe impact on the Chinese economy, with the output level reduced by more than 8 percent. Clearly China will not accept such a target. On the other hand, a target set according to the equal per capita emissions principle is the most favourable option for China. China will not have to do anything until 2040. Equally clearly, this target may not be acceptable to other countries. A better argument for China would be to adopt an emission control target which would bring about economic losses no larger than the developed countries. According to this principle, the experiment finds that China could start its control on CO_2 emissions between the end of the first commitment period and 2020 and gradually increase the reduction in emissions to about 10 percent in 2040. Consequently the required carbon tax to fulfil this task would be around US\$5–7 per tce in 2040.

Simulation also confirms that a differential international carbon tax system is better than a uniform one if wealth transfers are restricted. However, as the domestic economy is assumed to be integrated and transfers are not restricted within one country, a uniform domestic carbon tax achieves better results than a differential one. It is also found that international emission trading could improve the welfare even further than a differential tax system. However, the huge amount of wealth transfers brought about by the carbon emissions trading may cause resistance in the permit-buying countries.

9.2   THE DIRECTION FOR FUTURE WORK

The current work could be extended in the following aspects.

First, the empirical model could be improved to fully examine the theoretical findings made in this book. For example, the emission abatement activity could be explicitly modelled to facilitate the analysis of earmarking of emission tax revenues. Uncertainties about climate change effects and CO_2 emission control costs could also be introduced in the empirical model to examine the McKibbin–Wilcoxen Proposal. The model could be further disaggregated to accommodate the analysis of emission trading. In addition to the geographical allocation of permits, the allocation of permits over time, that is, permit banking, could also be explored.

In addition, efforts should be made to estimate more of the parameters used in the model. As mentioned previously, most behavioural parameters are estimated from the US data. Although calibration is a common approach, and the only feasible approach in many circumstances, direct econometric estimation of parameters on Chinese data should always be tried to increase the credibility of results. The first step forward would be to refine the estimation of elasticities of substitution between energy, labour, capital and materials as presented in Appendix 7.A.

Second, further effort should be put into the analysis of other economic instruments, for example, joint implementation and clean development mechanisms. They should be compared with an emission tax and/or a tradable permit system.

Moreover, the analysis of climate change policies should be linked to the discussion of other policies. An obvious extension would be to analyse policies addressing more local environmental problems from energy use, for example, acid rain. A climate change policy would have more chance of being adopted and succeeding if it could incorporate individual countries' domestic environmental policies. As the climate change problem affects the whole world, economic policies, such as trade policies, should also be considered when designing a global warming policy. World trade is not only affected by climate change policies, but it can also serve as a means of achieving international cooperation on global warming, as suggested by Babiker (2001).

Third, technological progress and resource endowment could be introduced in the analysis to better model energy production and consumption and greenhouse gas emissions. The current work covers only CO_2 emissions from energy use, and the analysis could be extended to cover other GHGs and those from other sources, for example, land use and land use change.

References

Abel, Andrew B. (1979), *Investment and the Value of Capital*, New York: Garland Publishing Company.

Adar, Zvi and James M. Griffin (1976), 'Uncertainty and the Choice of Pollution Control Instruments', *Journal of Environmental Economics and Management*, **3** (3), pp. 178–88.

Agras, Jean and Duane Chapman (1999), 'A Dynamic Approach to the Environmental Kuznets Curve Hypothesis', *Ecological Economics*, **28** (2), pp. 267–77.

Alcamo, J. (1994), *IMAGE 2.0: Integrated Modelling of Global Climate Change*, Dordrecht, Netherlands: Kluwer Academic Publishers.

Alcamo, J., A. Bouwman, J. Edmonds, A. Grübler, T. Morita and A. Sugandhy (1995), 'An Evaluation of the IPCC IS92 Emission Scenarios', in J.T. Houghton, L.G. Meira Filho, J. Bruce, Hoesung Lee, B.A. Callander, E. Haites, H. Harris and K. Maskell (eds), *Climate Change 1994: Radiative Forcing of Climate Change and an Evaluation of the IPCC IS92 Emission Scenarios*, Cambridge: Cambridge University Press, pp. 233–304.

Alcamo, J., E. Kreileman and R. Leemans (eds) (1998), *Global Change Scenarios of the 21st Century: Results from the IMAGE 2.1 Model*, London: Elsevier Science.

Andersen, Mikael Skou (1994), *Governance by Green Taxes: Making Pollution Prevention Pay*, Manchester and New York: Manchester University Press.

Asako, Kazumi (1980), 'Economic Growth and Environmental Pollution under the Max-Min Principle', *Journal of Environmental Economics and Management*, **7** (3), pp. 157–83.

Asian Development Bank (ADB), Global Environmental Facility and United Nations Development Program (1998), *Asian Least-cost Greenhouse Gas Abatement Strategy: People's Republic of China*, Manila, Philippines: Asian Development Bank.

Babiker, Mustafa H. (2001), 'The CO_2 Abatement Game: Costs, Incentives and the Enforceability of a Sub-global Coalition', *Journal of Economics and Control*, **25** (1–2), pp. 1–34.

Bagnoli, Philip, Warwick J. McKibbin and Peter J. Wilcoxen (1996), 'Global

Economic Prospects: Medium Term Projections and Structural Change', Brookings Discussion Papers in International Economics, 121, The Brookings Institution, Washington, DC.

Barrett, S. (1992), 'Reaching a CO_2-Emission Limitation Agreement for the Community: Implications for Equity and Cost-Effectiveness', *European Economy*, Special Edition 1, pp. 3–24.

Baumol, William J. and Wallace E. Oates (1988), *The Theory of Environmental Policy*, Cambridge, New York and Sydney: Cambridge University Press.

Baumol, William J., Wallace E. Oates and Sue Anne Batey Blackman (1979), *Economics, Environmental Policy and the Quality of Life*, Englewood Cliffs, New Jersey: Prentice-Hall.

Beaver, Ron (1993), 'Structural Comparison of the Models in EMF 12', *Energy Policy*, **21** (3: Special Issue on Policy Modelling for Global Climate Change), pp. 238–49.

Bergman, L. (1988), 'Energy Policy Modelling: A Survey of General Equilibrium Approaches', *Journal of Policy Modeling*, **10** (3), pp. 377–99.

Bertram, Geoffrey (1992). 'Tradable Emission Permits and the Control of Greenhouse Gases', *Journal of Development Studies*, **28** (3), pp. 423–46.

Blanchard, Oliver Jean and Stanley Fischer (1989), *Lectures on Macroeconomics*, Cambridge, Massachusetts: The MIT Press.

Bovenberg, A. Lans and Lawrence Goulder (1996), 'Optimal Environmental Taxation in the Presence of Other Taxes: General-Equilibrium Analysis', *American Economic Review*, **86** (4), pp. 985–1000.

Bromley, Daniel W. (1991), *Environment and Economy: Property Rights and Public Policy*, Oxford: Basil Blackwell.

Bruce, James P., Hoesung Lee and Erik F. Haites (ed.) (1996), *Climate Change 1995 – Economic and Social Dimensions of Climate Change: Contribution of Working Group III to the Second Assessment Report of the Intergovernmental Panel on Climate Change*, Cambridge, New York, Melbourne: Cambridge University Press.

Burniaux, Jean-Marc, John P. Martin, Giuseppe Nicoletti and Joaquim Oliveira Martins (1992a), 'The Costs of Reducing CO_2 Emissions: Evidence from GREEN', Economics Department Working Paper, 115, OECD, Paris.

Burniaux, Jean-Marc, John P. Martin, Giuseppe Nicoletti and Joaquim Oliveira Martins (1992b), 'GREEN – a Multi-Sector, Multi-Region General Equilibrium Model for Quantifying the Costs of Curbing CO_2 Emissions: A Technical Manual', Economics Department Working Paper, 116, OECD, Paris.

Byrd, William A. (1987), 'The Impact of the Two-Tier Plan/Market System in Chinese Industry', *Journal of Comparative Economics*, **11** (3), pp.

295–308.

Byrd, William A. (1989), 'Plan and Market in the Chinese Industry: A Simple General Equilibrium Model', *Journal of Comparative Economics*, **13** (2), pp. 177–204.

Caplan, Arthur J., Christopher J. Ellis and Emilson C. D. Silva (1999), 'Losers in a World with Global Warming: Noncooperation, Altruism and Social Welfare', *Journal of Environmental Economics and Management*, **37** (3), pp. 256–71.

Chan, Hing Lin and Shu Kam Lee (1997), 'Modelling and Forecasting the Demand for Coal in China', *Energy Economics*, **19** (3), pp. 271–87.

Chao, Hung-po (1995), 'Managing the Risk of Global Climate Catastrophe', *Risk Analysis*, **15** (1), pp. 69–78.

Chao, Hung-po and Stephen Peck (2000), 'Greenhouse Gas Abatement: How Much? And Who Pays?' *Resource and Energy Economics*, **22** (1), pp. 1–20.

Cline, William R. (1992), *The Economics of Global Warming*, Washington, DC: Institute of International Economics.

Cline, William R. (1996), 'The Impact of Global Warming on Agriculture: Comment', *American Economic Review*, **86** (5), pp. 1309–11.

Cline, William R. (1998), 'Climate-Change Damages: Comments', in William D. Nordhaus (ed.), *Economics and Policy Issues in Climate Change*, Washington, DC: Resources for the Future, pp. 257–61.

Coase, Ronald (1960), 'The Problem of Social Cost', *Journal of Law and Economics*, **3** (1), pp. 1–44.

Conrad, Klaus and Robert E. Kohn (1996), 'The US Market for SO_2 Permits: Policy Implications of the Low Price and Trading Volume', *Energy Policy*, **24** (12), pp. 1051–9.

Darwin, R., M. Tsigas, J. Lewandrowski and A. Ranese (1995), *World Agriculture and Climate Change: Economic Adaptation*, Report No. AER-709, Economic Research Service, US Department of Agriculture, Washington, DC.

Dasgupta, Susmita, Mainul Huq, David Wheeler and Chonghua Zhang (1996), 'Water Pollution Abatement by Chinese Industry: Cost Estimates and Policy Implications', *World Bank Policy Research Working Paper*, 1630, World Bank, Washington, DC, available at http://www.worldbank.org /nipr/work_paper/1630/.

de Bruyn, S.M., J.C.J.M. van den Bergh and J.B. Opschoor (1998), 'Economic Growth and Emissions: Reconsidering the Empirical Basis of Environmental Kuznets Curve', *Ecological Economics*, **25** (2), pp. 161–75.

de Jong, A. and G. Zalm (1991), 'Scanning the Future: A Long-Term Scenario Study of the World Economy', in OECD (ed.) *Long-Term Prospects of the World Economy*, Paris: OECD, pp. 27–74.

de Melo, J. (1988), 'Computable General Equilibrium Models for Trade Policy in Developing Countries: A Survey', *Journal of Policy Modeling*, **10** (4), pp. 469–503.

de Vries, Bert, Johannes Bollen, Lex Bouwman, Michel den Elzen, Marco Janssen and Eric Kreileman (2000), 'Greenhouse Gas Emissions in an Equity-, Environment- and Service-Oriented World: An IMAGE-Based Scenario for the 21st Century', *Technological Forecasting and Social Change*, **63** (2–3), pp. 137–74.

de Vries, Bert, Marco Janssen and Arthur Beusen (1999), 'Perspectives on Global Energy Futures: Simulations with the TIME Model', *Energy Policy*, **27** (8), pp. 477–94.

de Vries, H.J.M., J.G.J. Olivier, R.A. van den Wijingaart, G.J.J. Kreileman and A.M.C. Toet (1994), 'Model for Calculating Regional Energy Use, Industrial Production and Greenhouse Gas Emissions for Evaluating Global Climate Scenarios', *Water, Air and Soil Pollution*, **76** (1), pp. 79–131.

Demeritt, D. and D. Rothman (1999), 'Figuring the Costs of Climate Change: An Assessment and Critique', *Environment and Planning A*, **31** (3), pp. 389–408.

Devarajan, S. (1988), *Lecture Notes on Computable General Equilibrium Models*, mimeo, John F. Kennedy School of Government, Harvard University, Cambridge, MA.

Dinda, Soumyananda, Dipankor Coondoo and Manoranjan Pal (2000), 'Air Quality and Economic Growth: An Empirical Study', *Ecological Economics*, **34** (3), pp. 409–23.

Editorial Committee of China Environmental Yearbook (1993–98), *China Environmental Yearbook*, Beijing: China Environmental Science Press, in Chinese.

Edmonds, J., M. Wise and C. MacCracken (1994), *Advanced Energy Technologies and Climate Change: An Analysis Using the Global Change Assessment Model (GCAM)*, PNL-9798, UC-402, Pacific Northwest National Laboratory, Richland, WA.

Edmonds, J., M. Wise, H. Pitcher, R. Richels, T. Wigley and C. MacCracken (1996a), 'An Integrated Assessment of Climate Change and the Accelerated Introduction of Advanced Energy Technology: An Application of MiniCAM 1.0', *Mitigation and Adaptation Strategies for Global Changes*, **4**, pp. 311–39.

Edmonds, J., M. Wise, R. Sands, R. Brown and H. Kheshgi (1996b), *Agriculture, Land-use and Commercial Biomass Energy: A Preliminary Integrated Analysis of the Potential Role of Biomass Energy for Reducing Future Greenhouse Related Emissions*, PNNL-11155, Pacific Northwest National Laboratory, Richland, WA.

Edmonds, Jae A. and John M. Reilly (1983), 'Global Energy and CO_2 to the Year 2050', *The Energy Journal*, **4** (3), pp. 21–47.

Edmonds, Richard Louis (ed.) (1998), *Managing the Chinese Environment*, Oxford: Oxford University Press.

Ekins, P. (1999), 'Figuring the Costs of Climate Change: A Comment', *Environment and Planning A*, **31** (3), pp. 413–5.

Erkins, P. (1995), 'Rethinking the Costs Related to Global Warming: A Survey of the Issues', *Environmental and Resource Economics*, **6**, pp. 699–704.

Ezaki, Mitsuo and Lin Sun (1999), 'Growth Accounting in China for National, Regional and Provincial Economies', *Asian Economic Journal*, **13** (1), pp. 39–71.

Fankhauser, Samuel (1995), *Valuing Climate Change: The Economics of the Greenhouse*, London: Earthscan.

Fankhauser, Samuel and Richard S.J. Tol (1999), 'Figuring the Cost of Climate Change: A Reply', *Environment and Planning A*, **31** (3), pp. 409–511.

Fankhauser, Samuel, Richard S.J. Tol and David W. Pearce (1997), 'The Aggregation of Climate Change Damages: A Welfare Theoretic Approach', *Environmental and Resource Economics*, **10** (3), pp. 249–66.

Fishelson, Gideon (1976), 'Emission Control Policies under Uncertainty', *Journal of Environmental Economics and Management*, **3** (3), pp. 189–97.

Fisher, B.S., S. Barret, P. Bohm, M. Kuroda, J.K.E. Mubazi, A. Shah and R.N. Stavins (1996), 'An Economic Assessment of Policy Instruments for Combating Climate Change', in James P. Bruce, Hoesung Lee and Erik F. Haites (eds), *Climate Change 1995 – Economic and Social Dimensions of Climate Change*, Cambridge, New York, Melbourne: Cambridge University Press, pp. 397–439.

Fullerton, Don and Gilbert E. Metcalf (1997), 'Environmental Taxes and the Double-Dividend Hypothesis: Did You Really Expect Something for Nothing?' NBER Working Paper 6199, National Bureau of Economic Research, Cambridge, Massachusetts.

Garbaccio, Richard F. (1994), *Reform and Structural Change in the Chinese Economy: A CGE Analysis*, Ph.D. Dissertation, University of California, Berkeley.

Garbaccio, Richard F. (1995), 'Price Reform and Structural Change in the Chinese Economy: Policy Simulations using a CGE Model', *China Economic Review*, **6** (1), pp. 1–34.

Garbaccio, Richard F., Mun S. Ho and Dale W. Jorgenson (1999a), 'Controlling Carbon Emissions in China', *Environment and Development Economics*, **4** (4), pp. 493–518.

Garbaccio, Richard F., Mun S. Ho and Dale W. Jorgenson (1999b), 'Why

Has the Energy-Output Ratio Fallen in China?', *The Energy Journal*, **20** (3), pp. 63–91.

Garbaccio, Richard F., Mun S. Ho and Dale W. Jorgenson (2001), 'Modeling the Health Benefits of Carbon Emissions Reductions in China', *China Energy Efficiency Information Bulletin*, 7, no. 1, the Bulletin is published at http://www.pnl.gov/china/bulle7-1.htm and the article is in http://www.pnl.gov/china/healthmod.pdf, last accessed on 9 May 2001.

Goulder, Lawrence, Ian W.H. Parry and Dallas Burtraw (1996), 'Revenue-Raising vs. Other Approaches to Environmental Protection: The Critical Significance of Pre-Existing Tax Distortions', NBER Working Paper 5641, National Bureau of Economic Research, Cambridge, Massachusetts.

Goulder, Lawrence, Ian W.H. Parry, Roberton C. Williams III and Dallas Burtraw (1999), 'The Cost-Effectiveness of Alternative Instruments for Environmental Protection in a Second-best Setting', *Journal of Public Economics*, **72** (3), pp. 329–60.

Goulder, Lawrence H. (1991), 'Effects of Carbon Taxes in an Economy with Prior Tax Distortions: An Intertemporal General Equilibrium Analysis for the US', mimeo, Resources for the Future, Washington, DC.

Grossman, Gene M. and Alan B. Krueger (1993), 'Environmental Impacts of a North American Free Trade Agreement', in P. Garber (ed.), *The US–Mexico Free Trade Agreement*, Cambridge: The MIT Press, pp. 165–77.

Grossman, Gene M. and Alan B. Krueger (1995), 'Economic Growth and the Environment', *The Quarterly Journal of Economics*, **110** (2), pp. 353–77.

Gupta, Sujata and Preety M. Bhandari (2000), 'An Effective Allocation Criterion for CO_2 Emissions', paper presented at a Joint Meeting of EMF/IEA/IEW, 20–22 June 2000, Stanford University, CA, USA.

Hartwick, John M. (1977), 'Intergenerational Equity and the Investing of Rents from Exhaustible Resources', *American Economic Review*, **67** (5), pp. 972–4.

Hartwick, John M. (1978), 'Substitution Among Exhaustible Resources and Intergenerational Equity', *Review of Economic Studies*, **45** (2), pp. 347–54.

Hayashi, Fumio (1982a), 'The Permanent Income Hypothesis: Estimation and Testing by Instrumental Variables', *Journal of Political Economy*, **90** (5), pp. 895–916.

Hayashi, Fumio (1982b), 'Tobin's Marginal and Average q: A Neoclassical Interpretation', *Econometrica*, **50** (1), pp. 213–24.

Huber, Richard, Jack Ruitenbeek and Ronaldo Serôa da Motta (1998), 'Market Based Instruments for Environmental Policymaking in Latin America and the Caribbean: Lessons from Eleven Countries', World Bank Discussion Paper, No. 381, World Bank, Washington, DC.

Hufschmidt, Maynard M., D.E. James, A.D. Meister, B.T. Bower and J.A. Dixon (1983), *Environment, Natural Systems and Development: An*

Economic Valuation Guide, Baltimore: Johns Hopkins University Press.

IEDB, International Economic Data Bank, authorised ftp access at ftp://iedb.anu.edu.au.

Industry Commission (1997), 'Role of Economic Instruments in Managing the Environment', Staff Research Paper, July, Industry Commission, Melbourne, available at http://www.pc.gov.au/ic/research/information /ecoinstr/index.html, last accessed on 11 July 2001.

IPCC (2001), *Climate Change 2001 – Impacts, Adaptation and Vulnerability*, Cambridge, New York and Melbourne: Cambridge University Press, Summary for Policymakers available at http://www.usgcrp.gov/ipcc/ wg2spm.pdf, last accessed on 22 March 2001.

James, David (1997), 'Environmental Incentives: Australian Experience with Economic Instruments for Environmental Management', Environmental Economics Research Paper No.5, Environment Australia, Canberra, available at http://www.ea.gov.au/pcd/economics/incentives/, last accessed on 11 July 2001.

Jefferson, Gary H., Thomas G. Rawski and Yuxin Zheng (1996), 'Chinese Industrial Productivity: Trends, Measurement Issues and Recent Developments', *Journal of Comparative Economics*, **23** (2), pp. 146–80.

Jiang, Kejun, Toshihiko Masui, Tsuneyuki Morita and Yuzuru Matsuoka (1999), 'Long-term Emission Scenarios for China', *Environmental Economics and Policy Studies*, **2** (4), pp. 267–87.

Jiang, Tingsong (2001), 'Earmarking of Pollution Charges and the Sub-Optimality of the Pigouvian Tax', *The Australian Journal of Agricultural and Resource Economics*, **45** (4), pp. 623–40.

Jiang, Tingsong (2002), 'China in International Action on Climate Change', in Ligang Song (ed.) *Dilemmas of China's Growth in the Twenty-First Century*, Canberra: Asia Pacific Press, pp. 286–316.

Jiang, Tingsong and Warwick McKibbin (2002), 'Assessment of China's Pollution Levy System: An Equilibrium Pollution Approach', *Environment and Development Economics*, **7** (1), pp. 75–105.

Jin, Z., Daokou Ge and J. Fang (1994), 'Effects of Climate Change on Rice Production and Strategies for Adaptation in Southern China', in Cynthia Rosenzweig and A. Iglesias (eds), *Implications of Climate Change for International Agriculture: Crop Modeling Study*, US Environment Protection Agency, Washington, DC, pp. 1–24.

Johansen, Leif (1960), *A Multi-Sectoral Study of Economic Growth*, Volume 21 of Contributions to Economic Analysis, Amsterdam: North-Holland.

Jones, Tom (1994), 'Operational Criteria for Joint Implementation', in OECD and IEA (eds), *The Economics of Climate Change: Proceedings of An OECD/IEA Conference*, Paris: OECD Publication Service, pp. 109–25.

Jorgenson, Dale W. and Peter J. Wilcoxen (1991a), 'Reducing US Carbon

Dioxide Emissions: The Cost of Different Goals', in John R. Moroney (ed.), *Energy, Growth and the Environment*, Greenwich, Connecticut: JAI Press, pp. 125–58.

Jorgenson, Dale W. and Peter J. Wilcoxen (1991b), 'Reducing US Carbon Dioxide Emissions: The Effect of Different Instruments', mimeo, Harvard University, Cambridge, Massachusetts.

Kane, Sally, John Reilly and James Tobey (1992), 'An Empirical Study of the Economic Effects of Climate Change on World Agriculture', *Climatic Change*, **21** (1), pp. 17–35.

Kaufmann, Robert K., Brynhildur Daviddottir, Sophie Garnham and Peter Pauly (1998), 'The Determinants of Atmospheric SO_2 Concentrations: Reconsidering the Environmental Kuznets Curve', *Ecological Economics*, **25** (2), pp. 209–20.

Kaya, Y. (1990), 'Impact of Carbon Dioxide Emission Control on GNP Growth: Interpretation of Proposed Scenarios', paper presented to the IPCC Energy and Industry Subgroup, Response Strategies Working Group, Paris.

Kim, Jong Il and Lawrence J. Lau (1995), 'The Role of Human Capital in the Economic Growth of the East Asian Newly Industrialised Countries', *Asia-Pacific Economic Review*, **1** (3), pp. 3–22.

Kirschbaum, Miko U.F., Andreas Fischlin, M.G.R. Cannell, R.V.O. Cruz, W. Galinski and W.P. Cramer (1996), 'Climate Change Impacts on Forests', in Robert T. Watson, Marufu C. Zinyowera and Richard H. Moss (eds), *Climate Change 1995 – Impacts, Adaptations and Mitigation of Climate Change: Scientific–Technical Analysis*, Cambridge, New York, Melbourne: Cambridge University Press, pp. 95–129.

Kong, Xiang, Robert E. Marks and Guang Hua Wan (1999), 'Technical Efficiency, Technological Change and Total Factor Productivity Growth in Chinese State-Owned Enterprises in the Early 1990s', *Asian Economic Journal*, **13** (3), pp. 267–81.

Laffont, Jean-Jacques and Claudia Senik-Leygonie (1997), *Price Controls and the Economics of Institutions in China*, Paris: OECD Publications.

Lashof, D. and D.A. Tirpak (1990), *Policy Options for Stabilizing Global Climate*, 21P-2003, US Environmental Protection Agency, Washington, DC.

Leemans, R. and G.J. van den Born (1994), 'Determining the Potential Distribution of Vegetation, Crops and Agricultural Productivity', *Water, Air and Soil Pollution*, **76**, pp.133–61.

Li, Jingwen, Dale W. Jorgenson, Youjing Zheng and Masahiro Kuroda (1993), *Study on Productivity and Economic Growth in China, US and Japan*, Beijing: China Social Sciences Publishing House.

Li, Wei (1997), 'The Impact of Economic Reform on the Performance of

Chinese State Enterpirses, 1980–1989', *Journal of Political Economy*, **105** (5), pp. 1080–1106.

Lin, Erda (1996), 'Agricultural Vulnerability and Adaptation to Global Warming in China', *Water, Air and Soil Pollution*, **92** (1–2, Special Issue: Climate Change, Vulnerability and Adaptation in Asia and the Pacific), pp. 63–73.

Lucas, Robert E. Jr. (1967a), 'Adjustment Cost and the Theory of Supply', *Journal of Political Economy*, **75** (4, Part1), pp. 321–34.

Lucas, Robert E. Jr. (1967b), 'Optimal Investment Policy and the Flexible Accelerator', *International Economic Review*, **8** (1), pp. 78–85.

Luo, Qunying and Erda Lin (1999), 'Agricultural Vulnerability and Adaptation in Developing Countries: The Asia-Pacific Region', *Climatic Change*, **43** (4), pp. 729–43.

Lutz, Wolfgang (ed.) (1996), *The Future Population of the World: What Can We Assume Today?*, 2nd Edition, London: Earthscan Publications Ltd.

Ma, Jun (1997), *China's Economic Reform in the 1990s*, available at http://members.aol.com/junmanew/cover.htm.

Maddison, Angus (1998), *Chinese Economic Performance in the Long Run*, Paris: OECD Publications.

Manne, A. and L. Schrattenholzer (1995), *International Energy Workshop January 1995 Poll Edition*, Laxenburg, Austria: International Institute for Applied Systems Analysis.

Manne, A. and L. Schrattenholzer (1996), *International Energy Workshop January 1996 Poll Edition*, Laxenburg, Austria: International Institute for Applied Systems Analysis.

Manne, A. and L. Schrattenholzer (1997), *International Energy Workshop, Part I: Overview of Poll Responses, Part II: Frequency Distributions, Part III: Individual Poll Responses*, Laxenburg, Austria: International Institute for Applied Systems Analysis.

Manne, Alan S. (1992), 'Global 2100: Alternative Scenarios for Reducing Carbon Emissions', Working Paper 111, Department of Economics and Statistics, Organisation for Economic Co-operation and Development, Paris.

Manne, Alan S. (1996), 'Greenhouse Gas Abatement: Toward Pareto-Optimality in Integrated Assessments', in Kenneth J. Arrow, Richard W. Cottle, B. Curtis Eaves and Ingram Olkin (eds), *Education in a Research University*, Stanford: Stanford University Press, 391–405.

Manne, Alan S. and Richard G. Richels (1990), 'CO$_2$ Emission Limits: An Economic Analysis for the USA', *The Energy Journal*, **11** (2), pp. 51–74.

Manne, Alan S. and Richard G. Richels (1992) *Buying Greenhouse Insurance – The Economic Costs of CO$_2$ Emission Limits*, Cambridge, MA: The MIT Press.

Mansur, Ahsan and John Whalley (1984), 'Numerical Specification of Applied General Equilibrium Models: Estimation, Calibration and Data', in Herbert E. Scarf and John B. Shoven (eds), *Applied General Equilibrium Analysis*, Cambridge, New York: Cambridge University Press, pp. 69–127.

Martin, Will (1993), 'Modeling the Post-Reform Chinese Economy', *Journal of Policy Modeling*, **15** (5–6), pp. 545–79.

Martins, J.O., J.M. Burniaux, J.P. Martin and G. Nicoletti (1993), 'The Costs of Reducing CO_2 Emissions: A Comparison of Carbon Tax Curves with GREEN'', in OECD Economic Policy Committee (ed.), *The Costs of Cutting Carbon Emissions: Results from Global Models*, Paris: OECD, pp. 67–94.

McKibbin, Warwick J. (1997), 'Comment on Energy–Economy Interactions in Stabilizing CO_2 Emissions', in Y. Kaya and K. Yokobori (eds), *Environment, Energy and Economy*, Tokyo: United Nations University Press, pp. 171–80.

McKibbin, Warwick J. (1998), 'Greenhouse Abatement Policy: Insights from the G-cubed Multi-country Model', *Australian Journal of Agricultural and Resource Economics*, **42** (1), pp. 99–113.

McKibbin, Warwick J. and Yiping Huang (1997), 'Rapid Economic Growth in China: Implications for the World Economy', Brookings Discussion Papers in International Economics, 130, The Brookings Institution, Washington, DC.

McKibbin, Warwick J., Martin T. Ross, Robert Shackleton and Peter J. Wilcoxen (1999), 'Emission Trading, Capital Flows and the Kyoto Protocol', *The Energy Journal*, **20** (Kyoto Special Issue), pp. 287–334.

McKibbin, Warwick J. and Jeffrey D. Sachs (1991), *Global Linkage: Macroeconomic Interdependence and Cooperation in the World Economy*, The Brookings Institution, Washington, DC.

McKibbin, Warwick J., Robert Shackleton and Peter J. Wilcoxen (1999), 'What to Expect from an International System of Tradable Permits for Carbon Emissions', *Resource and Energy Economics*, **21** (3–4), pp. 319–46.

McKibbin, Warwick J. and Peter J. Wilcoxen (1992), 'G-Cubed: A Dynamic Multi-Sector General Equilibrium Model of the Global Economy (Quantifying the Costs of Curbing CO_2 Emissions', Brookings Discussion Paper 98, The Brookings Institution, Washington, DC.

McKibbin, Warwick J. and Peter J. Wilcoxen (1994), 'The Global Costs of Policies to Reduce Greenhouse Gas Emissions', Final Report on US Environmental Protection Agency Cooperative Agreement CR818579-01-0, The Brookings Institution, Washington, DC.

McKibbin, Warwick J. and Peter J. Wilcoxen (1997), 'A Better Way to Slow

Global Climate Change', *Brookings Policy Brief*, No.17, The Brookings Institution, Washington, DC.

McKibbin, Warwick J. and Peter J. Wilcoxen (1999), 'The Theoretical and Empirical Structure of the G-Cubed Model', *Economic Modelling*, **16** (1), pp. 123–48.

McKibbin, Warwick J. and Peter J. Wilcoxen (2000), 'Designing a Realistic Climate Change Policy that Includes Developing Countries', Paper presented at 2000 Conference of Economists, Gold Coast, Australia, 3–6 July 2000.

McKibbin, Warwick J. and Peter J. Wilcoxen (2002), *Climate Change Policy after Kyoto: Blueprint for a Realistic Approach*, Washington, DC: Brookings Institution Press.

Mendelsohn, Robert (1998), 'Climate-Change Damages', in William D. Nordhaus (ed.), *Economics and Policy Issues in Climate Change*, Washington, DC: Resources for the Future, pp. 219–36.

Mendelsohn, Robert, W. Morrison, M.E. Schlesinger and N.G. Andronova (1996), 'A Global Impact Model for Climate Change', draft.

Mendelsohn, Robert and William D. Nordhaus (1996), 'The Impact of Global Warming on Agriculture: Reply', *American Economic Review*, **86** (5), pp. 1312–5.

Mendelsohn, Robert, William D. Nordhaus and Daigee Shaw (1994), 'The Impact of Global Warming on Agriculture: A Ricardian Analysis', *American Economic Review*, **84** (4), pp. 753–71.

Messner, S. and M. Strubegger (1995), 'User's Guide for MESSAGE III', WP-95-069, International Institute for Applied Systems Analysis, Lazenburg, Austria.

Meyer, Aubrey and Tony Cooper (1995), 'Recalculation of the Social Costs of Climate Change', *The Ecologist*, an Occasional Paper in the Ecologist Series.

Mori, Shunsuke (2000), 'The Development of Greenhouse Gas Emissions Scenarios Using an Extension of the MARIA Model for the Assessment of Resource and Energy Technology', *Technological Forecasting and Social Change*, **63** (2–3), pp. 289–311.

Mori, Shunsuke and M. Takahashi (1999), 'An Integrated Assessment Model for the Evaluation of New Energy Technologies and Food Productivity', *International Journal of Global Energy Issues*, **11** (1–4), pp. 1–18.

Morita, Tsuneyuki (1999), 'IPCC SRES Database, Version 1.0', Emission Scenario Database prepared for IPCC Special Report on Emissions Scenarios, available at http://www-cger.nies.go.jp/cger-e/db/ipcc.html, last accessed on 2 May 2001, National Institute of Environmental Studies, Tsukuba, Japan.

Morita, Tsuneyuki and H.-C. Lee (1998a), 'Appendix to Emissions Scenarios

Database and Review of Scenarios', *Mitigation and Adaptation Strategies for Global Change*, **3** (2–4), pp. 121–31.

Morita, Tsuneyuki and H.-C. Lee (1998b), 'IPCC SRES Database, Version 0.1', Emission Scenario Database prepared for IPCC Special Report on Emissions Scenarios, National Institute of Environmental Studies, Tsukuba, Japan.

Morita, Tsuneyuki, Yuzuru Matsuoka, I. Penna and M. Kainuma (1994), 'Global Carbon Dioxide Emission Scenarios and Their Basic Assumptions: 1994 Survey', CGER-I011-94, Center for Global Environmental Research, National Institute for Environmental Studies, Tsukuba, Japan.

Nakićenović, Nebojsa and Rob Swart (eds) (2000), *Special Report on Emission Scenarios: A Special Report of Working Group III of the Intergovernmental Panel on Climate Change*, Cambridge: Cambridge University Press, available at http://www.grida.no/climate/ipcc/emission/index.htm, last accessed on 7 March 2001.

Nehru, Vikram and Ashok Dhareshwar (1993), 'A New Database on Physical Capital Stock: Sources, Methodology and Results', *Rivista de Analisis Economico*, **8** (1), pp. 37–59, data set is available at http://www.worldbank.org/research/growth/ddnehdha.htm, last accessed on 5 January 2001.

Neilson, R.P. (1993), 'Vegetation Redistribution: A Possible Biosphere Source of CO_2 During Climate Change', *Water, Air and Soil Pollution*, **70**, pp. 659–73.

NEPA (1993–97), *China Environmental Yearbook*, Beijing: China Environmental Science Press, in Chinese.

NEPA (1994), *The Pollution Levy System*, Beijing: China Environmental Science Press.

Nordhaus, William D. (1977), 'Economic Growth and Climate: The Carbon Dioxide Problem', *American Economic Review*, **67** (1), pp. 341–6.

Nordhaus, William D. (1991), 'To Slow or Not to Slow: The Economics of The Greenhouse Effect', *The Economic Journal*, **101** (407), pp. 920–37.

Nordhaus, William D. (1994a), 'Expert Opinion on Climate Change', *American Scientist*, **82** (1), pp. 45–51.

Nordhaus, William D. (1994b), *Managing the Global Commons: The Economics of Climate Change*, Cambridge, London: The MIT Press.

Nordhaus, William D. (ed.) (1998), *Economics and Policy Issues in Climate Change*, Washington, DC: Resources for the Future.

Nordhaus, William D. and Zili Yang (1996), 'A Regional Dynamic General-Equilibrium Model of Alternative Climate-Change Strategies', *American Economic Review*, **86** (4), pp. 741–65.

OECD (1989), *Economic Instruments for Environmental Protection*, Paris:

OECD Publication Service, written by Johannes B. Opschoor and Hans B. Vos under the supervision of the OECD Environment Committee's Group of Economic Experts.

OECD and NEPA (1997), *Applying Market-Based Instruments to Environmental Policies in China and OECD Countries*, Paris: OECD Publication Service.

Office of the US Trade Representative (2000), *2000 National Trade Estimate Report on Foreign Trade Barriers*, available at http://www.ustr.gov/html/ 2000_contents.html, last accessed on 7 November 2001.

Office of the US Trade Representative (2001), *2001 Trade Policy Agenda and 2000 Annual Report of the President of the United States on the Trade Agreements Program*, available at http://www.ustr.gov/reports/ 2001.html, last accessed on 7 November 2001.

Oglesby, R. J. and B. Saltzman (1990), 'Sensitivity of the Equilibrium Surface Temperature of a GCM to Systematic Changes in Atmospheric Carbon Dioxide', *Geophysical Research Letters*, July, pp. 1089–92.

Panayotou, Theodore (1994), 'Economic Instruments for Environmental Management and Sustainable Development', Report prepared for the United Nations Environmental Programme's Consultative Expert Group Meeting on the Use and Application of Economic Policy Instruments for Environmental Management and Sustainable Development, Nairobi, 10–12 August 1994, International Environment Program, Harvard Institute for International Development, Harvard University, Cambridge, MA.

Panayotou, Theodore (1995), 'Economic Instruments for Environmental Management and Sustainable Development', Revision of 1994 report, International Environment Program, Harvard Institute for International Development, Harvard University, Cambridge, MA.

Parry, Ian W.H., Roberton C. Williams III and Lawrence H. Goulder (1996), 'When Can Carbon Abatement Policies Increase Welfare? The Fundamental Role of Distorted Factor Markets', RFF Discussion Paper 97-18, Resources for the Future, Washington, DC.

Parry, Ian W.H. and Roberton C. Williams III (1999), 'A Second-Best Evaluation of Eight Policy Instruments to Reduce Carbon Emissions', *Resources and Energy Economics*, **21** (3–4), pp. 347–73.

Parry, M., T. Carter and N. Konijn, (ed.) (1988), *The Impact of Climate Variations on Agriculture*, Boston: Kluwer Academic Publishers.

Pearce, David (1991), 'The Role of Carbon Taxes in Adjusting to Global Warming', *The Economic Journal*, **101** (407), pp. 938–48.

Pearce, David W., William R. Cline, Amrita N. Achanta, Samuel Fankhauser, R.K. Pachauri, Richard S.J. Tol and P. Vellinga, (1996), 'The Social Costs of Climate Change: Greenhouse Damage and the Benefits of Control', in James P. Bruce, Hoesung Lee and Erik F. Haites (eds), *Climate Change*

1995 – *Economic and Social Dimensions of Climate Change*, Cambridge, New York, Melbourne: Cambridge University Press, pp. 179–224.

Pearce, David W. and Jeremy J. Warford (1993), *World without End: Economics, Environment and Sustainable Development*, Oxford: Oxford University Press.

Peart, R., J. Jones and R. Curry (1990), 'Impact of Climate Change on Crop Yield in the Southeastern USA', in *The Potential Effects of Global Climate Change on the United States*, Report to Congress, Volume 3, Washington, DC.

Peck, Stephen C. and Thomas J. Teisberg (1992), 'CETA: A Model for Carbon Emissions Trajectory Assessment', *The Energy Journal*, **13** (1), pp. 55–77.

Peck, Stephen C. and Thomas J. Teisberg (1995), 'International CO_2 Emission Control: An Analysis Using CETA', *Energy Policy*, **23** (4–5), pp. 297–308.

Peck, Stephen C. and Thomas J. Teisberg (1997), 'International CO_2 Emissions Targets and Timetables: An Analysis of the AOSIS Proposal', *Environmental Modeling and Assessment*, **1** (4), pp. 219–27.

Peck, Stephen C. and Thomas J. Teisberg (1999), 'CO_2 Emissions Control Agreements: Incentives for Regional Participation', *The Energy Journal*, **20** (Kyoto Special Issue), pp. 367–90.

Pepper, W.J., W. Barbour, A. Sankovski and B. Braaz (1998), 'No-Policy Greenhouse Gas Emission Scenarios: Revisiting IPCC 1992', *Environmental Science and Policy*, **1**, pp. 289–312.

Pepper, W.J., J. Leggett, R. Swart, J. Wasson, J. Edmonds and I. Mintzer (1992), 'Emissions Scenarios for the IPCC. An Update: Assumptions, Methodology and Results: Support Document for Chapter A3', in J.T. Houghton, B.A. Callandar and S.K. Varney (eds), *Climate Change 1992: Supplementary Report to the IPCC Scientific Assessment*, Cambridge: Cambridge University Press.

Perman, Roger, Yue Ma and James McGilvray (1996), *Natural Resources and Environmental Economics*, London and New York: Longman.

Pezzey, J.C.V. and N.R. Lambie (2001), *Computable General Equilibrium Models for Evaluating Domestic Greenhouse Policies in Australia: A Comparative Analysis*, Report to the Productivity Commission, AusInfo, Canberra.

Pigou, Arthur Cecil (1920), *The Economics of Welfare*, London: MacMillan, 1938 Fourth Edition.

Pigou, Arthur Cecil (1928), *A Study in Public Finance*, London: MacMillan, 1949 Reprint of 1947 Edition.

Pizer, William A. (1997a), 'Optimal Choice of Policy Instrument and Stringency under Uncertainty: The Case of Climate Change', RFF

Discussion Paper 97-17, Resources for the Future, Washington, DC.

Pizer, William A. (1997b), 'Prices vs. Quantities Revisited: The Case of Climate Change', RFF Discussion Paper 98-02, Resources for the Future, Washington, DC.

Pizer, William A. (1999), 'The Optimal Choice of Climate Change Policy in the Presence of Uncertainty', *Resource and Energy Economics*, **21** (3–4), pp. 255–87.

Prentice, I.C., W.P. Cramer, S.P. Harrison, R. Leemans, R.A. Monserud and A.M. Solomon (1992), 'A Global Biome Model Based on Plant Physiology and Dominance, Soil Properties and Climate', *Journal of Biogeography*, **19**, 117–37.

Qu, Geping (1991), *Environmental Management in China*, Beijing: China Environmental Science Press.

Qu, Geping (1992), *Environment and Development in China*, Beijing: China Environmental Science Press, in Chinese.

Reilly, John (1995), 'Climate Change and Global Agriculture: Recent Findings and Issues', *American Journal of Agricultural Economics*, **77** (3), pp. 727–33.

Reilly, John (1998), 'Climate–Change Damages: Comments', in William D. Nordhaus (ed.), *Economics and Policy Issues in Climate Change*, Washington, DC: Resources for the Future, pp. 243–55.

Reilly, John, W. Baethgen, F.E. Chege, S.C. van de Geijn', Erda Lin, A. Iglesias, G. Kenny, D. Patterson, J. Rogasik, R. Rötter, C. Rosenzweig, W. Sombroek and J. Westbrook (1996), 'Agriculture in a Changing Climate: Impacts and Adaptation', in Robert T. Watson, Marufu C. Zinyowera and Richard H. Moss (eds), *Climate Change 1995 – Impacts, Adaptations and Mitigation of Climate Change: Scientific–Technical Analysis*, Cambridge, New York, Melbourne: Cambridge University Press, pp. 427–86.

Reilly, John M. and D. Schimmelpfennig (1999), 'Agricultural Impact Assessment, Vulnerability and the Scope for Adaptation', *Climatic Change*, **43** (4), pp. 745–88.

Riahi, Keywan and R. Alexander Roehrl (2000), 'Greenhouse Gas Emissions in a Dynamics-as-Usual Scenario of Economic and Energy Development', *Technological Forecasting and Social Change*, **63** (2–3), pp. 175–205.

Ritchie, J., B. Gaer and T. Chou (1990), 'Effects of Global Climate Change on Agriculture: Great Lakes Region', in *The Potential Effects of Global Climate Change on the United States*, Report to Congress, Volume 3, Washington, DC.

Roberts, Marc J. and Michael Spence (1976), 'Effluent Charges and Licenses under Uncertainty', *Journal of Public Economics*, **5** (3–4), pp. 193–208.

Rose, Adam, Juan Benavides, Dongsoon Lim and Oscar Frias (1996), 'Global Warming Policy, Energy, and the Chinese Economy', *Resource and*

Energy Economics, **18** (1), pp. 31–63.

Rosenzweig, Cynthia (1990), 'Potential Effects of Climate Change on Agricultural Production in the Great Plains: A Simulation Study', in *The Potential Effects of Global Climate Change on the United States*, Report to Congress, Volume 3, Washington, DC.

Rosenzweig, Cynthia and Daniel Hillel (1993), 'Agriculture in a Greenhouse World', *Research and Exploration*, **9** (2), pp. 208–21.

Rosenzweig, Cynthia and Martin L. Parry (1994), 'Potential Impact of Climate Change on World Food Supply', *Nature*, **367** (13 January), pp. 133–8.

Rothman, Dale S. (1998), 'Environmental Kuznets Curve – Real Progress or Passing Buck? A Case for Consumption-based Approaches', *Ecological Economics*, **25** (2), pp. 177–94.

Rutherford, Thomas F. (1992), 'The Welfare Effects of Fossil Carbon Restrictions: Results from a Recursively Dynamic Trade Model', mimeo.

Sankovski, Alexei, Wiley Barbour and William Pepper (2000), 'Quantification of the IS99' Emission Scenario Storylines Using the Atmospheric Stabilization Framework', *Technological Forecasting and Social Change*, **63** (2–3), pp. 263–87.

Santer, B. (1985), 'The Use of General Circulation Models in Climate Impact Analysis – A Preliminary Study of the Impacts of a CO_2 Induced Climate Change on West European Agriculture', *Climatic Change*, **7** (1), pp. 71–93.

Schimmelpfennig, J., J. Lewandrowski, J. Reilly, M. Tsigas and I. Parry (1996), 'Agricultural Adaptation to Climate Change: Issues of Longrun Sustainability', Report No. AER-740, Economic Research Service, US Department of Agriculture, Washington, DC.

Schmutzler, Armin and Lawrence H. Goulder (1997), 'The Choice between Emission Taxes and Output Taxes under Imperfect Monitoring', *Journal of Environmental Economics and Management*, **32** (1), pp. 51–64.

Selden, Thomas M. and Daqing Song (1994), 'Environmental Quality and Development: Is There a Kuznets Curve for Air Pollution Emissions?' *Journal of Environmental Economics and Management*, **27** (2), pp. 147–62.

Shafik, Nemat (1994), 'Economic Development and Environmental Quality: An Econometric Analysis', *Oxford Economic Papers*, **46** (Supplementary, Special Issue on Environmental Economics), pp. 757–73.

Shibli, A. and A. Markandya (1995), 'Industrial Pollution Control Policies in Asia: How Successful Are the Strategies?' *Asian Journal of Environmental Management*, **3** (2).

Shogren, Jason and Michael Toman (2000), 'Climate Change Policy', RFF Discussion Paper 00-22, Resources for the Future, Washington, DC.

Sicular, Terry (1988), 'Plan and Market in China's Agricultural Commerce', *Journal of Political Economics*, **96** (2), pp. 283–307.

Sims, Holly (1999), 'One-fifth of the Sky: China's Environmental Stewardship', *World Development*, **27** (7), pp. 1227–45.

Smil, Vaclav (1998), 'China's Energy and Resource Uses: Continuity and Change', in Richard Louis Edmonds (ed.), *Managing the Chinese Environment*, Oxford: Oxford University Press, pp. 211–27.

Solomon, Allen M., N.H. Ravindranath, R.B. Stewart, M. Weber, S. Nilsson et al. (1996), 'Wood Production under Changing Climate and Land Use', in Robert T. Watson, Marufu C. Zinyowera and Richard H. Moss (eds), *Climate Change 1995 – Impacts, Adaptations and Mitigation of Climate Change: Scientific-Technical Analysis*, Cambridge, New York, Melbourne: Cambridge University Press, pp. 487–510.

Solow, Robert M. (1974a), 'The Economics of Resources or the Resources of Economics', *American Economic Review*, **64** (2), pp. 1–14.

Solow, Robert M. (1974b), 'Intergenerational Equity and Exhaustible Resources', *Review of Economic Studies*, **41** (Symposium), pp. 29–45.

Song, Jian (1988), 'Speech in the National Committee of Environmental Protection', *Huan Jing Gong Zuo Tong Xun* (*Newsletter of Environmental Protection*), no. 10, in Chinese.

SSB (1990–98), *China Statistical Yearbook*, various issues, Beijing: China Statistical Publishing House, in Chinese.

SSB (1999), *China Statistical Yearbook 1999*, Beijing: China Statistical Publishing House, in Chinese.

SSB (2001), 'The First Communiqué of Main Results of the Fifth National Census', *People's Daily*, 29 March 2001.

SSB Department of National Accounts (1999), *1997 Input–Output Table of China*, Beijing: China Statistical Publishing House, in Chinese.

Stavins, Robert N. (1995), 'Transaction Costs and Tradable Permits', *Journal of Environmental Economics and Management*, **29** (1), pp. 133–48.

Stavins, Robert N. (1996), 'Correlated Uncertainty and Policy Instrument Choice', *Journal of Environmental Economics and Management*, **30** (2), pp. 218–32.

Stavins, Robert N. (2000a), 'Experience with Market-Based Environmental Policy Instruments', RFF Discussion Paper 00-09, Resources for the Future, Washington, DC.

Stavins, Robert N. (2000b), 'Market-Based Environmental Policies', in Paul R. Portney and Robert N. Stavins (eds), *Public Policies for Environmental Protection*, Resources for the Future, Washington, DC, pp. 31–76.

Suri, Vivek and Duane Chapman (1998), 'Economic Growth, Trade and Energy: Implications for the Environmental Kuznets Curve', *Ecological Economics*, **25** (2), pp. 195–208.

Tao, Z. (1992), 'Influences of Global Climate Change on Agriculture of China', in *Climate Biosphere Interactions*, New York: John Wiley and Sons.

Tian, Xueyuan (1998), 'Report of China's Development Study: Population and Sustainable Development', in Chinese Academy of Social Sciences Institute of Population Study (ed.), *China Population Yearbook 1998*, Beijing: China Civil Aviation Publishing House, pp.119–61.

Tietenberg, Tom, M. Grubb, A. Michaelowa, B. Swift and Z.X. Zhang (1999), *International Rules for Greenhouse Gas Emissions Trading: Defining the Principles, Modalities, Rules and Guidelines for Verification, Reporting and Accountability*, UNCTAD/GDS/GFSB/Misc.6, United Nations, New York and Geneva.

Titus, J. G. (1992), 'The Cost of Climate Change to the United States', in S.K. Majumdar, L.S. Kalkstein, B. Yarnal, E.W. Miller and L.M. Rosenfeld (eds), *Global Climate Change: Implications, Challenges and Mitigation Measures*, Easton, PA, USA: Pennsylvania Academy of Science.

Tobin, James (1969), 'A General Equilibrium Approach to Monetary Theory', *Journal of Money, Credit and Banking*, **1** (1), pp. 15–29.

Tol, Richard S.J. (1995), 'The Damage Costs of Climate Change Toward More Comprehensive Calculation', *Environmental and Resource Economics*, **5** (4), pp. 353–74.

Tol, Richard S.J. (1998), 'Climate-Change Damages: Comments', in William D. Nordhaus (ed.), *Economics and Policy Issues in Climate Change*, Washington, DC: Resources for the Future, pp.237–42.

Tol, Richard S.J. (1999), 'The Marginal Cost of Greenhouse Gas Emissions', *The Energy Journal*, **20** (1), pp. 61–82.

Torras, Mariano and James K. Boyce (1998), 'Income, Inequality and Pollution: A Reassessment of the Environmental Kuznets Curve', *Ecological Economics*, **25** (2), pp. 147–60.

Treadway, A.B. (1969), 'On Rational Entrepreneurial Behavior and the Demand for Investment', *Review of Economic Studies*, **36** (2), pp. 227–39.

Ulph, Alistair (2000), 'Harmonization and Optimal Environmental Policy in a Federal System with Asymmetric Information', *Journal of Environmental Economics and Management*, **39** (2), pp. 224–41.

UNFCCC, *Greenhouse Gas Inventory Database*, available at http://ghg. unfccc.int/, last accessed on 5 January 2001.

United Nations (1992), *Rio Declaration on Environment and Development*, available at http://www.unep.org/documents/default.asp?documentid=78& articleid=1163, last accessed on 5 January 2001.

United Nations (1998), *World Population Projections to 2150*, Doc. No. ST/ESA/SER.A/173, Population Division, Department of Economic and Social Affairs, United Nations, New York.

United Nations (2000), *Long-Range World Population Projections: Based on the 1998 Revision*, ST/ESA/SER.A/189, Population Division, Department of Economic and Social Affairs, United Nations, New York.

Unruh, G.C. and W.R. Moomaw (1998), 'An Alternative Analysis of Apparent EKC-type Transitions Environmental Kuznets Curve', *Ecological Economics*, **25** (2), pp. 221–9.

US Bureau of the Census (1999), *World Population Profile: 1998*, Report WP/98, US Government Printing Office, Washington, DC, available at http://www.census.gov/ipc/www/world.html, last accessed on 7 May 2001.

US Bureau of the Census (2000a), *International Data Base*, available at http://www.census.gov/ipc/www/idbsum.html, last accessed on 7 May 2001.

US Bureau of the Census (2000b), *NP-T1 Annual Projections of the Total Resident Population as of July 1: Middle, Lowest, Highest and Zero International Migration Series, 1999 to 2100*, available at http://www.census.gov/population /projections/nation/summary/np-t1.txt, last accessed on 7 May 2001.

US Bureau of the Census (2000c), *Total Midyear Population for the World: 1950 to 2050*, available at http://www.census.gov/ipc/www/worldpop.html, last accessed on 7 May 2001.

US Bureau of the Census (2001), *US Trade Balances by Country*, available at http://www. census.gov/foreign-trade/balance/index.html, last accessed on 11 December 2001.

Uzawa, Hirofumi (1969), 'Time Preference and the Penrose Effect in a Two Class Model of Economic Growth', *Journal of Political Economy*, **77** (4, Part 2: Symposium on the Theory of Economic Growth), pp. 628–52.

Vermeer, Eduard B. (1998), 'Industrial Pollution in China and Remedial Policies', in Richard Louis Edmonds (ed.), *Managing the Chinese Environment*, Oxford: Oxford University Press, pp. 228–61.

Wang, Hua and David Wheeler (1996), 'Pricing Industrial Pollution in China: An Econometric Analysis of The Levy System', World Bank Policy Research Working Paper 1644, World Bank', Washington, DC, available at http://www.worldbank.org/nipr/work_paper/1644/.

Wang, J.H. and E.D. Lin (1996), 'The Impacts of Potential Climate Change and Climate Variability on Simulated Maize Production in China', *Water, Air and Soil Pollution*, **92** (1–2, Special Issue: Climate Change, Vulnerability and Adaptation in Asia and the Pacific), pp. 75–85.

Wang, Jinnan and Xingyuan Lu (1997), 'Economic Policies for Environmental Protection in China: Practice and Perspectives', in OECD (ed.), *Applying Market-Based Instruments to Environmental Policies in China and OECD Countries*, Paris: OECD Publications.

Watson, Robert T., Marufu C. Zinyowera and Richard H. Moss (eds) (1996),

Climate Change 1995 – Impacts, Adaptations and Mitigation of Climate Change: Scientific–Technical Analysis, Contribution of Working Group II to the Second Assessment Report of the Intergovernmental Panel on Climate Change, Cambridge, New York, Melbourne: Cambridge University Press.

Watson, William D. and Ronald D. Ridker (1984), 'Losses from Effluent Taxes and Quotas under Uncertainty', *Journal of Environmental Economics and Management*, **11** (4), pp. 310–26.

Weitzman, Martin L. (1974), 'Prices vs. Quantities', *Review of Economics Studies*, **41** (4), pp. 477–91.

Weitzman, Martin L. (1978), 'Optimal Rewards for Economic Regulation', *American Economic Review*, **68** (4), pp. 683–91.

Weyant, John P. (1993), 'Costs of Reducing Global Carbon Emissions', *Journal of Economic Perspectives*, **7** (4), pp. 27–46.

Whalley, John and Randall Wigle (1990), *The International Incidence of Carbon Taxes*, mimeo.

White, Kenneth J. et al. (1997), *SHAZAM, the Econometric Computer Program: User's Reference Manual*, Version 8.0. New York: McGraw-Hill.

Wirl, Franz, Claus Huber and I.O. Walker (1998), 'Joint Implementation: Strategic Reactions and Possible Remedies', *Environmental and Resource Economics*, **12** (2), pp. 203–24.

World Bank (1994), *China: Issues and Options in Greenhouse Gas Emissions Control*, Washington, DC: World Bank.

World Bank (1997), *Clear Water, Blue Skies: China's Environment in the New Century*', Washington, DC: World Bank.

World Bank (2000), *World Development Indicators 2000*, Washington, DC: World Bank, some indicators available at http://www.worldbank.org/data/wdi2000/index.htm, last accessed on 5 January 2001.

World Bank (2001), *World Development Indicators 2001*, Washington, DC: World Bank, some indicators available at http://www.worldbank.org/data/wdi2001/index.htm', last accessed on 11 May 2001.

Wu, Baozhong, Kebin He, Yuansheng Fan and Weijun Zhao (1998), 'The Status and Trend of China's Policies on Climate Change', in Michael B. McElroy, Chris P. Nielsen and Peter Lydon (eds), *Energizing China: Reconciling Environmental Protection and Economic Growth*, Cambridge, Massachusetts: Harvard University Committee on Environment, pp. 541–56.

Xie, Jian (1996), *Environmental Policy Analysis: A General Equilibrium Analysis*, Aldershot: Avebury.

Xie, Jian and Sidney Saltzman (2000), 'Environmental Policy Analysis: An Environmental Computable General-Equilibrium Approach for

Developing Countries', *Journal of Policy Modeling*, **22** (4), pp. 453–89.

Xu, Dianqing (1990), *The Transition Process from Planning to Markets. A CGE Analysis of the Chinese Economy*, Ph.D. Dissertation, University of Pittsburgh.

Xu, Dianqing (1993), 'Price Distortion in the Transition Process: A CGE Analysis of China's Case', *Economics of Planning*, **26** (2), pp. 161–82.

Xu, Dianqing (1996), 'A Chasm in the Transition: A CGE Analysis of Chinese Economic Reform', *Journal of Policy Modeling*, **18** (2), pp. 117–39.

Yamaji, K., R. Matsuhashi, Y. Nagata and Y. Kaya (1991), 'An Integrated System for CO_2 Energy GNP Analysis: Case Studies on Economic Measures for CO_2 Reduction in Japan', Paper presented at Workshop on CO_2 Reduction and Removal: Measures for the Next Century, 19–21 March 1991, International Institute for Applied Systems Analysis, Laxenburg, Austria.

Yang, Jintian, Jinnan Wang et al. (1998), *Reform and Design of Pollution Levy System in China*, Beijing: China Environmental Science Press, in Chinese.

Yohe, Gary W. (1976), 'Substitution and the Control of Pollution: A Comparison of Effluent Charges and Quantity Standards under Uncertainty', *Journal of Environmental Economics and Management*, **3** (4), pp. 312–24.

Zhang, H. (1993), 'The Impact of Greenhouse Effect on Double-Crop Rice in China', in *Climate Change and Its Impact*, Beijing: Meteorology Press, pp. 131–8.

Zhang, Xiaoguang (1998), 'Modeling Economic Transition: A Two-Tier Price Computable General Equilibrium Model of the Chinese Economy', *Journal of Policy Modeling*, **20** (4), pp. 483–511.

Zhang, ZhongXiang (1998a), *The Economics of Energy Policy in China: Implications for Global Climate Change*, Cheltenham, UK and Northampton, MA, USA: Edward Elgar.

Zhang, ZhongXiang (1998b), *Is China Taking Actions to Limit its Greenhouse Gas Emissions*, available at http://www.weathervane.rff.org/refdocs/zhang_china.pdf, last accessed on 5 January 2001.

Zhang, ZhongXiang (1998c), 'Macroeconomic Effects of CO_2 Emission Limits: A Computable General Equilibrium Analysis for China', *Journal of Policy Modeling*, **20** (2), pp. 213–50.

Zhang, ZhongXiang (1999), 'Should the Rules of Allocating Emissions Permits Be Harmonised?' *Ecological Economics*, **31** (1), pp. 11–18.

Zhang, ZhongXiang (2000a), 'Can China Afford to Commit Itself An Emission Cap? An Economic and Political Analysis', *Energy Economics*, **22** (6), pp. 587–614.

Zhang, ZhongXiang (2000b), 'Decoupling China's Carbon Emission Increase from Economic Growth: An Economic Analysis and Policy Implication', *World Development*, **28** (4), pp. 739–52.

Zhang, ZhongXiang (2001), 'Meeting the Kyoto Targets: The Importance of Developing Country Participation', *China Energy Efficiency Information Bulletin* 7, no. 2 (April/May 2001), the Bulletin is published at http://www.pnl.gov/china/bulle7-2.htm and the article is available at http://www.pnl.gov/china/ feemzxz3.pdf, last accessed on 9 May 2001.

Zuidema, G., G.J. van den Born, J. Alcamo and G.J.J. Kreileman (1994), 'Simulating Changes in Global Land Cover as Affected by Economic and Climatic Factors', *Water, Air and Soil Pollution*, **76**, pp. 163–98.

Index